AN END TO ORDINARY HISTORY

A NOVEL BY

MICHAEL MURPHY

AN END TO ORDINARY HISTORY

J. P. TARCHER, INC.
Los Angeles
Distributed by Houghton Mifflin Company
Boston

ACKNOWLEDGMENTS

My thanks to Jim Hickman, whose understanding and love of the Soviet Union have informed all my work on this book; to George Leonard, Fred Hill, Mary Payne, Roger MacDonald, Anya Kucharev, Keith Thompson, and Steve Donovan for their suggestions and encouragement; to Digby Diehl for excellent advice and for making the writing more fun; and to Jeremy Tarcher, whose devotion to this project has permanently enlarged my sense of what a publisher can be.

Library of Congress Cataloging in Publication Data

Murphy, Michael.
An end to ordinary history.

Includes index.
I. Title.

| PS3563.U745E5 | 813'.54 | 81-51040 |
| ISBN 0-87477-179-X | | AACR2 |

Requests for such permissions should be addressed to:
J. P. Tarcher, Inc.
9110 Sunset Blvd.
Los Angeles, CA 90069

Library of Congress Catalog Card No.: 81–51040

Design by Miki Jackson

MANUFACTURED IN THE UNITED STATES OF AMERICA

S 10 9 8 7 6 5 4 3 2 1

First Edition

For Dulce

AUTHOR'S NOTE

In the Soviet Union, the Mysteries have not died: so begins a CIA memorandum dated April 19, 1973. The pages that follow tell a fantastic story. A Soyuz spaceship crashed when its two pilots saw an apparition; the Soviet government commissioned a study of the cosmonauts' visions and their relation to UFO reports; and as a result the Soviet Academy of Sciences was torn by controversy. A cousin of Sergei Kirov, Stalin's rival for power in the 1920s, was involved, along with Ivan Strelnikov, Russia's great pioneer of laser research.

The memorandum was released in 1979 under the Freedom of Information Act, with a few sections deleted for security reasons. Across one of its margins are scribbled the words "file in looney bin with other UFO reports," a phrase that reflects our government's attitude toward the whole affair. Neither the CIA nor State Department has answered my inquiries about it.

In spite of initial skepticism, I have come to believe the story. My judgment is based to some extent on my travels in the Soviet Union, but also on my faith in Darwin Fall, an American who was involved in the events described by the CIA memo. His detailed account has convinced me that the Soviet peoples' fascination with the Mysteries has not abated during the Communist era.

This fascination is not limited to orthodox faiths, however, and is far deeper and more complex than an interest in UFOs or parapsychology. While embracing wisdoms of the past, it inspires new explorations, some of them highly experimental. The issues it raises are often debated, sometimes in the Soviet press. In 1981, for example, *Komsomol Pravda* proposed that a national institute be formed to study psychic healing, only to be criticized by *Literaturnaya Gazeta* for its promotion of superstitious beliefs. Similar debates go on between scientific institutes and government bodies. Within the labyrinthine structures of the Soviet academic and government bureaucracies, the reality of precognition, clairvoyance, telekinesis, and mystical illumination are much discussed. As you will see, even their Academy of Sciences figures in these controversies.

Until 1972, Darwin Fall owned and ran the Greenwich Press in San Francisco. His central interest, though, has been a comparative study of the human body's supernormal capacities, a project that led to his meeting Jacob Atabet, the strangely gifted artist you will meet in these pages, and to their adventures with Vladimir Kirov, the Soviet Union's leading expert on parapsychology.

Kirov, around whom this story revolves, was an initiate of a mystic school in Central Asia and an agent of the KGB. He introduced Fall to his school's secret doctrine that our planet is part of a "larger Earth," the "Earth of Hurqalya," in which the human body becomes a luminous form of the soul.

During the autumn of 1979, I met Fall twice a week to hear about his adventure. From those conversations I learned that Kirov's passion to join the mystic quest with the ideals of socialism had been awakened and shaped by his broken family. His maternal grandfather, Ali Shirari, the seer who gave the Way of Hurqalya its modern expression, had been publicly condemned by Kirov's father, a prominent Bolshevik. By showing that spiritual exploration is a part of social progress, Kirov hoped to heal the schism his family exemplified. His strange destiny separated him from both friends and enemies, but joined him paradoxically to most of the Soviet people he knew. For most of his fellow citizens carry a similar chasm in their heart. Nearly all of them must reconcile the separate worlds they are born to, worlds that come into conflict, it seems, in the halls of the Kremlin itself.

1 The town of Olema sits on Highway 1 north of San Francisco. Bordered on the west by the wooded ridges of a federal recreation area and on the east by rolling hills and meadows, it has a general store, a real estate office, and two bars catering to people driving through on the two-lane highway. Late one afternoon in August 1972, three men sat in the Rodeo Bar and Grill lingering over drinks. One was a college student who lived behind the general store, but the others were newcomers to Olema. The two strangers sat in silence at a table by the door. They were Mexican farm workers, guessed Billy Garcia, the bar's proprietor. For the last two weeks they had come into the place each afternoon, wearing the same jeans and work shirts, to drink a single beer apiece.

They were out of work, Garcia thought, judging from their lazy manner, but something seemed peculiar about them. Though they looked like the Mexicans who worked the farms around town, they had an unfamiliar air, a look that made certain customers uneasy It occurred to him that they might be selling drugs. Were they using the bar for their rendezvous?

"You guys live around here?" he asked.

One was bigger and rougher-looking than the other. They lived down the road, he said.

That his voice had no trace of a Mexican accent surprised Garcia. In these last two weeks the man had never spoken to him. As he polished glasses at the bar, the proprietor decided the man was Basque. But the other had to be a Mexican Indian. With his high cheekbones and hooked nose, he looked like one of Garcia's cousins.

"We like the smell in here," said the man with Indian looks. "We like the shade. You keep it nice and cool."

Garcia sensed a challenge. "The smell?" he asked. "What smell?"

"Wooden walls," said the man in broken English. "They've got resin. Resin clears the head."

Garcia shrugged and turned away, annoyed by the man's odd manner.

"He's right!" said the student brightly. "I smell it too." Like Garcia, he was puzzled by the men in working clothes. A disciple

9

of the occult, he read Carlos Castaneda devoutly and wondered if the Indian-looking man might be Castaneda's sorcerer, Don Juan. Rumors were going around that Don Juan worked as a gardener incognito for a rich lawyer nearby. The man's brooding presence fit his picture of the old *brujo* exactly.

In fact, the man was an immigrant Tibetan lama named Kazi Dama. His friend, Jacob Atabet, was an American of Basque descent.

"That kid thinks we have occult powers," Kazi Dama murmured to Atabet. "And he's making up a story about us. I think he's had too much acid."

They both looked down at their table, withdrawing from the others. "We'll make people wonder, if we come here too much," said Atabet. "Maybe we've used the place up."

"Drink your beer," the Tibetan said abruptly. "But don't look up. I think our friends have come."

Two husky men, one wearing a seersucker suit with tie, the other in slacks and a sweaty white shirt, had taken seats at the bar. "Two beers," said the man in seersucker.

"We're out," said Garcia. "I'm sorry."

"Then vodka and Sprite," the man answered, wiping his face with a handkerchief. "Andrew, what do you want?"

"The same," the other said hoarsely.

Neither spoke as Garcia poured the drinks, but the man in the seersucker suit turned to look at the student. His companion sat listlessly, staring at his reflection in the mirror behind Garcia.

The Tibetan picked up a newspaper and opened it to hide his face. Atabet picked up the paper's sport page. In the shadows where they sat, they were almost invisible to the men at the bar.

As the two men downed their second drinks, Billy Garcia went into the kitchen to see if his cook had arrived. Speaking in Russian, the man in seersucker told his companion that they shouldn't have any more drinks.

Both Atabet and Kazi Dama overheard the remark. "Wait outside," the Tibetan whispered. "I'll stay and watch."

Atabet nodded, standing up with his back to the bar. As Garcia emerged from the kitchen, he went out through the restaurant door.

"Looks like the Point Reyes National Seashore is buying up all the land around here," said the man in the sweat-stained shirt. "The real estate people say there's nothing for sale."

"That's right," said Garcia. "Everyone's angry about it."

"Nothing for sale at *all* ?" the man asked, in what Garcia took to be a Texas drawl. "We're lookin' for somethin' small. A house for me and my wife, maybe a couple of acres with it. Know if there's anything for rent?"

"You'll have to ask the salespeople," Garcia said politely. "They have an office across the highway."

"I know," said the man with the drawl. "We talked to the lady there. She says there's nothin'. Has anyone rented here lately?"

"I don't keep track. There are houses stuck away in the woods from here to Inverness, places no one's ever heard of. Sorry I can't help you."

The Tibetan sank into his chair as the man in the seersucker suit scanned the restaurant. These were the men who had been watching their farm, he decided. Half-closing his eyes, he listened to the sounds they made and felt their restlessness. They were on the hunt, and one was Russian. They were the men who had planted the bug.

"Who might help us besides the real estate people?" the man with the Texas accent was asking. "Any of the farmers around here?"

"You'd be wasting your time," Garcia said. "You might ask at the Stewart farm a mile down the road. Or the ranger station. But I doubt they can help you. Have you tried the real estate people in Inverness?"

"Tried 'em all," the man said wearily. "There's nothin' on the market, for sale *or* rent." He got off his barstool and went to the door, the man in the seersucker suit beside him. "Thanks for your help," he said. "I'll ask at the ranger station."

Through a window Kazi Dama saw them get into a Chevrolet station wagon. It was not the car that had parked each night near the farm. As they headed south on Highway 1, he stood and paid his bill. Atabet was outside. A moment later, they followed the strangers in their pickup truck.

"It's not the same car," the Tibetan said. "But one of them's Russian."

"It's them," Atabet said with a nod. "They're the ones who planted the bug."

Atabet had enjoyed this adventure, the Tibetan thought, ever since the surveillance of their farm had begun. Five minutes later they saw the station wagon turning onto the access road that led up a hill toward the farm.

"They must be lousy spies," said Atabet, "making themselves so visible. Let's watch from the horse trail."

The horse trail was just wide enough for their truck. Crossing a field that bordered the farm, they drove to the crest of a hill from which they could see the station wagon parked on a rise two miles away. In the valley below stood the farmhouse, half hidden by a stand of eucalyptus.

"Watch from here," said the Tibetan. "I'll go around behind their car. Maybe I can find out more about them."

Kazi Dama circled the farm and found a hiding place some thirty yards above the station wagon. Sitting cross-legged behind a tree, he could see the two men gesturing in the car's front seat. It was getting cooler now and his mind began to quiet. In the deepening silence he could barely hear them above the buzzing of insects in the grass. They seemed to be arguing. With a concentration he had learned in his long monastic training in Tibet, he focused on their gestures and shifting inflections, and his mind became quieter still. Their voices gradually grew more distinct, and suddenly he could make out their words. Now they seemed just a few yards away.

Kazi Dama let their presence fill his mind. They were angry, tired, and confused, their voices contrasting harshly with the serenity of the valley below. A long moment passed, and the stillness of his mind grew deeper.

In spite of the strangers' bad mood, the entire vista renewed itself endlessly. Everything he looked at—the hills, the sky, the summer grass—formed a single field of delight.

From across the little valley, Atabet watched the strangers too. As the minutes passed he felt a state like his friend's. A stillness pervaded the hills, a presence in which everything seemed to float. Letting his excitement subside, he felt a subtle pleasure streaming through the countryside.

An hour passed, and the sun began to sink behind the hills. The wooded ridges turned to blue and purple. Only distant traffic broke the silence.

In the farmhouse below, Darwin Fall sat by his bedroom window. From the moment Atabet had phoned from Olema, he had watched for the men in the car. But the call had come an hour ago and the waiting was getting painful. Unlike his friends, Fall wasn't used to such vigils. Moving away from the window, he turned on his radio and found an FM station playing a Tschaikowsky symphony. He began to hum in syncopation with the orchestra until a pulse of static interference nearly drowned out the music. He slowed his beat, and the pulse of static slowed. He went faster and it went faster. For the third day in a row, this test of eavesdropping devices worked. The tiny transmitter that the strangers had attached to the house was sending its signal to a receiver somewhere within a twenty-mile radius—so an expert in bugging techniques had told him. Was the signal going to an office of the FBI?

Unlike his friends, Fall was not convinced that Russians had planted the bug. For two years, both the CIA and the FBI had worried about his studies of Soviet parapsychology. Maybe their worries had turned to paranoia. Unless Vladimir Kirov was involved. Kirov so obsessed him now that he was sometimes inclined to agree with his friends that the Russian spy was behind this surveillance.

He stood impatiently. Clearly, Kirov's haunting presence was his own projection. He had always carried a fantasy of the Russian Magus, of a Rasputin or Gurdjieff, into his studies of Soviet parapsychology, and now the rumors about Kirov gave his fantasy a plausible shape. His friends in Prague had described Kirov's occult powers, and the amateur psychic researchers in Moscow claimed that the famous spy was an initiate of the Mysteries. Such stories fed his fantasy, Fall told himself, but they were almost certainly misleading.

If the strangers tried to approach the farm on foot, Atabet would not see them now in the darkness. Releasing the emergency brake, he let his truck coast downhill. Then he turned on the engine and drove across an open field to the farm's garage. Quietly, he got out of the truck and went up to his bedroom on the second floor of the Victorian farmhouse.

Driving up Highway 1 from San Francisco, Corinne Wilde reviewed her day's adventure. The CIA people had told her that Soviet intelligence might be interested in Darwin Fall, but she had trouble believing it. Would his studies of Russian parapsychology warrant a bugging device?

She thought of Atabet and smiled. Though some of her adventures with him had been strange beyond belief, this was the silliest yet. Having moved to Olema for seclusion, they might now have attracted KGB men in search of military secrets! Tossing her hair across her shoulders, she laughed out loud. Would there be strangers in the bushes again tonight?

And yet, she could see how intelligence people might get interested in this unlikely group. No one knew more about supernormal powers than Darwin, who had made a lifelong study of them. And who actually possessed them like Jacob? Kazi would attest to that: Atabet, he said, was a religious genius unlike any he had known in Tibet. Yes, it was conceivable that Soviet intelligence wanted to know what their group was doing. Where else were people gathering so much information about the power of mind over matter?

She parked her car in the garage, crossed the yard to the house, and went up to the second-floor bedroom she shared with Atabet. "Jacob?" she said through the door to his studio. There was no response. The three men had walked to Olema, she thought, to get the easel Atabet had ordered through the general store.

Atabet sat behind her in the darkness, watching her start to undress. Against the light from the stairwell, her figure formed a sensuous silhouette, and as she took off her skirt her skin gave off a faint luminescence. She tossed back her long hair, took off her brassiere, and stretched up toward the ceiling. Ever since leaving San Francisco, she had wanted to stand naked like this.

The smell of her body filled the room, still sweet after a day in the city. Reaching out silently, Atabet pulled her onto his lap.

"Oh, God!" She slid through his legs. "This isn't fair!"

"What a body!" he whispered. "What an aura!"

"I'll get even," she said with exasperation. "You could've given me a heart attack!"

Holding her on his knees, Atabet let the light around her turn to violet. In it, the contours of her face were softened, giving prominence to her bright green eyes. "Kazi's outside looking for the guys who planted that bug," he said. "We followed them from Olema."

"You're kidding!" She stood abruptly. "This thing's getting crazy. How long have they been out there?"

"Since about six o'clock."

"I met Natalie Claiborne." She put on a robe. "The CIA knows something about us."

"The image of Kirov came up," he whispered. "His name, his presence, even a sense of his face."

She turned on a lamp by their bed. In the dim light, his dark Basque looks were pronounced. "I don't understand your obsession," she said. "But Natalie Claiborne has a lead to him."

"I think I just heard Kazi." He stood and went to the window. "Come down and tell us about her."

Fall was building a fire in the kitchen's metal hearth. Cursing to release his tension, he turned as Kazi Dama and Atabet entered.

"Don't say it," he said, his face bright red from exertion. "You could hear me grumbling. Well, damn it, I don't have a woman to remind me of the Godhead."

In this mood of controlled frustration, he sometimes reminded Atabet of a picture depicting an angry Samuel Johnson. Fall poured himself a glass of wine and turned to the Tibetan. "Kazi," he said, "are you okay?"

Picking up a notepad, the Tibetan wrote "One Russian, one American spy outside."

Atabet sat by the hearth. "Where are they now?" he asked, forming the words silently.

"In their car," Kazi wrote. "Shall we stop the bug?"

"If we stop it they'll know," Fall whispered. "But it's screened off by the hearth. Just stand over here and keep your voices down."

The three men gathered by the fireplace, keeping its metal chimney between them and the window. Perspiration covered the Tibetan's forehead. "I heard them talking," he whispered. "They have a camera, but they're confused. They argued the whole time I was near them. I got their license, though. Maybe we can find out where they came from."

Corinne had come downstairs. "We might have a lead to Kirov," she said, taking a seat by the hearth. "Natalie Claiborne admitted she works for the CIA, collecting information about parapsychology and altered-states research in California. She knows about Boone's Foundation."

"She told you that?" Fall asked with surprise.

"Yes. She said that the CIA's funding Boone's parapsychology project. But here's the best part. Lester Boone, our famous American patriot, has friends in Germany who are friends of Kirov. She said there is some kind of network—as you guessed, Darwin—that includes Boone and a German industrialist and scientists in Vienna, all working outside their governments to harness psychokinesis. At least *certain* CIA people believe that."

Fall sat down beside her. "Incredible," he whispered. "How did you get her to talk?"

"I did what you said—told her we correspond with Soviet parapsychologists. I told her you and I were friends, and that you wanted to meet her. Now get this. She said there's a man at the Stanford Research Institute who might be part of Boone's network. He sounds like the one who came to see you in November, the one who said he was inquiring about Kirov for the Department of Defense."

"God! I wonder," Fall said. "An independent network after all!

What the hell are they up to? But why would she tell you about it?"

"She was very low key, but interested in the Greenwich Press and your translations of the Russian stuff. She wanted to hear about your experiments with Gorski. She was dangling bait, of course, when she said that Boone and Kirov might be connected. I think she believed me, though, when I said we knew nothing about it."

"I think you ought to see this lady," Atabet said, turning to Fall. "Maybe you could trade her something for news about Boone. And maybe . . ." he paused. "Maybe we ought to look for Kirov after all. His image came up tonight. Again and again. Kazi, this Kirov obsession is the damnedest thing. Where does it come from?"

The Tibetan's face reflected the stillness that had gathered around him through the afternoon. "Listen!" he whispered. "Can you hear their car?"

Only Atabet could hear it. An automobile was moving off the access road half a mile away. He nodded at the others.

Kazi Dama closed his eyes. "Vladimir Kirov?" he asked. "It's only a name to me. But *someone* Russian is bugging this house and trying to take pictures of us. If not Kirov, then some other Soviet wants to know us better."

2   The third-story room on an alley in the outskirts of Vienna had been Vladimir Kirov's European hideaway for the last three months, his retreat from both Western and Soviet surveillance. His special position in the Scientific and Technical Directorate of the KGB and his Order of Lenin allowed him such a place, but as he sat on a wooden chest looking at the deserted alley below, he was aware that his freedom might be ending. His superiors in Moscow were questioning his months alone in Europe, his erratic travels, his failure to demonstrate a significant effort in the West to harness parapsychology for military purposes. Kirov sensed growing suspicions when he reported each Monday to the Vienna Rezident. The queries from Directorate T were getting more urgent, as if someone sensed his failing morale. Did they suspect his thoughts of defection?

He got up from the chest, took off his gray, tailored suit, and hung it in the closet, brushing it carefully. Inanimate objects, he believed, had a dim consciousness that responded to human feelings toward them. In some subtle way his suit would respond with gratitude to this loving attention.

Dressed in a T-shirt and undershorts, he did a series of stretching exercises. He was five feet eight inches tall, weighed 155 pounds, and was built like a well-conditioned gymnast. His fair complexion reddened as he did the exercises, and his blue eyes lost their haunted look. This ritual, based on dervish movements that conditioned the body for meditation, always gave him a physical lift.

He sat on the wooden chest again and picked up a brochure that lay there. During the last few weeks this unlikely document had obsessed him.

The brochure's title, "Books from the Greenwich Press," was printed unobtrusively along the cover's lower edge, as if to make room for the picture above it. The picture, from a painting by Jacob Atabet, showed a winter sun rising through the hills of San Francisco. Kirov shook his head with wonder: the image was identical to his secret order's most important icon. The contours of the city, the sense of living tissue in the hills, and the sun's cool deadliness were the same in both pictures, as if the painter had copied some forgotten reproduction of the old mosaic. The similarity was more than coincidence, all his instincts told him, but the sources of the American artist's inspiration remained a mystery.

He turned to the brochure's account of Darwin Fall's book, the second layer of the mystery. But he sensed he would find nothing new. He had studied it for more than three months, had sent a Soviet undercover man to study Fall and his friends, and had traced Fall's movements in Russia without understanding him. It was clear from the KGB files that these Americans didn't work for the CIA. During his trip to the Soviet Union in 1969, Fall had met the amateur parapsychologists foreigners were permitted to visit, but he had not asked to see the people an agent would look for in getting leads. Fall had gone to Russia for some other reason, and Kirov could not tell why.

He turned to the third perplexity: the description of Fall's telepathic experiment with Nikolai Gorski, the famous Russian clairvoyant—an experiment that indicated Fall might have discovered the Soviet Union's largest parapsychology project. Were there connections between it and the painting?

He looked again at the brochure's description of Fall's research. If it was accurate, Fall's project was unique. Nowhere else had Kirov seen such a thorough study of the body's supernormal powers and their connection to spiritual practice. Conceivably,

Fall had made important discoveries about the human body's future transformation. Yet he had completed much of his study before meeting Atabet, his teacher. If Fall was only thirty-two, as the surveillance people said, he must have been twenty when his research started. Where had his vision come from? Kirov was convinced that these Americans were seeking a mutation of human flesh into the Earth of Hurqalya.

"Identity and embodiment" was the title of a chapter in Fall's book. It was followed by a rare Sufi adage: "A sea of centers is the One, not annihilation." Kirov's school had used the same sentence for centuries to describe a fundamental connection between flesh and the soul. Fall's summary of the chapter said that humans would grow into their luminous and eternal bodies. Everywhere in this extraordinary catalogue there were coincidences with the witness of his teachers.

3 From his second-story office at the Greenwich Press on upper Grant Avenue in San Francisco, Darwin Fall looked down at tourists crowding into the restaurants below. It was Friday night, and the noise was worse than ever. Seeing a passerby stop to watch him, he closed the windows and shutters. Selling this place and retiring completely from the city would be a relief.

He surveyed the paneled room. Research papers covered a long wooden table. The latest version of his book was arrayed in stacks of binders on his desk. Files lined an entire wall. In this sanctuary he had established the foundations for his life's intellectual work. In these last five years he had made this office the world's largest archive of lore about the human body's supernormal capacities.

A daguerreotype of his great-grandfather, Charles Fall, hung on the wall behind his desk. Tonight, the proud, silver-maned face seemed full of anticipation, as if the old man were excited about meeting the CIA lady. He made a bright contrast to Ezra Pound and Sigmund Freud, who flanked him. Fall looked at the desk again. His manuscript, now 2,500 pages long, would demonstrate the range and thoroughness of his work to the Agency's Life Sciences Division. He would show it to Ms. Claiborne first, with the supporting documents he had collected during the last twelve years.

Fall opened a drawer and found the file on Bernadine Neri. It contained articles about the Italian saint from European medical journals, with testimony about her healing force that Fall had collected in 1965 at her home in the Arno valley. Six photographs showed the physical changes that accompanied her ecstasy: though they did not reveal her stigmata, they recorded her transformation from a pinched little peasant woman to a robust beauty. Natalie Claiborne would be impressed.

Or would she? Fall's Stanford advisers had rejected these documents, arguing that Bernadine Neri's followers had mythologized her life and works. Studying the saint had cost Fall the support of his doctoral committee. The uncontrollable energy that shone through Bernadine's face disturbed most academics, he had concluded. Natalie Claiborne, he hoped, would be more open. The CIA, after all, had made its own studies of the powers that accompanied illumination.

Placing the Neri file on his desk, Fall remembered the letter he had written to his professors in 1967 informing them that he was giving up his Ph.D. work. He would continue his studies, unburdened by their demands for statistical evidence and more clinical evaluations of his cases. Fall remembered his joy at the decision. The week after he made it, he had founded the Greenwich Press with money his parents had left him and had begun his life's work with a passion. In the five years since, this room had become his place of vindication.

From another cabinet he took a file on an Indian runner who had completed the Bombay Marathon ten minutes faster than the world record. Photographs taken before and after the race showed a change in the runner's looks as remarkable as Bernadine Neri's. While running, he had entered a *nirvikalpa samadhi*, the man had told the press, in which his mind had "vanished." Three watches gave the same time for his run, and a check of the course had confirmed its length exactly. But the International Amateur Athletic Federation would not recognize the event, and most sports experts dismissed it by saying that Indians couldn't count. Like many extraordinary athletic feats, this would be discounted by the sports establishment. Its persuasiveness depended upon its similarity in crucial details to other cases in Fall's collection.

Fall laid the photographs of the Indian runner and the Italian saint beside the transcripts of his experiment with Nikolai Gorski. Natalie Claiborne would be impressed most of all with the Russian's responses during their telepathic exchange. Finally she would see that Fall knew more about the human organism's hidden powers than the Agency's leading experts. After seeing this archive, she might be tempted to trade him information about Vladimir Kirov.

There was a knock on the door, and Natalie Claiborne entered. She was blonde, slightly taller than Fall, and more attractive than he had expected. He took her coat and poured her a glass of wine while she looked around the office. "Ezra Pound!" she exclaimed, going to the gallery of faces. "And Freud. Who's the man in the middle?"

"Charles Fall, my great-grandfather. He and Henry James, Senior, were friends. They worked together on a theory of man's future evolution."

"Henry James Senior." She leaned forward awkwardly to study the pictures. "What a glorious man! Have you read his books?"

"Just the manuscript he and Charles Fall began." Fall handed her the wine. "It helped inspire my study."

She was five feet ten, but seemed even taller in her black sheath skirt and sleeveless overblouse. Her carriage and cultured inflection suggested an Eastern finishing school, he thought. Had she gotten her job through family connections?

"I read your report on the Gorski experiment," she said, sitting on the room's only couch. "Corinne Wilde must've told you I'm curious about it."

"Gorski and I saw it as a gesture for peace," he said, as he sat down on a chair across from her. "But we had another idea, a crazy one, I guess. We thought we could start a Soviet-American project to study telepathy. I thought my report would stir up more attention than it did."

Natalie Claiborne was surprised by the man she faced. Instead of the cool intellectual her director had told her about, Fall seemed ill-at-ease. His rough florid complexion and unguarded responses did not fit the man she had pictured.

"How did all this get started?" she asked, indicating the crowded desk and shelves. "It looks like you've been gathering material for an awfully long time."

"For twelve years, since I was in college."

"But you must have a staff," she said with admiration. "How can you run a press and do so much research?"

"I started collecting some of it when I was in high school," Fall said, nodding toward the row of files that lined the wall behind her. "I've been interested in the body's powers since I recovered from polio when I was a kid. Getting over it taught me some things about mind over matter."

With his arm bent at the elbow, Fall rotated his left shoulder stiffly. "I still can't move my shoulders right," he said. "But they're improving. I've been recovering my movement for more than twenty years, if you can believe it." He hesitated, considering whether she would be bored with his medical history. "All of this, my book, this archive, my trips to Russia, started when I saw how much capacity for change we have, how much reserve. You know the Soviet term, I suppose—'hidden human reserves.'"

"Yes," she nodded. "My boss in Washington talks about it all the time. He thinks the Soviets are the world's leading experts!"

"That's one reason I went there," Fall said. "To see if I could loosen up these shoulders more. And to learn about their theories. Mind over matter is one of their great frontiers."

"And that led to your experiment with Gorski?"

"It's led to that and a great deal more." He paused. "Have you read the Greenwich Press catalogue?"

"Your description of the Gorski experiment was fascinating. Did he really get the images you sent?"

"Some of them. You read my account. It was something, wasn't it, how he saw the elephant? He thought it had a 'movable nose dropper,' just like the trunk on the model I used. I was amazed he was so accurate. There was absolutely no way he could cheat, given the fact that he was in Moscow and I was in San Francisco."

It was more than coincidence, she reminded herself, that "elephant" was the KGB code word for the largest Russian project in parapsychology, a project her superiors had taken pride in discovering. Were he and Gorski flaunting their knowledge of it? This experiment and Fall's reports on Soviet research had to be related. There was more to it all than a gesture for peace.

"A professor friend of mine chose the targets," he said, "using a random-number table. Each object had to be small enough to hold in my hands, like the toy elephant with the movable trunk. We used the same four objects every Monday, Wednesday, and Friday at noon—which was eleven at night in Moscow."

Were Fall and Gorski part of some dissident scheme? she wondered. It was hard to believe that they had chosen an elephant as their first target by coincidence. "Did he get any of the others right?" she asked, feigning a look of innocence.

"Look." He leaned toward her. "I think we'll save time by avoiding formalities. I'll tell you everything I'm doing. As far as I know, none of it has anything to do with national security. If it does, I want you to tell me. But I'd like to find out about Vladimir Kirov. Corinne Wilde told you the rumors I've heard about him."

Startled by his sudden directness, she sat back on the couch. "I told Corinne Wilde everything I know about Kirov," she said evenly. "I've only heard rumors that he might know Lester Boone. Rumors, mind you—only rumors. The Agency's baffled by Soviet parapsychology because we hear so many conflicting reports."

"You know I published a report on the Starr Foundation." Fall stood to refill his glass. "I was down at Boone's lab in El Paso a couple of years ago and met his Argentine research man, Isaac Cruz. You read what I wrote."

"Yes," she said. "I've read all your catalogues. What do you think of their experiments?"

"They've gotten pretty good results. I saw one of their subjects—a boy Cruz found in Buenos Aires—score thirty straight runs that were two or more standard deviations from chance. Cruz had him making love to their random-event machines. That's their secret, I think—getting good subjects excited. I heard Cruz tell the boy to get an erection if he wanted to. He said it plainly, right in front of me!"

"My goodness! What a creative approach!" she said ironically. "How did you meet this Isaac Cruz?"

"Wrote to Boone, then went to see them in El Paso. We talked for a couple of hours and Boone got interested in my book. But what do *you* think they're up to? The CIA still funds their work."

"I don't know what Boone's about," she said. "But we know he goes to Vienna twice a year and sees a German businessman named Wessig who's got a lab like his. The German knows Kirov."

"And Kirov? What do you know about him? Is he really involved in parapsychology?"

"We're not sure, at least that's what my boss says. If anyone in the Agency were certain, I'd know."

For a moment they studied each other's expressions. "I heard about him from some Russians I met," Fall said with hesitation, "but none of them was sure whether he worked for the KGB, or was a double agent, or an American mole, or simply a fanatic believer in psychic research. Some people from Novosibirsk said he helped get the Soviet military interested in the field using his own occult powers. None of my Russian friends had ever met him, though. I'm sure they were telling the truth. The man's completely hidden from the people in parapsychology who meet foreigners."

Fall leaned back in his chair, uncertain how to proceed. If she knew anything more about Kirov, she wasn't going to tell him—that much was certain now. And she wasn't going to give him more reasons for the CIA's curiosity about his experiments with

Gorski. To get more leads to Kirov's network, he would have to get to know her better.

The restaurant stood high on Telegraph Hill, and on a night like this you could see the lights of several cities across San Francisco Bay. From Tiburon to the north down to Hayward, the East Bay hills were covered by a long electric negligee. But the water between looked cavernous. Staring into its uncertain depths, Natalie Claiborne wondered why she had come here. She had not planned to do so, and had even canceled another engagement. This was not her way at all!

But the man was transparent, she reassured herself—it would be easy to spot any attempt he might make to get past her defenses. And she might learn something. Clearly, he knew more about Lester Boone, and he might know more about Kirov. That must be the reason she had agreed to this dinner so quickly—to get more information. And yet she was puzzled . . .

"Do you practice hypnosis?" she asked him. "I had another date tonight, you know."

Fall wagged his head to suggest that he might have practiced something, and she smiled playfully. Their exchange was becoming erotic. As their waiter poured them each a glass of wine, he studied her face. Her strong features had softened in the lamplight, giving her new appeal. It would take a deliberate decision to resist her, for the game they were playing gave an extra dimension to this meeting, a subtle charge that heightened her attractiveness.

As they ate they each put forth a theory about Kirov's notoriety. Fall said he must operate an espionage network to keep track of Western research on exotic powers of the mind, and Boone might cooperate to get information for his own work.

"That's one rumor," she said, turning her gray eyes toward him. "But I think there's more. Kirov might be using his knowledge of parapsychology to camouflage his military interests. Lester Boone is a weapons tycoon. There's no telling what games the Soviets might play to approach him. Kirov might give him harmless stuff about psychic research, throwing in stuff like virtual-state engineering to win his confidence, hoping that Boone will let slip some things about the planes he builds. God knows how Kirov works, but if half the stories about him are true he must be pretty good. Why don't you ask Boone himself? Does he trust you enough to talk about his Russian connections?"

"He might. Could I tell him you told me all this?"

"That might alarm him." She frowned. "If you do, say that these are *my* speculations. He's suspicious about the Agency, even though it funds him."

Fall studied her handsome face, so cool in this exchange. Could she be making this suggestion on Agency orders? "How do you know about virtual-state engineering?" he asked. "You've done your homework well."

She shrugged. "Isn't it well-known among parapsychologists?"

"Not really. Who have you talked to about it?"

For an instant, his widely set blue eyes seemed forbidding. She would have to be careful. "Who was it?" She paused, pretending to remember. "I'm bad with names. There were some people at the Psychical Research Society in Berkeley. And Schroeder and Ostrander's book, their stuff about psychotronics and Pavlita."

From her uncertain response Fall saw she was concealing something, perhaps items she had read about Pavlita in a CIA report. He also saw that she perceived his suspicion. As he sipped his wine, he felt an intimate and strangely familiar mood. He wondered where he had felt it before . . .

And then he remembered.

This feeling had appeared with Russian friends like Gorski when they shared their intimate thoughts. The mood, he had decided, came from the complexities involved in friendships with Soviets, complexities that gave drama to the simplest events. But there must be more than that, more to this sense of a secret connection. For when suspicion built upon suspicion without driving two people apart, the essential mystery of the other could become more intensely attractive. Both partners in such an encounter might feel their practiced responses collapsing into a naked unity. . . .

"Pavlita," he murmured, turning to avoid her glance. "I met him once in Prague. He's a strange old bird."

"Do you think his generators work?" She pretended amusement. "His ideas sound pretty farfetched."

"Can the mind pass into matter?" He peered into his glass. "Can I fill this wine with my bioplasma, like Pavlita says? Some Soviet researchers think so. There's interest there in his machines." He paused as a new insight dawned. "But yes—maybe that's what Boone is up to! He's interested in a new kind of weapon, something like Pavlita's psychotronic generator. I think I should try to find out."

"You'd better be careful," she cautioned. "I understand he's vindictive. How would you go about it?"

"Go down to El Paso and see him." Fall shrugged. "I'll see if he wants me to publish some of their work."

Natalie Claiborne felt a sudden sympathy for the complex man she faced. "Why do you take these risks? With all your research work, your publishing, your book, why go running after Boone and Kirov? You could get into trouble."

For an instant, a helpless expression crossed Fall's face. "It might seem crazy," he said, "but I think the Soviets are doing things that are crucial for my work. The study of the human biofield is more complex over there than it is anywhere in the West. Marxist dogma forces them to look for the material causes of psychic events, to look for subtle energies like 'bioplasma' to account for ESP and spiritual illumination. Their thinking converges with my interest in bodily transformation. I believe that out of Russia will come new insights about the relation of spirit to matter."

Fall's already ruddy complexion had grown even redder, and his blue eyes more intense. "Their therapies and parapsychology alone wouldn't've attracted me," he said. "That's only the excuse I give. It's their drive to understand the mysteries, especially the mystery of matter and consciousness." He paused. "So many of them think about it. I guess their history has forced them to. Gorski, for example, when we planned our experiment, said it might show that the earth is in the soul! 'The body's in the soul,' he said, 'so the earth is in the world-soul.' Nearly all the parapsychology people I met there had some kind of vision like that."

"But how does that lead to Kirov and Boone?" she asked with a look of concern. "Why get involved in these spy games?"

"They're not spy games!" Fall said with a pained expression. "According to the rumors, Kirov is the Soviets' leading expert in parapsychology. He might teach me something, and Boone could lead me to him. Isn't that reason enough?"

"Maybe." She remained unconvinced. "But I hope you're careful. People like Lester Boone play for keeps."

4 The decrepit warehouse stood between three fields of hay and an empty parking lot ten miles from downtown El Paso. Nothing had been done to improve the building's exterior since Fall's visit two years before. The same *for sale* sign,

battered by wind and rain, was attached to a pole in front. The same windows on the side were broken. The place needed a fresh coat of paint. Fall wondered if Boone deliberately left the warehouse in disrepair to conceal the experiments inside.

Fall drove his rented car down the narrow approach road into the parking lot. Before getting out, he reviewed the story he would tell, rehearsing his answers to Boone's questions about Stefan Magyar and their mutual acquaintances in Prague. Withholding the CIA's suspicions about Boone would be his only duplicity, he told himself, and a small one. His story was consistent in all details.

Following Cruz's instructions, he went to the back of the warehouse and found Boone's silver Mercedes. A driver sat behind the wheel. "You the man from San Francisco?" he asked with a flat Texas drawl. "Mr. Boone's been waitin' for you. He said he'd meet you in the lab."

Opening an unmarked door the driver pointed to, Fall stepped inside. Few changes had been made here, too. Computers and workbenches lined the fiberboard walls, and sunlight streamed through windows fifteen feet above him. In the middle of the long, narrow room stood Cruz's random-event machines. There were six he recognized, and seven new ones, the largest collection like this outside the Soviet Union. Housed in shining metal cases, they were covered with colored windows and painted displays like slot machines in a gambling casino. Fall remembered Cruz describing them with pride, explaining that each contained an electronic noise generator that triggered lights in the colored windows. In his psychokinesis experiments, subjects tried to order these random signals through a power of their mind. Fall found the machine he had worked with two years before. He had spent an hour with it, rooting for a flashing light to move across a dark green window toward a yellow target. The Argentinian researcher had urged him on excitedly, cheering his successes with with loud olés. Afterward both had been exhausted.

Fall scanned the room. The place felt clammy, as if it contained something sick. Had Cruz's experiments left a presence here? Suddenly Fall was self-conscious. Was someone watching? He remembered Cruz saying there was a hidden window.

Then he jumped back in alarm.

Hanging directly above him was a body, its feet dangling limply toward the floor. But backing away, he saw that the thing was a dummy. The harness it hung in was a Witch's Cradle, a metal swing Cruz used to rock his subjects into a hypnotic trance.

Leaning against a wall, Fall waited for the sense of shock to pass. The dummy swung slowly above him as if caught in a dizzy reverie. Fall wiped perspiration from his lips, then turned and left the room. As he did, Isaac Cruz came down the corridor.

Fall followed him back to the laboratory. "Boone will be here soon," Cruz said with a Latin accent. "We are both interested in news of Magyar."

His dark eyes had a bright intensity, a light without compassion, Fall thought, or any trace of humor. Gravely Cruz showed him the latest versions of the random-event machines. Unfortunately, he said, they had not found enough talented subjects to achieve the results they hoped for.

Isaac Cruz might have been painted by El Greco, Fall thought. His long otherworldly face seemed twisted toward an interior light. "What about that awful thing?" he asked, pointing to the Witch's Cradle. "What are you doing with it?"

Cruz raised his hands in a Latin gesture of disgust. "Nothing!" he said. "Not a single thing. It is hard to find people who can use them, people with courage enough to lose their minds! You know Ramón has disappeared. Ramón, our very best subject. He could make these generators dance."

Through some intangible power of the mind, a gifted subject could bring order to the random events that these machines produced. Fall thought of the handsome boy from Buenos Aires stroking and kissing these metal boxes as if they were his lovers, passionately urging their flashing lights to move as Cruz directed. It had been a grotesque sight, leaving him uneasy for days.

"Yes, Ramón was our best until he vanished," Cruz sighed. "He threw himself into this with all his energy. But it is a problem, keeping good subjects."

At these words, Lester Boone came through the door. He made a tall, kindly contrast to his otherworldly associate. "Well, Darwin!" he said with a deep Texas drawl. "It's about time you got down here again to see us. We've been keepin' up with you." His blue eyes suggested a depth of intelligence and humor. "I'm gonna' hold you to that promise you made me, about that book of yours. When are we gonna' see it?"

"No one's seen a copy yet. It may take ten more years to finish."

"Well, what's in it? We read your catalogues, and ask ourselves, 'Now what's he up to?' Sounds like you're gonna' finish the skeptics off once and for all!" He squeezed Fall's shoulder and gestured grandly toward the random-event machines. "Has Isaac shown you our latest ghost traps?"

"Ramón liked this one most of all." Cruz pointed to a tall white box with a display of red lights shaped like a Valentine heart. "This is the machine he did best on. He thought it was alive."

Experimenting with such devices, Fall had sometimes felt a mysterious connection with them. As he studied the heart-shaped display, he remembered that a similar device had seemed to smile at him as he tried to move it telepathically. A bond of reciprocal feeling could develop between man and machine, it appeared.

"Ramón scored better than four standard deviations from chance on over a hundred straight runs," Cruz said, stroking the graceful box. "And for days this machine kept scoring like that *no matter who* the subject was. Ramón made a field in it that worked for everyone. He invested this machine with a soul!" He paused. "It is still hard for us to get a series of random numbers from it. I think it is crying for its friend."

"Ah, Ramón," Cruz sighed. "He made these boxes *dance*. And still they pine for him. Fall, do you believe me?" There was a challenge in his voice. "You know about the linger effect, how the results of psychokinesis stay in a particular spot. I remember your articles about it. Didn't you say there was a connection between it and psychotronic machines? Or did the Czechs say that?"

"The Czechs are making a breakthrough," Fall said. "Some friends of mine say they have a machine that will hold a mind's force for months. I think they're trying to scramble computers and disrupt satellite codes. Their work has caught the Soviets' attention."

"Darwin," said Boone, placing a hand on Fall's shoulder. "We've been friends too long to play games. Now who are these friends of yours? Someone you've met since '69?"

"They're friends of Magyar's. Georgi Latko, Stanislaus Kocek—I think you know most of them."

"Yes, I know them," Boone drawled. "So you've been stayin' in touch with Stefan. I hadn't heard about their smearin' satellite codes."

"That's what's gotten the Soviets interested. That and Pavlita's new work. But maybe you know one of the Russians they're dealing with." Fall pulled away from Boone's controlling grip. "Vladimir Kirov. Didn't you meet him in Prague?"

The tall gray figure frowned. "Let's go upstairs, Isaac," he said. "I think our friend has something to tell us."

They followed Boone up a flight of stairs into Cruz's office. Boone poured himself a glass of seltzer water, then sat in a reclining chair. Fall sat on a couch to face him. For a moment the silence was broken only by the sound of Cruz stacking papers on his desk.

"So Kirov..." Boone sighed, as if the subject drained his energy. "What do you know about him?"

"Not much," Fall said, choosing his words with care. "What I know comes through Magyar's people, and they've sworn me to secrecy. Some say you're working with him."

"That I'm working with Kirov! Well, fuck! Your people in Prague told you that?"

Fall shrugged. "There are all sorts of stories going 'round."

Boone looked at Fall with amusement. "Now where do you think they'd come up with a story like that? He's a member of the KGB, isn't he? How the hell would I work with someone from the KGB?"

"Magyar's people think the KGB's everywhere," Fall said impassively. "Some of them think Kirov has a network that involves the Starr Foundation. They think you're part of it."

"Well, I'll be damned!" Boone slapped his knee. "Didn't know I was gettin' that famous." He paused, then leaned toward Fall. "There's something to those rumors, though. I *did* meet Kirov once. That must've started the stories. But *look!*" He glanced around the room as if an outsider might be listening. "No money, no secrets, no plans passed between us. I hope you believe that."

"So you did meet him!" Fall pretended surprise. "I only half-believed it. You know he's Russia's biggest mystery man in parapsychology."

"I've heard the stories," Boone whispered. "Some people say he's running all of Soviet psychic research, but that's a pile of crap. Most of the stories about him are crap. Has someone from the CIA talked to you about him?"

"Yes," Fall said. "I checked Magyar's stories through them. An officer in the Life Sciences Division said Kirov won an Order of Lenin for espionage work in the sixties. The Agency wants to know more about him."

"More about what? More about his work in parapsychology?"

"Yes," Fall nodded. "And why he's stirred up these rumors. They wonder if he's tapping Americans for espionage work. He's supposed to be a star recruiter."

Boone leaned close to Fall. "Well," he said, "he's one tough son of a bitch, I can tell you that. A real tough son of a bitch. But not like you might think. On the surface he doesn't seem tough at all. Now I don't want you tellin' people about this. I'd be awfully unhappy if I knew you'd let this out." His clear blue eyes were filled with menace. "You understand? I'll tell the CIA myself about it."

"Who would I tell?" Fall said. "The last thing I want to be is a CIA scout."

"All right," Boone said, holding up a hand in warning. "I'm telling you this to set the record straight. But you keep it to yourself, you hear? The only reason I met him was curiosity. I was just plain curious about someone who could stir up those stories."

"What did you talk about?"

"We talked about everything—and nothing. That son of a bitch didn't tell me a thing, but when it was all over I realized what he'd squeezed *out of me*. No secrets, mind you, but all kinds of information." He shook his head with disgust. "First time someone ever did that. I think he hypnotized me. But that's all that passed between us. You tell our friends in Czechoslovakia that. There's no deal between us. No secrets. No money. No nothing. *Nothing*, you hear?"

Fall nodded his agreement as he studied the stern, rugged face. Boone could be telling the truth, judging from his expressions and gestures. Maybe the stories had come from their single meeting.

"But he never mentioned Soviet parapsychology," Boone said. "I tried to angle around to the subject, but he kept sliding off. He's a real smoothy. Didn't ask me anything, though, about the Starr Foundation." Boone stretched his legs on the footrest. "But you know—I don't think he's really that interested in pscyhic research. I think those stories about him are some kind of front. It's military secrets he's after, and information about our electronics industry. Your Silicon Valley out in California, that's what he's curious about. That's the kind of thing he got from me, I realized later, damn it! He got the name of an alloy we're using in one of our planes, something I never should've mentioned. He made a fool of me."

Fall was changing his mind about Boone's connection to the Russian spy. Though the old man was probably veiling some of the facts, maybe they had met just once. The CIA might be as mistaken as his friends in Prague.

"But Darwin, you don't believe these rumors, do you?" Boone asked with a fatherly look. "You know me too well to think I'm run by Kirov. That has to be a pile of shit."

"I believe you," Fall said. "Magyar's group is a rumor machine. The poor bastards live in fear half the time, trying to keep their research going with Army support. Paranoia's their way of life."

Boone leaned back in his chair. "But why did you want to see us?" he asked. "Comin' all the way down here like this, I figured you didn't trust the telephone. You got someone on your tail? Wouldn't be surprised after your last catalogue."

"What do you mean?" Fall asked with surprise.

"Hell. You know! That Gorski thing. Your Russian translations. Some jackass in the CIA might be alarmed. They're always after *us*." He glanced at Cruz. "They always think we know something they don't. Shit! And they don't do a thing about it. Don't talk to Russian immigrants who've worked in the psychology labs. Don't do any research."

"But they're funding your work, I thought."

"You call that funding? Thirty, forty thousand a year? Hell, that barely pays Isaac's salary! But let's forget them. You and I know more about the Russian work than the Agency's whole Life Sciences Division put together. Tell us what you've heard about Pavlita and his psychotronic machines, and I'll tell you what we've heard from Magyar."

The bargaining had started, Fall thought. Boone would trade information item for item as if this were a business deal upon which his fortune depended. "Here are some new descriptions of work in Prague that should interest you," Fall said, taking a folded paper from a jacket pocket. "Kocek sent them to me. They're results from his new psychotronic generator."

"Pretty good. Yeah, not bad." Boone passed the paper to Cruz. "You're good at collecting this stuff, young man. I think they trust you more than me. What else you got?" A sly, genial smile crossed his face. "You must have something more."

"I've got some more of their reports at my office. Maybe I can send them. There's one especially you will like—a diagram of their new machine."

"So we're bargaining, are we?" Boone grinned. "I thought we'd gotten beyond that. What do you think of that, Isaac? He's gettin' some of my bad habits. Darwin, what can we tell you? You've seen our random-event machines. What else would you like to know?"

"Whatever you're doing, but Kirov first of all. He's the main reason I'm here. Magyar's people say he knows more about bodily transformation than anyone else they know. He could help my work."

Boone seemed genuinely puzzled. "You know anything about it, Isaac?" he asked.

"*Nada*. Not a thing." Cruz folded his hands in front of his face. "I think he is mainly a legend. A mystical James Bond, incorporating us all in his network. A Rasputin from the KGB."

Cruz's dark, narrow face, half-concealed behind his folded hands, had a masklike impassivity. In contrast, Boone's feelings seemed transparent. "Isaac's right," he said, slapping his chair. "This business generates so goddamned many rumors! Hell, I don't know. Maybe he *does* know something about your bodily transformation, but don't ask me about it. I hope you're not going to all this trouble because of Magyar's people. I hope you have more sources than that."

"All right." Fall lowered his voice. "Can we agree to keep this quiet? Some of it sounds crazy."

Boone glanced at Cruz, then nodded. "A promise," he said. "Nothing goes beyond this office."

Fall told them about the surveillance of the farm in Olema and their intuition that Kirov was involved. "It sounds paranoid," he said, "but we think the man is reaching out to us. God knows why. It sounds so crazy I'm embarrassed to tell you. But that's the extent of it—the stories from Prague, the CIA rumors, and our sense he's watching us."

"It sounds crazy, all right," Boone said. "Chasin' down here with so little to go on. I wish we had more to tell you."

Fall sensed this was the truth. "Damn it! This trip's all for nothing, I guess. You got anything else I can see? Any new projects I can report on?"

Boone rose from his chair with energy. "Come on, Isaac. Let's show him the shop."

"There is not much that is new," Cruz said with displeasure. "But if you like, we can look around." He led the way out the door and down a flight of stairs to a room that Fall hadn't seen in his previous visit. Two men worked on a small computer. "They are making a program for our random-event machines," Cruz said. "A good program, I think. It is a shame we have so few good subjects."

"Are they working full time?" Fall asked. "They weren't here before."

"They came last month," Boone whispered so the men couldn't hear. "I'm gettin' extravagant, Isaac says. We'll have to let 'em go pretty soon."

"This is our machine shop." Cruz gestured toward benches covered with tools and spare parts. "We have a lot of gadgets, in spite of our talent shortage." He seemed bored by the subject now and turned to lead them from the room. Crossing the corridor, they went into a white-walled laboratory filled with animal smells.

A row of cages covered a long, narrow bench. "Mice and guinea pigs," Cruz said. "For our experiments with psychic healing. Some of them have tumors that people in Dallas and Houston are praying for. But the results are not very good. We need more people like Ramón. He would heal all these tumors in a day." He picked up a swollen mouse. "This one is almost dead now, in spite of our prayers for it." Cruz tossed the mouse into its cage and headed toward the door. "The people in the experiment come from church groups. Mainly ladies in the Texas Society for Psychic Research. We don't have to pay them." As they left the room Cruz explained that every participant had a picture of the animal he was trying to heal. A pity, he said, that so many would have to die for such a small experimental result.

Boone seemed ill-at-ease with his research man's account. "Come on, Isaac," he objected. "We're gettin' some great results. Let's show him the Red Lab."

Cruz made a gesture of disgust. The Red Lab, he said, was closed for repairs. "This is really all we have to show you," he said with weariness. "A few random-event machines waiting for a subject. Some mice and guinea pigs, and two electronics men who will soon be fired. With thirty or forty thousand, you cannot do very much."

"That's right," Boone sighed. "That's about all there is. Darwin, I'm sorry we haven't more to show you. Poor pickin's for a trip to El Paso." He looked down at Fall with regret. "I'll tell you what, though. After you send us those diagrams, I'll send you some new stuff from Prague. There might be something in it you haven't seen before."

Fall was surprised by this sudden end to their meeting. "So!" Boone slapped his shoulder. "Let me walk you out."

The commanding figure gently turned Fall around and guided him toward the exit. Outside, the chauffeur still leaned against the silver Mercedes. "Have a good trip back," Boone said with energy. "And keep up the good work. When your book is done, you send it down here!"

Lester Boone strode down the corridor with an energy beyond his sixty-eight years. Taking three stairs at a stride, he went up to Cruz's office. The research man was pacing back and forth behind his desk, cursing softly in Spanish. "Boone!" he exclaimed. "What were you thinking, having him see the Red Lab? You were playing with dynamite!"

"Now, Isaac," Boone said, extending his arm in a pacifying

gesture. "Calm down! He doesn't suspect a thing. Not a thing." He locked the door behind him. "Let's talk about this without getting upset. Isaac, he didn't see enough to get suspicious."

"He is an expert in these matters," Cruz said, sitting behind his desk. "He is one of the few people in the world who could estimate how much we are spending. If he had seen the other labs, he would have known at once. And he might have seen the Russian machines. It would ruin everything for us if anyone learned about that!"

"I got carried away," Boone said apologetically. "You were right to steer him out. But don't worry. He saw two of our people, out of how many? Sixteen? He saw just about forty thousand dollars' worth."

"But I do not like it. He did not tell us all his reasons for coming here. Boone, do you believe his story—asking us about Kirov like that? What does he suspect?"

"Isaac, he told us the truth." The old man waved impatiently. "I've known him long enough to tell. He doesn't have a clue about our arrangement with Kirov. But I'll tell you what does intrigue me. It's him and Atabet. They're on to something, I think. This Atabet might be for real. The way they've psyched out Kirov's interest is amazing. It's the damnedest thing. Somehow, someway, they've felt his interest in them. I told Kirov he shouldn't have bugged their place. You can't deal that way with clairvoyants." He slapped his knee. "Shit! These spy wars take the damnedest turns. No wonder those chicken-hearted bastards at the Agency don't want to play. This kind of stuff is way over their heads."

"Boone, I don't like it." Cruz scowled. "What did he come here for? You don't think he's looking at us for the CIA?"

"Isaac, will you stop that? He came for the reasons he said. And I'm *glad* he did, because he's got a talent we can use. Isaac, I'm gonna' offer to pay his way to Prague to see what Magyar's up to. If Magyar's told them about my meeting Kirov, we've got to know why."

"You mean we'll get Edvard Hus to watch them?"

"Yes. And Kirov, too!" Boone said. "He can meet them with an alias."

Cruz leaned back from his desk. "Yes," he whispered, "it might work. But what reason will you give him for the offer?"

"The real one." The old man smiled wickedly. "That we're interested in Magyar's work. Then we'll tell our master spy. Kirov will finally meet his American face to face. Hus can watch them and tell us about the meeting. Maybe we can find out what Kirov sees in Fall and Atabet."

There was silence as they considered the plan. "Yes," Cruz said at last. "It is a good idea. We can solve three mysteries at once: what Magyar's group is thinking, what Kirov sees in Fall, what Fall and his friends want from Kirov. You are a clever man, señor."

Boone lowered his voice. "And no one at the CIA will know. They've let us down too long to share this."

"We shouldn't be too hard on them," Cruz said. "Losing two subjects in a Witch's Cradle will not make them many friends in Congress. But when we perfect our Red Lab, they will be back with their grants and more."

As Fall walked toward his car, a station wagon drove off the access road and stopped beside the warehouse. Three women came out of the building and walked toward the parking lot. Through the large open door behind them, Fall saw five more people standing in a lab Boone hadn't shown him.

The three women got into the station wagon and drove down the road toward El Paso. Fall hesitated, his heart beating rapidly. If there were eight people at work in addition to the men Cruz had shown him, Boone—or the CIA—must be supporting a million-dollar project. A chill ran up his back. Boone had said something about a Red Lab and Cruz had changed the subject. Had they been hiding the most sensitive part of their work? He approached the door, then stopped. On a bench inside the lab stood models of a satellite, and near it hung a Witch's Cradle like the one he had seen before.

Another woman came out of the door. "Where's the road to El Paso?" Fall asked her.

"Down there." She pointed toward the highway. "What are you doing here? You here on business?"

"I'm a friend of Boone's. I've published his work in parapsychology."

She was a thin, intense-looking woman in her forties, dressed in a trench coat and jeans. "Take that road toward the highway," she said, turning back into the lab and shutting the door behind her.

Fall quickly got into his car and drove out of the parking lot. Cruz hadn't wanted him to see the Red Lab, he thought, because they had lied to him about the size and nature of their project. They were developing psychokinesis as a weapon of war, and the satellite models must help them focus on Soviet spacecraft, while the Witch's Cradle helped their subjects work up energy. There was no telling what other rituals and devices they used. Random-event machines shaped like Valentine hearts, erotic dances and voodoo ceremonies: Cruz would use anything that summoned an extra psychic force. Catching a last glimpse of the broken-down warehouse through his rearview mirror, Fall felt a sense of disgust. Boone's decrepit building had become one of the world's most unlikely factories of war.

5 An hour after his return from El Paso, Fall sat alone in his Greenwich Press office. Everyone else had gone home for the night, and the place was unusually quiet. Even the street outside was silent. Taking off his shoes, Fall lay on the couch. After five hours traveling, he could finally relax.

But as he lay down the phone started to ring. It was Corinne or Atabet, he thought, wanting to know when he would come to Olema.

When he picked up the phone, however, the voice had a deep Texas drawl. "Lucky to get you, Darwin!" said Lester Boone. "I had to call you right away after our talk this morning. I've got a proposal for you. You got a minute to listen?"

Startled, Fall sat up. "Yes, I've got some time," he said. "What's on your mind."

"Good!" Boone said warmly. "That stuff you gave me this morning's *good.* So good in fact that I want to make you an offer. I'll pay your way to Prague to find out more about those psychotronic machines. Would you like that? I'll cover all your expenses with five thousand dollars on the side."

Fall was stunned by the offer. The materials he had given Boone must hold more information than he'd realized. "When would you want me to go?" he asked with hesitation. "My schedule's crowded now."

"Whenever you say. You get things from them I can't, so the fee's worth it to me. And I'll try to get my friends in Prague to set up a meeting with Kirov."

"I'm definitely interested, but let me call you back. Will you be at the lab tomorrow?"

"I'll be there all day expecting your call. But you better take me up on this, young man. If you don't, I'll go see Magyar myself!"

Fall hung up and sat back exhausted. He needed to sort out his feelings about this, he thought. It was good he was seeing his friends in Olema that night.

At 9:00 that night, Fall met Atabet and the Tibetan at the Rodeo Bar in Olema. For two hours they reviewed Fall's trip to El Paso, coming gradually to agree that Lester Boone was running a research enterprise with a million-dollar budget. But the CIA, they decided, was giving him only thirty or forty thousand dollars a year, just as Boone had said. The project was essentially his own adventure.

"Given all the disclosures about their work with LSD and hypnosis," Fall said, "our intelligence agencies wouldn't touch a project with psychics and Witch's Cradles. They probably pay for the random-event machines, but that's the extent of it. Boone covers the rest of the bill himself. No wonder the CIA wants to know more about him. If our guess about his project is right, he's the largest supporter of parapsychology in the world, with the exception of the Soviet government. The largest in history, I guess. There can't be more than fifteen full-time people in all the other U.S. labs combined, so he must employ half the parapsychology people in the country!"

Kazi Dama was troubled. "The man is frustrated by the government," he said, "because they will not back his research. He wants to beat the Russians, and he knows that psychic power works. That is a bad combination." He turned to Fall. "I don't think you should take his offer. You don't need his money, do you? You could go to Prague on your own."

"It's not the money," Fall responded slowly. "It's the connections he'll make for me. He's given Magyar and Kocek money for their work, and they owe him a favor. Maybe they can lead me to Kirov."

Atabet was worried about the trip. There was a chance it might raise suspicions in the CIA about Fall's dealings with Boone and the Czechs. Yet the pull he felt toward Kirov was inescapable. His fascination with the Russian spy had lasted for more than nine months, and he was now convinced that Kirov was behind the bugging of their house. "The CIA might wonder," he said, "but finally I think you should do it. Magyar will think you're after research for your book. You'll be telling the truth, after all, when you say that."

"You don't think Magyar will know that Boone's paying my bill?" Fall asked. "It would be bad if they thought I was being paid, even indirectly, by the CIA."

"Have Boone make out a check to the Greenwich Press. He can claim the money was spent to pay for more Russian translations. It's all out in front about his wanting you to meet his friends there. And you can share our suspicions about him, though you'd better not tell them about that secret lab. If your telling them got back to Boone, we would be in trouble. He's not the kind of man we want for an enemy."

"That settles it," Fall said. "What have we got to lose? Boone will pay my way, and what if the CIA wonders? We're not doing anything illegal."

Neither Atabet nor Kazi Dama answered. In spite of Fall's confidence, they felt a vague apprehension. It was conceivable that a KGB officer in Prague, suspecting Fall to be a CIA man, might hold him for interrogation. And there was no telling what Kirov would do.

But Fall had made up his mind. "Let's go home," he said. "In the morning we'll all feel braver."

6 In the distance, Prague Castle rose above the Moldau as if it might be a passageway out of this lovely but poisonous ambience. Sitting so splendidly in this valley, Fall thought, under thermal inversions that trapped its smoke for days, the city dazzled you in a golden suffocation. No wonder it gave rise to so many dreams of transcendence. The Golem-magic of Rabbi Lev, the Great Work of the alchemists, and now the psychic research of Stefan Magyar were part of a long, sustained effort to rise out of this stifling air toward the beauty that Prague always promised. Fall remembered the way Franz Kafka had voiced this contradiction: to him "this dear mother had claws."

Magyar embodied the city's paradoxical forces. His loneliness and secret enthusiasms, his idealism in the midst of disasters, his fascination with the transmutation of the body were more comprehensible when you understood Prague's haunting effect. This city was the encircling net of golden dreams a poet once had called her, and Magyar was fatefully trapped.

The Communist regime only sweetened his conflicts—Fall had seen that in 1969. He recalled their raucous trip to Brno with four other disaffected Czechs, the five of them still celebrating the freedoms of the previous year. Though they had lost out in the Soviet suppression of the Dubček regime, they still had hopes for another Prague Spring. Magyar had gone to work for Czechoslovakian army intelligence because it would sponsor his psychotronic research, but he had regaled Fall with his plans for converting his superiors to a belief in the soul. His friends worked for government agencies, clinics, or schools while pursuing their mystical interests in secret. It was an ancient tradition in Central Europe, they said, living dangerously, and during their five days together they introduced Fall to other members of their circle—including a group of twenty dowsers in Brno and friends in Bratislava who practiced forms of white magic. Socialist oppression only heightened their metaphysical drama. The tight golden circle of the city dramatized the whole world's plight, they said, forcing them toward a marvelous transcendence.

Fall remembered Magyar's boast that he and his friends would wear down their suppressors because they "stood on a more durable truth" than Soviet-style socialism. They had all lifted their glasses to that. But he wondered if the State had won out. Would the man he saw be the Magyar he remembered?

Fall found Magyar's house, the same one he had lived in before, and knocked on its tall, black door. There were footsteps inside, then the sound of locks being opened. With a nervous smile, Magyar said his colleague was waiting upstairs.

He was not the man that Fall remembered. Magyar was thirty pounds lighter, and his once cheerful face had lost its rosy complexion. His six-foot frame was bent and his big green eyes looked hollow. At the top of the stairs, a short, husky man stood waiting. "Darwin Fall," said Magyar, "this is Edvard Hus. Mr. Hus is an expert on psychotronics and came here especially to meet you."

In contrast to Magyar, Hus seemed completely at ease. He gestured toward an armchair as if he were the master of the house.

"Are you well?" Magyar asked, his hands fluttering nervously. "How is the Greenwich Press?"

"I've sold the Press," said Fall, "to work full time on my book and research. That allows me to come here, to see what you are doing!"

Magyar turned to Hus. "You see! I told you what an admirer he is of our psychotronics. Darwin, Edvard here is an expert in these things. Perhaps the new owners of the Press will want to publish his papers!"

"No," Hus frowned. "My work in these fields is modest. Stefan, you get too excited."

Magyar forced a smile, but Fall could see he was easily intimidated by his colleague. Was Hus here to watch them for Czech intelligence?

"Are you a parapsychologist?" Fall asked.

"I am engineer," Hus said impassively. "For building projects here in Prague. Psychotronics is my hobby."

Fall sensed that he was lying. "Have you written anything?" he asked. "The Greenwich Press will be publishing another collection of East European and Soviet papers in parapsychology. Maybe they could publish some of yours."

"Please." Hus made a chopping motion with his hand. "My papers are too boring. Full of numbers and diagrams. You don't want them."

"He is too modest." Magyar waved his hands expansively. "Edvard has designed some machines like Pavlita's. They are the best we have."

"No," Hus said firmly, his small eyes narrowing. "Stefan, that is enough."

Covering his embarrassment, Magyar offered Fall a drink.

"No, thanks," Fall said, masking the sadness he felt for his friend. "I just had lunch. Did Lester Boone write about my coming? He's interested in the things you're doing. When he heard I was coming, he wanted me to bring his greetings."

"I have his letter." Magyar wiped his hands with a handkerchief. "He is eager for news of our work, and insists we give you everything we have. I am afraid he is used to ordering people around! It must be nice to have someone so rich in parapsychology. We hear he has a big lab."

"I saw it about four weeks ago," Fall said. "He has two or three people and said they're running on a forty-thousand-dollar budget. It's not as big as I expected, but I'm amazed at how interested he's gotten."

"A real student." Magyar glanced at Hus. "You know he comes here once a year to see us. It makes our intelligence people nervous, having an American weapons maker look at our psychotronic machines. But in the interest of science we share everything that is not military." He smiled unctuously. "Our government allows us that freedom."

In 1969, Fall thought, Magyar had been cynical about government censorship of his work. He must be talking now for Hus's benefit.

"Yes," Hus said. "They let him come and look around. It shows the free exchange that is possible between our countries."

"Who else will you see on this trip?" Magyar asked, moving closer to Fall. "Georgi Latko and Stanislaus Kocek?"

"I haven't called them yet, but I'd like to. Are they in town?"

"I think so," Magyar answered. "We will have to see. But tell us about your new work."

They talked for fifteen minutes more, Fall and Magyar holding back the sensitive items they had shared during their previous visit. Fall guessed that Magyar would not mention Kirov as long as Hus was present.

"But enough!" Fall said, signaling an end to their talk. "I'm meeting some American friends for dinner. Stefan, can we meet tomorrow?"

"Good!" said Magyar. "Call me tonight when your plans are set and we will make a time."

Hus rose impassively to say good-bye, then stood at the top of the stairwell watching Magyar show Fall out. "Next time we'll talk longer," Magyar said. "I know a restaurant you will like." He hesitated, as if he wanted to say something more, then waved nervously and closed the door.

Later that afternoon Hus and Magyar sat in their Army Intelligence office discussing Boone's recommendation that they arrange a meeting between Kirov and Fall. Hus hadn't revealed Boone's other message, though, in which he had expressed suspicions about Magyar.

"He wants to know the reasons for Kirov's fascination with Fall and his friends," Hus said, pretending dismay. "He says we might want to arrest Fall, then have you arrange his release to establish yourself as his friend. He is an unpredictable man, this Boone. Sometimes I wonder whose side he's on."

"He is on the American side," Magyar said without emotion. "He thinks he is using the KGB to help his psychic research. Loaning that Argentine boy to Project Elefant was a transparent move. He thinks he has penetrated the Soviets' secret work in parapsychology."

Magyar's vacant look pleased Hus. Lying to Fall was part of a process that had numbed his conscience step by step over the last three years. Being a connoisseur of such changes, Hus knew that Magyar would do what he wanted. "Kirov will call at seven," he said. "What do you think he will say?"

"He will ask us whether Fall knows about our connection with him," Magyar answered with a flat inflection. "He may already know the answer of course, but he will test us. Beyond that, I don't know. This is a strange affair."

Hus nodded his agreement. There *was* something in this situation that was hard to calculate. No one in their office knew why the Russian master spy had spent so much time abroad these last twelve months or why the KGB had started so many rumors to take Western intelligence off his track. Hus himself had been ordered to plant a story with the CIA that Kirov had been called back to Moscow in disgrace. Only the most important KGB operation would warrant such disinformation, so Hus wondered why Kirov had spent so much time and effort tracking Fall and his friends. Their Washington informants had told them that Fall did not work for the U.S. government. He had published reports of Soviet parapsychology, but the information they contained could be found in all sorts of journals. His importance to Kirov was a mystery.

Magyar, however, had a clue to Kirov's thinking, an item he had kept to himself. He thought of the questions Kirov had asked during their meeting two months before: How did Fall carry himself? What did he laugh at? What was his complexion like? Then Kirov had done an astonishing thing. With complete gravity he had asked whether Fall possessed "a true enlightenment." When Magyar asked what he meant, Kirov had gently rebuked him. Was Fall *odukhotvoryonniy?*—the question was as simple as that. *Erleuchtung*, he had said, giving the German word; and *moksha*, the Sanskrit term for liberation. Magyar had studied these things enough to know what Kirov was asking, but he could only give a vague reply, saying finally that Fall's theories were stronger than his practice of the mystical life.

The exchange was still perplexing. Had Kirov dropped a veil for him, revealing his understanding of the soul? Had their conversation been a test? There were rumors, after all, that the Russian master spy was an initiate of the Mysteries. Remembering the incident now, Magyar guessed what Kirov would say. They could not touch Fall until Kirov met the man himself. Magyar would arrange the meeting. What would happen after that, however, was hard to predict.

As he crossed the lobby of the Alcron hotel, Fall was stopped by a man dressed in jeans and a turtleneck sweater. Would he like to change American dollars for Czech korunas at the black market rate? Fall waved him away, but the stranger followed him into the elevator. Abruptly it stopped between floors. They could exchange money now, the man said, placing a hand on Fall's shoulder. It was apparent he worked with the elevator attendant. Intimidated, Fall took out his wallet and exchanged a twenty-dollar bill; then the elevator went up to his floor. He stepped out into the hall slightly shaken.

Maids had rearranged his desk, and he looked for his book of addresses. His hands trembled as he looked for the telephone numbers of Kocek and Latko. The unexpected encounter had triggered a fear he could not account for.

He copied the two numbers on a slip of paper and sat down to calm himself. Had the money exchange been a deliberate setup?

If the Czechoslovakian police took him into custody, Magyar might not protect him. He put the address book in a jacket pocket. Maybe the room had been bugged. It suddenly occurred to him that Hus had placed him under surveillance.

As he and Hus waited for Kirov's call, Magyar felt a growing anxiety. He was willing to betray his friend, willing to comply with his torture, conceivably—but *for what*? For the cause of psychotronics? Was that the reason for these deceits? How had it all begun? When had he taken the first step into this world of lies and betrayals?

"You are brooding," Hus murmured. "What are you thinking, Stefan?"

"That I have so little time to study philosophy," he answered listlessly. "We are so busy, I haven't opened a book for months."

"Is that all?" Hus asked. "Does capturing Fall upset you?"

"If Kirov wants it, it must be necessary. Who am I to say? We are not that close, after all." They sat in the shadows for a half-hour more, Hus occasionally breaking the silence with a question, while Magyar felt a growing helplessness. Then a red light went on below the telephone and Hus picked up the receiver. "Yes, office 123," he said to the special operator. "Magyar's here. No one else is in the office. Yes, the lines are closed." Then he sat in silence waiting for connections on the KGB line to Vienna.

Kirov came on the phone and Hus took notes as they talked. Magyar leaned forward to listen, his heart beating rapidly.

"Yes," Hus said at last. "I understand. You want to meet him yourself, under normal circumstances. We will arrange a meeting at the Press Club. Just Magyar, you, and me."

The voice in the receiver continued, too faintly for Magyar to hear. Hus nodded and wrote down a message, then quietly said good-bye as the phone's red light went out. "You will ask Mr. Fall," he told Magyar, "to meet us tomorrow night. Kirov will join us at the Press Club, but you will say that he is a Soviet engineer with an amateur interest in psychical self-regulation. Under no circumstances is Fall to be arrested. I don't know what this means. Your American friend must be very important."

Magyar turned away to hide his relief. "I will call him now," he said, pretending weariness. "None of this makes sense."

Fall left the Alcron Hotel and walked casually toward Wenceslaus Square. At a corner he stopped and looked back for the man who had followed him from the lobby. Having established the fact that he was being watched, he set out briskly for the United States Embassy in the Malá Strana. The people there might give him a better sense of the risks he was running.

Forty-five minutes later, Fall explained his situation to William Morton, the embassy's chief intelligence officer. A CIA career man in his fifties, Morton had a thin, unlined face and close-cropped hair that made him look younger to Fall. "So you know Lester Boone," he said with a faint Boston accent. "And you've published some of his work in parapsychology?"

"Yes," Fall answered. "He likes to keep track of psychic research over here. That's why he paid for my trip."

"Let's see if I've got this right." Morton put on a pair of steel-rimmed glasses to review the notes he had made. "You think that Edvard Hus is having you followed because Czech intelligence suspects you're working for the CIA, possibly in concert with Boone. And you think they might've set you up in case they want to compromise you."

Fall nodded.

"Okay." Morton studied his notes. "Tell me how you got involved with Boone and these people in Prague."

Fall described his 1969 trip to Prague and Russia, and his meetings with Lester Boone. There were two reasons for this second trip, he said: to learn about Czech parapsychology, and to track down rumors about Vladimir Kirov.

"Vladimir Kirov?" Morton asked. "That's the second time this week I've heard his name. What do you know about him?"

"Rumors mainly." Fall chose his words carefully. "Some people say he's the Soviets' leading parapsychologist. In Moscow, there were all kinds of stories about him: that he got the Soviet government interested in psychic research, that he's a KGB hero, that he's a double agent, even. A CIA man in Washington told me he'd won the Order of Lenin."

"And you're here looking for him?" Morton frowned. "That doesn't sound very smart."

"After seeing the change in Magyar today, I agree." Fall let Morton see his embarrassment. "I don't think the Czechs are going to lead me to Kirov now."

"They can't," Morton said gravely. "Kirov's been hauled back to Moscow. Seems he's in trouble with the KGB bosses. We've heard that from two sources here. You'd better check him off your program, because it looks like he won't be around for a while."

Stunned by the revelation, Fall did not answer.

"We've been tracking him," Morton continued, "ever since his meeting with Boone. The Agency's worried about them. Do you know what they talked about?"

"Just what Boone told me." Fall made a helpless gesture to cover the shock he felt at this news about Kirov. "He said Kirov's after military secrets, and uses parapsychology as a front to approach Westerners. They didn't trade any secrets or make any deals. I think Boone told me the truth about the meeting, though I wouldn't swear to it. I don't know him very well."

"Why's he so interested in parapsychology?" Morton asked. "You'd think he'd have better ways to spend his time."

"I'm not sure." Fall shrugged. "He's fascinated with the field certainly, but more than that, maybe he thinks he can make some kind of weapon using the power of mind over matter. Maybe he wants to build some kind of psychotronic gun. The Czechs are doing work that might develop into something like that. I've published some of it, in case you want to read it."

"I would be very interested in seeing it. Have you got any papers with you?"

"I've got some in my suitcase at the Alcron," Fall said apprehensively. "If no one's taken them. Hus might've had my rooms searched by now."

"Okay," Morton leaned forward with a look of concern. "You're sure you were followed here? Followed all the way from the hotel?"

"All the way. The guy kept ducking into doors, but he followed me down every alley and side street."

After a silence, Morton switched on an intercom. "Helen," he said to the woman in charge of the embassy's maintenance staff. "Do we have a room for a friend? He's a guest of the State Department."

"Oh, my!" she answered plaintively. "All we've got is the room with the cot. He isn't royalty?"

"He's young." Morton smiled at Fall. "The bed's hard, but he'll like the view."

Morton leaned back in his chair. "I think you'll feel better here. Hus can't bug your room, and we'll put him on notice that you're not to be tampered with."

The offer startled Fall. "Do you do this often?" he asked. "This is instant service!"

"Rarely." Morton lit a cigarette. "But there aren't many people with a story like yours. I've never heard of Hus or Magyar, and I don't know anything about their psychotronics, but let's stay on the safe side. How long are you going to be here?"

"Three or four days. I can tell you exactly after I call my other friends."

"Good." Morton smiled through the cigarette smoke. "Let me know what your plans are, and I'll start to check on Hus. Meanwhile, you can use that cot and make your calls downstairs. It's not fancy here, but the canteen serves real hamburgers. Bring your stuff from the Alcron, and let's meet here at eight in the morning. We should know more by then. And I'd appreciate seeing that stuff you published. It might help me understand Boone."

Morton led Fall to the guest room on the floor above. "They'll give you a pass downstairs to let you come and go," he said.

"I'd like to rest a while," Fall said with gratitude. "I really appreciate this."

Morton strode off down the corridor, and Fall looked around the room. It had two windows with views of the Malá Strana. Between the windows hung a photograph of Richard Nixon and a painting of Neil Armstrong stepping onto the moon. Suddenly discouraged, he stretched out on the cot. Now that Kirov was in Moscow, he thought, the trip had lost most of its purpose. And if he were followed by the Czech police, Latko and Kocek wouldn't want to see him. If Hus's surveillance continued, he would go back to the States as soon as he could.

His discouragement turned into depression. Finding Kirov seemed impossible now, and Magyar could not be trusted. This trip was beginning to seem like a waste of time and money.

Downstairs, Bill Morton dialed his assistant. They had a man in the embassy, he said, who might help them solve the mystery of Lester Boone. He gave the assistant Fall's description of Magyar and Hus. "Look at our files on Czech army intelligence," he said. "See if we've got anything on a project there with psychotronics. What a godsend if this guy's for real!"

The weapon maker had been a problem for the embassy staff. He always refused Agency protection abroad, and his trips to Czechoslovakia raised questions about his parapsychology work. Though Boone always checked in with Morton, the Agency wondered why he risked being compromised in Prague. His refusal to name his Czechoslovakian contacts added to the government's worries about him.

"Hurry on this," Morton said. "I'd like to know about Magyar and Hus by eight tomorrow morning."

Fall's room at the hotel had been searched. Two books he had left side by side had been separated, and an entire stack of research papers was upside down. A maid had done it, he guessed, but she hadn't been trained for this kind of work. He hoped this indicated his low priority with Czech intelligence.

Fall carried his suitcase to the lobby. At the check-out window, the woman recognized his name. There was a message, she said, handing him an envelope. It had been delivered a half-hour before. The message was from Magyar, asking Fall to phone him as soon as he could.

At eight o'clock the following morning, Fall met Morton in his office. The intelligence man looked weary. "No leads to Hus," he said. "There's nothing in our files. I wonder if he used an alias with you."

"I don't know," Fall said, handing Morton his message from Magyar. "What do you think I should do about this?"

Morton read the note. "I think you should call him," he said. "Tell him you're suspicious and scared. If you want, I'll listen in. Maybe I can figure him out."

"But this isn't Magyar's private number. If it's his office, they'll have us bugged."

"Good. We want them to know we're tracking this. That's your best protection."

"Okay," Fall said. "Let's make the call."

Morton dialed his assistant and asked him to ring Magyar's number. "Tape the conversation," he said. "And see if we can trace it."

A moment later, Magyar was on the line, sounding miles away. He seemed to be shouting. "Darwin, can you hear me? I tried to reach you at the Alcron!"

"I'm at the American Embassy," Fall said loudly. "I came here because I was followed. I thought that I might be arrested."

"Arrested!" Magyar's voice came close. "But that is crazy! Why did you think that?"

"Because of Hus, Edvard Hus. I don't trust the man."

"Darwin, I'm surprised! I promise you, there is nothing to fear. But look, I want you to meet another friend of mine, a Russian parapsychologist. He's read your catalogues. I have arranged a meeting at the Press Club for tonight. Ah, Darwin, this is absurd what you think about Hus!" Magyar sounded completely sincere. "Please believe me. You will laugh at this tomorrow. Will you come?"

"I'm sorry, Stefan," Fall said. "I don't want to be followed like some kind of spy. I'm going back to the States tomorrow."

"But Darwin, this is crazy! Please, you cannot leave. This man is very important to you. He knows about all the Soviet parapsychology work. It would be crazy for you to miss him."

"How does he know so much about Soviet parapsychology?" Fall asked suspiciously.

"He is an old friend of mine named Sergei Aitmatov. Darwin, don't be stupid. Hus and I will prove to you that you have not been followed."

Fall glanced at Morton, who was listening on another line. "Go," Morton whispered. "They know you have our protection."

"All right, Stefan," Fall said reluctantly. "What time do you want me there?"

Magyar gave him the time and place. "Promise you will be there?" he asked. "I know you will enjoy this."

Fall agreed and hung up the phone. "It sounds alright," Morton said with amusement. "He certainly wants you there. But he knows we were listening. I could tell they were monitoring the call. You're safe now that they know you're here." He paused. "One favor though. If we could photograph Magyar and Hus, it could help answer our questions about Boone."

"How can you do that?" Fall asked with apprehension.

"It won't be easy, but we have ways. It won't reflect on you since they know you're not CIA now. Not the way you're acting."

"Go ahead," Fall nodded. "If they're going to follow me, take all the pictures you can."

7 An attendant in a white linen jacket waited at the top of the stairs on the second floor of the Press Club. Saying in broken English that Magyar and his friends were about to arrive, he ushered Fall to a spacious room set up for a small reception. On the oak-paneled walls a picture of Marx hung next to large color photographs of Prague. Bottles were arranged on a portable bar: Stolichnaya vodka, a Czechoslovakian Pilsner, and wine from Soviet Georgia. It looked like a club for the privileged, judging from the quality of the liquor and the deference of the attendant.

"You like a drink?" the attendant asked.

"A vodka," Fall said, thankful for this chance to ease his nervousness. "What is this place used for?"

"Partees. How do you say—marriages! People come here to have a good time!" The man made an apologetic gesture for his English.

"Is Dr. Magyar a member?"

"A member? No. There are no *members*." He laid out dishes of caviar. "Everyone come here when they will be married!"

Fall surveyed the room. It was about twenty feet by thirty with a ceiling, also of oak, some twelve feet high. He pressed his foot into the deep red carpet. Except for the portrait of Marx, the room might belong to an exclusive club in London or New York. He went to a mirror and straightened his tie. Lack of sleep the past three nights had left him hollow-eyed. He finished the vodka and asked the attendant for another.

Magyar came into the room, his arms outstretched. "Darwin! I'm glad you got here early! Hus and my Russian friend will be here soon." He poured himself a glass of wine. "I'm glad we can talk alone. Your suspicions have upset me!"

Whether from the vodka or from Magyar's ebullience, Fall felt a sudden confidence. "But I *should have been* suspicious." He playfully grabbed Magyar's arm. "You know I was followed when I left the hotel. Hus thinks I'm here to get articles from your friends about the new regime. Now tell me—that's what happened."

"That is crazy!" Magyar looked hurt. "Hus will laugh when you tell him. I promise—we have nothing to do with state security. We don't work for the police, but the Army. Now, please, you must believe me." He pressed a finger to his lips. "But let's not talk about this with my friend. He is a fan of yours. He knows something about the Soviet work with psychic self-regulation."

This was the Magyar Fall remembered, ebullient and impatient, always promoting the cause of psychic research. Fall finished his second glass of vodka. As he did, Hus came into the room with Kirov.

Magyar introduced them. "Darwin Fall, this is Sergei Aitmatov. He has read your catalogues."

The Russian was pale and slightly withdrawn, a small figure next to Magyar and the dark, stocky Hus. He shook Fall's hand and turned to take a glass of wine from the attendant.

Fall felt an urge to laugh. Magyar, Hus, and he were part of a gigantic comedy reaching from America to the USSR. He laughed aloud as he thought of Atabet listening for spies in Olema. Hus watched him with apparent good humor while Kirov spread a piece of bread with caviar. Magyar forced a smile to cover his embarrassment. Fall put down his glass and wiped his face with a napkin. "I'm sorry," he said. "I don't do this very often. Don't ask me to explain it."

The Russian seemed distracted, but Magyar's rosy face turned crimson. "Edvard," he said, "he thinks you had him followed. I think he has been under pressure. Is that what you're laughing at, Darwin?"

"Not exactly," Fall answered, reaching for a third glass of vodka. "What's funny is that we're all so suspicious. Now, Hus, you did have me followed. They told me that at the embassy. But why? Why are we all so suspicious? Isn't that right, Aitmatov?" Fall asked, turning to the Russian. "We should laugh at these cold-war suspicions. Isn't it stupid that friends like Magyar and me should play these games of cops and robbers?"

Kirov shrugged. He looked almost invisible to Fall, as if his body were made of ectoplasm. Was he suffering from a blood deficiency?

"We are driven," Kirov said in a slow but excellent English. "Driven to do these things. We act like living machines."

His voice grew softer as he talked, yet his words had a strange penetration. Again Fall felt like laughing. The combination of depth and vulnerability in Aitmatov's manner seemed as humorous as Hus's game of cops and robbers.

But the Russian might think he was mocked, so Fall raised his glass in a toast. "To brotherhood!" he said. "And transparency!"

"And to your work," Kirov answered. "It interests me very much."

For the first time Kirov smiled. It was a faint but complex expression. The man was born to an unusual family, Fall could see—the charm in the curl of his lip must come from centuries of breeding. Was he descended from aristocrats?

There was silence as they drank. Fall imagined that the Russian enjoyed his challenge.

"So you have read his catalogues?" Magyar asked Kirov to break the silence.

"Just this one." Kirov pulled the Greenwich Press brochure— limp from much perusal—from a jacket pocket. "You can see I've studied this," he said to Fall. "I am a student of psychic research. An amateur, but faithful student."

Because the man's blue eyes had a slightly Oriental tilt, Fall wondered if some of his ancestors were Central Asians.

"Sergei dabbles in many things," said Hus. "But in only one of them well. He is an expert in hydroponics. You should see the cabbages he grows on his roof in Moscow!"

Kirov bowed in response. "Hus is jealous of my cabbages," he said with quiet irony. "And he knows that if he makes fun of them too much, he will not be invited to dinner. But here!" He opened the catalogue to the description of Fall's book. "Your study of 'supernormal physicality.' That is something our sports establishment would like to know about." He moved lightly on the balls of his feet, as if he were gesturing with his entire body. "But I am not certain I understand what you mean by 'supernormal.' Your study of stigmata, for example?"

"They are examples of our body's ability to manifest an ideal. Our cells conform to our passions, as mine are conforming to this vodka . . ."

"Aitmatov will be interested in your analysis," Magyar said, putting a solicitous hand on Fall's shoulder. "But first we should have something to eat."

Fall's confidence had turned to a sense of the grotesque. Magyar's big green eyes seemed to protrude from his head, and Hus looked like a gangster. The two Czechs formed a startling contrast to the elegant, evanescent Russian.

Kirov moved closer to Fall. "Is your study the only one of its kind? I don't know of anything like it in the Soviet Union."

The man came in layers, Fall thought—now he had a subtle but unmistakable radiance. "I don't know," he answered. "I've been at it twelve years and I'm only scratching the surface."

"He is modest," Magyar said to Kirov. "His study *is* unique. We are all waiting to see it. You must encourage him to publish it soon!"

Kirov held up the catalogue. "This cover," he said, "is it connected to your book?"

In the reproduction of Atabet's painting on the catalogue cover, a winter sun was rising through the hills of San Francisco. A chill ran up Fall's back. He had looked at it countless times before, but it had never occurred to him that the image might represent the central aspect of his theory. Suddenly the picture seemed alive. Its brightness was upsetting.

"This vodka!" Fall looked to Magyar. "Stefan, you're right, I think I'd better have something to eat." He stepped to the bar, steadying himself, and spread caviar on a biscuit. But the painting still turned in his mind, upsetting his concentration.

The Russian put the catalogue in his pocket, then placed his glass on the bar. Though Fall could not be certain, it seemed that the man had hypnotized him. He felt a rush of fear. The three were watching him now, and not one was reaching out to help.

"Now what were we saying?" Fall asked. "About that painting? Stefan, you've got me drunk!"

"I asked if there was a connection between the painting and

your book," Kirov said. "You had them side by side in a way that might suggest it."

"Is there a place I can sit down?" Fall reached for Magyar's shoulder. "I think I'm getting sick . . ."

The attendant's face showed concern and amusement. "Too much vodka," he said. "You must drink this coffee."

Though the room was still turning, Fall sat up to take the cup. "A taxi is coming," the man said. "Dr. Magyar will take you to your hotel."

A uniformed taxi driver came in from the street. Fall drank some coffee and got up unsteadily. Slipping into his overcoat, he walked out to the cab. Magyar and Hus got into the back seat with him.

"I should have warned you," Magyar said with a solicitous look. "Three glasses of vodka so fast when you are not used to it! Then *poof*!"

As the car moved away from the curb, Fall slid down in the seat and waited for the spinning to stop. If he did not hold a center, it would turn to nausea. When they reached the embassy, Hus got out and rang the bell. Magyar put a hand across Fall's chest. "Wait here until someone comes to the gate," he said.

A cold sweat covered Fall's lips, and he felt the afterglow of shock. "What happened to Aitmatov?" he murmured. "He's an interesting man."

"He stayed at the club," Magyar said distractedly. "We are going to have dinner there."

Hus came back to the cab. "Here," he said with disgust. "Let us help you inside to make sure you are not arrested. I hope you will trust me now." He and Magyar helped Fall to the gate. A Marine guard led him through a courtyard to the main door while the Czechs said good-bye and drove off.

The man on duty walked Fall up the stairs to his room. "Too much vodka?" he asked. "They apologized for the party."

Fall nodded apologetically and asked to see Bill Morton. "He won't be back until tomorrow," the man replied, "but I'll leave him a note."

Fall lay on the bed and focused on the ceiling. He felt a glow of relief, and saw an image of Atabet's painting. What had Aitmatov meant about its connection to his book? His brain would not respond, however, to a call upon it. Gradually, inexorably, he sank into a heavy sleep.

8 Sunlight streamed through a window as Fall rose from his bed. Bill Morton was calling from the hallway. Moving carefully, Fall stood to let him in. "I hear you tied one on last night." The intelligence man smiled broadly.

Apologizing for his appearance, Fall went into the bathroom. The face in the mirror was pale and splotchy. "Anything suspicious happen?" Morton asked from the bedroom. "They didn't roll you, did they?"

"What an evening!" Fall groaned. "But it didn't last long, I tell you. That vodka sneaked up on me fast. That Russian was a strange one, though, *real* strange. Christ! I can barely remember what we were talking about. I must've passed out cold."

"Did they try to find out much about you?"

"Their friend was interested in something I published. He seemed to be fascinated with it." Fall paused, remembering the way the Russian had pointed to the brochure cover. "He's a strange guy, that Aitmatov."

"What was his name? Did you say Aitmatov?"

"Yes. Do you know him?"

"No, but someone by that name left a message for you this morning. With a number."

"You're kidding! It must be him. Well, I'll be damned!"

"What was your impression of Magyar and Hus?" Morton stood in the bathroom door. "We haven't been able to trace them."

"I got drunk too fast to tell," Fall said, coming into the bedroom. "Maybe they're part of some occult underground group. Maybe Aitmatov's one of the members. I'm sorry, Morton." He shook his head ruefully. "Maybe I've been imagining things. They all seemed harmless last night."

"So you're not worried now about the KGB?"

"No, I don't think so. Magyar's probably working for Army intelligence with his psychotronics, just like he says. Aitmatov is probably part of his circle. And Hus? God, I don't know. He could be watching Magyar, but maybe he's part of their circle too. God knows, they've got to keep their mysticism hidden. The poor bastards, forced to sneak around like that."

"Did you talk about Lester Boone?"

"No. His name didn't come up. But everything happened so fast."

"Why don't you see what the Russian wants?" Morton said, moving to the door. "Then let me know what you're doing. I want to talk to you some more about Boone."

When Fall dialed the number Kirov had left, a man answered in

Czech, then switched to broken English. "Yes, there is an Ait-matov here," he said. "Will you wait, please?"

He came back on the line. "Are you there? Aitmatov is coming. Please wait." The Russian's voice came on. "Fall, are you there?" he asked softly.

"Sixty percent. I'm sorry about last night."

"We have a saying in Russian," Kirov's voice came closer. *"On svoy paren vdosku,* 'a trustworthy man can get drunk with his friends.' But I would like to see you today. There is more to talk about."

There was velvet in his voice, and urgency. "I'd like to," Fall said. "Is Magyar coming?"

"No. Let's talk alone. Is lunch good for you? I know a restaurant in the Malá Strana." They agreed on a time and the Russian gave him directions. As he hung up, Fall felt an unexpected excitement. There was something strangely attractive about this Aitmatov, a combination of intelligence and urgency that promised an interesting meeting.

Below the walls of Prague Castle stands the Malá Strana, a maze of buildings and crooked streets dating from the seventeenth century. Crossing the Charles Bridge into its labyrinth, Fall found the square that the Russian had described. In an alley above it he found the wooden sign: *deus est spiritus.* Above the words two figures faced a tiny tree growing from a well. Following Kirov's instructions, he continued up a shadowed passageway between buildings that looked like apartments. Another sign appeared: *Zlatá Studné,* Czech for "golden well." This was the restaurant he was looking for.

A waitress led him to a balcony from which diners looked out on the red-tiled roofs of the Malá Strana. Mr. Aitmatov would be here in a moment, she said. He had reserved this seat with a view.

Fall's curiosity about the Russian had grown. Was he carrying a message from Soviet dissidents? Did he belong to a religious underground? Or was he part of the loosely formed network that included Magyar and Boone? When he had held Atabet's painting in his outstretched hand, it was as if he was displaying a jewel, turning it slowly to show its various facets. Had the gesture been some kind of signal?

Several minutes passed while Fall's fantasies about the Russian faded into the city's golden vista. Then he saw him coming through the entrance to the balcony, dressed in a gray windbreaker jacket and slacks. He approached the table with the same anonymity that he had displayed the night before. The plainness of his manner and dress made a striking contrast with the richly textured voice on the phone.

Not until the waitress had taken their orders did the Russian look Fall in the face. When he did another contrast appeared. Up close, his blue eyes were remarkably iridescent, with an intensity that would be hard to forget. Fall guessed that he avoided eye contact with people he wanted to keep his distance from.

For a while they talked about the restaurant. The Russian liked its prospect overlooking the Moldau and the red rooftops of the Malá Strana. The name was charming, too, he said: "Golden Well" had an alchemical reference.

"What brings you to Prague?" Fall asked.

"A factory they're building here. I am a consulting engineer. It is boring work."

"Have you been to the States? Your English has an American inflection."

"Yes, America." Kirov smiled wistfully. "I don't have permission to go there. It is one of my sadnesses. You see, I chose my accent for the time I could. Learning English at our language institutes, one must choose the American or the British inflection."

"You have mastered it," Fall said. "You sound like you were born in California."

"I listened to tapes of Americans for hours," Kirov said, looking away toward the river. "But it has been a wasted effort. Someday, perhaps I will visit your country. I would like to see San Francisco and visit the Greenwich Press!" He looked Fall in the face. "But I have a confession to make. After looking through your catalogue I thought you might work for U.S. intelligence. I see I was mistaken."

The waitress brought them wine, and Kirov lifted his glass. "Let us dissolve our suspicions," he said. "After your performance last night I could see I was greatly mistaken."

"But what made you think that? My report on Soviet parapsychology?"

"No, your brochure. I imagined that its cover was a signal to someone here about your work. That cover—you know it contains a remarkable coincidence. Remarkable. It is almost identical to a mosaic hidden in a mosque near Samarkand. Did you know that?"

"No, I didn't. Jacob Atabet, the man who painted it, must've seen a reproduction of it."

"No," Kirov said. "It has *never* been photographed. The mosque was closed by the government in 1939, and no one had photographed it before then. I wondered if some Soviet dissident had taken a picture of it. Someone, perhaps, from a dissident Islamic group in Central Asia."

"But are you sure the two paintings are identical? When did you see the mosque last?"

"Many years ago. But one does not forget it. According to legend, it shows an important prophecy. Do you think that someone told Atabet about it?"

Aitmatov was like Gorski's Moscow friends, Fall thought, grasping for hidden connections. It was one of the bizarre effects of Soviet religious suppression. But ridiculing his suspicions would not help. "No," he said quietly. "It's impossible. Atabet did the painting on his own. But you know a curious thing? Last night, at the Press Club, there was a moment when I thought the painting showed the secret of my work."

"Are there words for the secret?" Kirov smiled.

"I really can't remember. But there seemed to be things I hadn't realized." He paused, startled by a sudden recognition. "There were Japanese faces looking into the sun. The sun in the painting looked like an atom bomb. But yes! It seemed for a moment that our research might undo the bomb. Finding the body's secret would begin to remove the threat of nuclear warfare!" For a moment they were silent while Fall searched for connections to this grandiose thought.

"Is there something in your work about atomic physics?" Kirov asked. "It is hard to see the connection."

"You read the catalogue. There's nothing about physics in it. No, it must've been the vodka."

"Your work might undo the bomb," Kirov murmured. "That's interesting. Because I was going to ask you a question that bothers me. In the description of your book, there is no mention of a world to support the transformed body you seek. Such a body, if I understand you, would have a new relation to time and space, a new power to ease the shock upon the world it inhabits. It would need the sort of secret space that certain mystics speak of."

"Secret space?"

"The Earth of Hurqalya. Have you heard the phrase?"

"No," Fall said. "What mystics use it?"

"It is an expression they use in the mosque where that mosaic is buried. It means the larger Earth that contains this planet, connecting us to the larger life of the universe. Only it can support the power of angels."

Suddenly and irrationally, it seemed to Fall that he had known this Russian for years. He seemed to remember their discussing this very subject . . . .

"Perhaps your thought last night was connected," Kirov said, "to a subconscious idea that in this larger Earth a balance can be made between our supernormal energies and their perverse expression through the Bomb."

Fall looked away from the table in an effort to grasp the thought. "A larger Earth?" he asked. "Do you mean something beyond the electromagnetic spectrum?"

"I mean something beyond all the spectra our science has named. It is the Earth we would grow into if our bodies developed in the way your book suggests. The Earth of Hurqalya is the wider, freer atmosphere such a body, such a life would require."

Before Fall could reply, the waitress brought them bowls of dumpling soup. "But maybe the day is too lovely for these difficult matters," Kirov said. "These dumplings are the best in Prague."

As they ate, Fall felt divided. Aitmatov seemed sophisticated about the interior life. He would like to tell him about his work with Atabet, but there might be dangers in such a disclosure, given the man's friendship with Magyar. "For the ancient Greeks," he said, "the body was in the soul. The Earth of Hurqalya sounds like soul in that conception."

"The Greek *psyche* was like the larger Earth," Kirov said without looking up. "But the Greek philosophers didn't have a way that was strong enough to enter Hurqalya directly."

"If it isn't *psyche* then, is it equivalent to the One, or Atman or Brahman? Is it our spiritual source?"

"I think you know the answer to that." Kirov carefully split a dumpling with a fork and spoon. "Our Source is everywhere, but transcends time and space. The larger Earth has extension, even more than this universe. And duration. It comes *from* the Source, like every moment and location."

Fall was startled by the Russian's grasp of these ideas. He must have studied philosophy for years or practiced some mystical path.

"But you might like to hear one of the prophecies concerning that mosaic." Kirov sat back from the table. "An old Iranian legend says that a sun would rise in the west. That was what the picture showed. And, the legend continued, there would be a way through which that backward rising sun could be brought to its true Orient. You have never heard that?"

Fall shook his head emphatically.

"You have never read it in a Sufi book? Neither you nor Atabet?"

"But Atabet's painting," Fall protested, "there must be dozens like it. All it shows is an ordinary sun rising through the hills of San Francisco."

"Then let me ask you this. Your experiment with Gorski. Did you know that *elefant* is the code name for the largest Soviet project in parapsychology?"

Sophisticated as he might be, Aitmatov was slightly paranoid, Fall thought, to make these bizarre connections. He felt a surge of sympathy for him. "I promise you I never knew that," he said. "And neither did Gorski. We talked for days about what the Soviet military might be doing, and he didn't know a thing."

"Well," the Russian whispered. "You see how suspicious one can get." A light perspiration had broken out along his upper lip, and he wiped it away with his napkin. "But here," he said, lifting his glass. "To your health. I see you are sipping today!"

On his way to the restaurant Fall had vowed to stay sober through this meeting. But he drank anyway. Aitmatov was wound tight, he thought, and maybe their drinking together would help ease his tension.

The waitress brought their entree. "You really seem to know your philosophy," Fall said. "Have you studied the ancient Greeks?"

"A little. It is one of my hobbies, like parapsychology, and like the American language. But look!" he said abruptly. "One reason I wanted to see you was this." He took his Greenwich Press catalogue from a jacket pocket and laid it between them. "I am fascinated by this Atabet. I would guess he's a gifted clairvoyant, that he is extremely vigorous for a man so sensitive, that he is passing through a spiritual crisis. Am I right?"

"You sound clairvoyant yourself! How do you see all that?"

Kirov pointed to the catalogue's worn cover. "This sun. It is breaking loose inside the world, like an atom bomb perhaps. He has painted it from experience. That is how I see his spiritual crisis, a crisis that has lasted for years. But the sun is contained by the strong composition of the work, the muscularity of it. That suggests his physical vigor. And these little buildings resemble living cells. The image comes from his clairvoyance, in this case, a clairvoyance turned to his own body."

Fall put down his fork. The accuracy of the Russian's analysis was amazing. Aitmatov had seen more about Atabet in the painting than he had.

"My work takes me to Central Asia," Kirov went on. "To places where people still study these things. Many people in the Soviet Union would be interested in Atabet."

Kirov sipped from his wine glass. For a moment he seemed distracted.

"It's impressive what you see in this painting," Fall said. "What do you know about bodily clairvoyance?"

"You are the one to tell me," Kirov said. "Atabet seems to be the master."

"It's hard to talk about him. His experience is very strange."

"It is embarrassing, I know," Kirov said with a look of understanding. "Our culture does not prepare us for these mysteries."

"Your understanding is remarkable!" Fall said. "I would like to tell you more about him."

"And I would like to hear. It is a privilege to learn about someone with his gifts."

"You see . . ." Fall hesitated. "His clairvoyance takes some crazy turns. Sometimes he sees with symbols, sometimes directly. When he sees into the body, his own or mine or yours, he might see animals or human faces. Or cells and organs as they look in a medical book. When it happens, it's not very pleasant. And to make matters worse, his seeing brings up powers." He paused. "They're harder to explain than his clairvoyance."

"It is amusing, isn't it?" Kirov smiled. "How hard it is to talk about these matters. But you must continue. The cat is struggling to get out of the bag!"

"It *is* struggling! You're right." Fall laughed, glancing around to see if anyone was listening. "The changes he goes through don't last very long. You might see a light around him or a change in the texture of his skin. There have even been times when he seemed to disappear! Disappear *physically*, for a split second, like he's passing to some other vibrancy." *siddhas*

"And how long has all this been happening?"

"He was born with these gifts, I think. But he's had to find a way to integrate them. We have a Tibetan friend who's helped, and my scholarly work." Fall paused. "And we think there might be people in Russia like us. That's the reason I've studied Soviet parapsychology."

"In that school in Central Asia," Kirov said quietly, "you would find support for your work. They say, for example, that there are degrees of translation into the larger Earth. At first, only part of the body crosses, the surface of the skin or the eyes or the brain. That is the reason, perhaps, why Atabet seems to disappear. It

→ *Gaia &*
how the soul 59
contains the body
the Earth of Hurqalya

takes many years to translate the body, even for a second. And there are different kinds of crossing over. Some cross only through perception, seeing into the Earth beyond, while others alter their elements completely. But this is not the place to talk. Unfortunately, someone is watching us."

Startled, Fall sat back.

"It's all right," Kirov said casually. "Please don't look around."

A woman in her forties, seated at an adjoining table, was listening to their conversation. "We will pay the bill," Kirov said, "and I will phone you when I find a safe place to meet. Can I reach you at the embassy?"

Fall nodded and signaled the waitress. Waiting for the bill, they finished their wine in silence. "When we meet next," Kirov stood, "I would like to hear about your work in detail. Then I will tell you how it compares to the understanding of that school in Central Asia. You will hear from me tonight."

They walked casually out of the restaurant and down the alley into the Malá Strana. No one followed them. "Until later then," Kirov said, disappearing into a crowd of passersby.

9 On the edge of Old Prague there was a house for KGB agents in which Kirov kept a special room. On his bed there, a newly pressed shirt and several European newspapers were laid out in the way he liked. These were the only personal favors the man in charge of the house could do for him, given Kirov's ascetic habits, but they were done with ritual care. For Kirov was a legend to his peers. His role in the KGB espionage triumph at Orly Field in 1963, and his survival of torture by the French police, brought him uncommon respect. Most KGB men agreed that the Orly Field coup would not have succeeded without his efforts. Kirov's work of recent years, moreover, had added stature to his reputation. Few other intelligence people had created a new field of espionage all their own. And yet, his special role in the Scientific and Technical Directorate placed him apart: no one else made an entire career of watching Western parapsychology and altered-states research, and his reports could not be easily assimilated into the KGB's normal channels of information gathering. For these reasons, he was free from the controls placed on most agents abroad. Though his superiors in Moscow had begun to question his erratic travels, they seldom queried

agents in the field about him. Consequently, no one in this house watched him closely enough to perceive his growing despair or suspect his thoughts of defection.

Kirov changed into the newly pressed shirt, then sat to meditate. Was it right to his inner eye, was it right before God, to seek his home in the West? Would Atabet and Fall accept him as a friend?

But meditation only heightened his conflict. For it showed him more clearly that his intuitions were right about these Americans. Jacob Atabet was the religious genius he had guessed, and his project with Fall was momentous. Everything Fall had said confirmed that. Kirov opened the Greenwich Press catalogue and read Fall's essay again. It revealed an understanding of the body's mysteries that could have come from Kirov's school. Reading it, he felt a new despair. His work for Soviet intelligence was leading him away from his vows, while Americans like Atabet and Fall developed the Way he had given his life to. The irony of it caused a pressure in him that was near the bursting point.

As often happened in crisis Kirov saw the mosque again, then an image of his grandfather's face. They had spent the night in the ancient retreat, and as the famous mosaic caught the rays of a worshipper's torch, he had been swept into ecstasy. In that blazing moment, more than twenty years before, he had vowed to join his grandfather's mystic vision to his father's Communist ideals. In the transformation of the State, the Earth of Hurqalya would blossom.

Kirov had reviewed the event for months, but understanding it brought little relief. For his despair about Russia didn't come from regrets about his past: his career had unfolded in a way to make him believe in a guardian angel. His position in Directorate T gave him power to protect his friends, and a place to encourage ideas that might enlarge the vision of the Soviet leadership. He wouldn't have that position without the Orly Field coup. Without his efforts, the Soviet Union wouldn't have discovered so many weaknesses in the NATO armed forces; it wouldn't have known where the United States placed its nuclear weapons in Europe; it wouldn't have broken all those American codes. The NATO losses he had helped to cause were "irreparable and incalculable" according to an American spokesman. Because of his success there was more chance for peace. That alone justified the path he had taken.

Still, his work seemed meaningless now. The intelligence he was gathering for Directorate T had become increasingly trivial.

More studies of parapsychology would not provide the vision his country needed.

He looked out the window. Only in the West was there freedom enough to pursue the insights he treasured. The discoveries that Atabet and Fall were making seemed impossible now in Russia. And these Americans needed him. They were destined, it seemed, to work together. By joining their separate perspectives they would open a way into the larger Earth.

A Russian guard sat by the telephone downstairs. Kirov asked him for a secure line, then phoned the American Embassy. A moment later he talked to Fall in English. "I must see you," he said. "This afternoon if possible. There is an emergency."

Fall hadn't expected the call so soon. "Are you all right?" he asked with alarm.

"I am fine," Kirov said calmly. "There is a café near the Charles Bridge. Can we meet there at four o'clock?"

Kirov gave him the address and handed the phone to the guard. "This is an important contact," he said in Russian. "He will give us something important."

In his room, Kirov gathered up his papers. One in particular would certify his authenticity to Western intelligence: the letter that had accompanied his Order of Lenin. Folding it into an inside jacket pocket, he remembered the secret ceremony . . .

"Vladimir Mironovich Kirov!" the Chairman of the KGB had intoned his name. "Another Kirov to distinguish the State! Another hero of this remarkable family!" The Chairman had praised his father's exploits, then he had talked for ten minutes more about Kirov's own sacrifice at Orly Field. Five other KGB people secretly received the same honor that day for the triumph, but none had been praised with such fervor. It had been a special vindication, Kirov remembered, for as he took the medal he had said the holiest prayer of his grandfather's school, had repeated it silently as he bowed to each KGB boss.

Then he remembered his imprisonment and torture at the hands of the French. His scars were a badge he would carry all his life. Crisscrossing his ankles and calves were sharp red ridges left by the tourniquet wires. No longer so visible, but more painful, were the scars on his groin and testicles, left there by electric prods the police had used to force his confession. Kirov had said the same prayer during the torture that he had repeated while receiving his medal. With both groups, he had silently retaken his vows.

But for twenty years he had worked to implement his vision,

and now it seemed more impossible than ever. The heads of the Party and government, the leading philosophers and scientists he knew, were no closer to understanding him. More and more it appeared that the Soviet Union would not open to its higher destiny. That an American should recreate his school's most sacred symbol—while finding a way into the Earth of Hurqalya—was the final indication that it was time to carry the vision abroad.

Walking toward the Charles Bridge, Fall felt a sadness for the Russian that deepened when Kirov appeared, affecting a jaunty savoir faire. The man was clearly in trouble.

They would go to a café where no one could hear them, Kirov said, for he had a confession to make. A confession and a proposal. When they reached their destination, Fall could see the American Embassy down the street.

Kirov gestured toward a table by the window. "Sit here," he said. "We will have a nice view of the river." He nodded toward a thin figure outside watching the restaurant intently.

When the waitress came, Kirov fixed his attention on her. Her solid, heavily lined face formed a stable point of reference. Defection was evil, he thought—evil and absurd. How could he turn on Baranov, who had protected him for twenty years, and Umarov, his beloved friend, and their comrades in Samarkand? All of them risked their lives to preserve the order's teaching. And how could he abandon his nation? With all its flaws, with all its suffering, it was still accomplishing much of its promise. As Fall ordered coffee, Kirov turned to see the man outside. If he were going to seek asylum in the American Embassy, this was the time to do it.

"You have a proposal?" Fall whispered.

"I have knowledge that will help your work. Some insights that will surprise you." In a low voice, Kirov started to describe the mosque near Samarkand. But as he did, he saw the horror his defection would cause. There would be reprisals and the mosque would be closed. Baranov and his friends would be in jeopardy.

As he talked, a second self began to form—a consciousness detached from the scene around them. Suddenly his true self was stationed in perfect clarity above this chain of events. A presence that contained his entire field of vision could see that the person talking now would retreat from this encounter.

The larger self in which Kirov's consciousness centered had formed a resolution. There would be no defection now, or ever. With all its problems, the Soviet Union had a stupendous destiny. The vows that had shaped his life would hold.

And then, as if in answer to this clear decision, a man from the

KGB safehouse came out of the crowd toward the window signaling that he had an important message.

He was in and out before the other diners noticed. The envelope he left on their table might have been dropped by a ghost.

Kirov was talking about the mystery schools of Central Asia, about the spread of the Zoroastrian religion into the great oases of Samarkand and Bukhara some two thousand years ago. But he also opened the envelope and scanned the note inside. It was from Baranov. He must return to Moscow, it said. There was a crisis that called for his presence, a "crisis of angels."

Kirov looked at Fall with composure. "You must think this is madness," he sighed. "But a most extraordinary thing has happened. I will have to phone you at the embassy. Will you forgive this rudeness?"

Then he had a daring idea. "Would you be willing to meet me in Moscow?" he asked. "I may have to go there today. I can arrange a room for you at the National Hotel. I will see that you get a room in front with a view of Red Square. We can meet there sometime next week."

"But why? You can't tell me what's happening?"

"No, I can't," Kirov whispered. "I am not sure myself. But there are things you can learn from me. I know about secret Soviet work in parapsychology. And more. Things are happening there that will help your work."

Alarmed and dismayed, Fall nodded. Kirov paid the waitress, and they went outside.

"I will send you a message at the embassy," Kirov said. "You must not be worried. I was going to invite you to Moscow anyway, but events have only speeded the invitation!" His intense blue eyes suddenly brightened. "I promise you an interesting time," he said, turning away among the passersby.

Walking toward the embassy, Fall felt a sudden excitement. Given his remarkable sophistication about the body's transformation, Aitmatov almost certainly belonged to a school with aims like his and Atabet's. Such a school, if it existed, might confirm and illumine their work.

And yet, the Russian's inconsistency disturbed him. Would the man follow through on his offer? And if he did, would it be safe to visit his school's retreat? Since travel to most Central Asian deserts was forbidden to foreigners, wouldn't they break Soviet law by visiting the secret mosque? As he went into the embassy, Fall decided to share his doubts with Morton.

10

In his room, Kirov packed his suitcase and wrote this message for Fall:

I will reserve rooms for you in the National Hotel, beginning tomorrow. You will enjoy the Moscow circus, especially the elephant. Perhaps we can travel to Novosibirsk to see your colleagues there. And to Samarkand to look for mosques.

Sergei Aitmatov.

The message was delivered to the American Embassy an hour later, and Fall reviewed it that afternoon with Morton. The intelligence man was puzzled. "The elephant?" he said. "That refers to your experiment with the Russian? I'm sorry, Fall, but this is way off my beat. I don't think I can help you."

Morton's check on Magyar and Hus had produced nothing beyond the information Fall had given him. "Aitmatov just sounds like someone eager to connect with Americans," he said. "Though he's more original than most. Inviting you to Central Asia's an unusual trick. Do you want to go?"

Fall was embarrassed by the trouble he had caused the embassy staff. "I don't know. Maybe he does have a school there. And Samarkand would be an adventure. It makes me nervous, though, that he can get a room so easily at a place like the National."

"That's no big deal," Morton said with a shrug. "But if you're nervous, I'll give you a letter to a friend at the embassy in Moscow. You can check with him if you like. And I'm sure he can get you permission to see his mosque. Tourists in Samarkand can go out to the desert. The only thing that worries me is Boone's involvement. We'd appreciate your telling us anything else you learn about his activities here. You're not going to see Magyar again?"

"I can't. His housekeeper said he's left town for a two-week vacation, but she doesn't know where. And I don't want to visit with Hus. Magyar must have orders to avoid me."

"What about your other friends, Latko and Kocek?"

"They're not answering, either. Maybe they think I'll get them into trouble."

"Could be. Your staying here at the embassy might have worried them. Hus must know we're checking on him and could've told the others. I'm sure Boone knows what he's doing, though. He's not about to give away items about his fighter planes, no matter how much he wants their psychotronics. But I'll be damned if I know why the State Department lets him come here all alone. Makes a lot of trouble for us."

Morton looked at his desk, searching for anything he might have overlooked. "When do you want to leave?" he said at last.

"The day after tomorrow. I have a ticket to Moscow on Aeroflot. When can I get that letter?"

Morton promised to write it in the morning and stood to shake Fall's hand. "Good luck," he said. "Keep an eye on that elephant."

A group of army officers sat in front of Kirov on the Aeroflot passenger plane, and seven KGB men sat behind him. There were few other people on this flight, and the seats beside him were empty. Relaxing into his seat, Kirov reread the note from Moscow.

In Baranov's code, "angels in crisis" meant that people in high places were having problems that required help. Which angels? Kirov asked himself. Members of the government's Committee for Science and Technology, for which Baranov worked? Was there debate about Baranov's proposal that an institute be formed to study the paranormal powers of the mind? Kirov checked his excitement as he weighed the possibility. If the Committee included supporters for the proposal, his and Baranov's ideas were gaining legitimacy in the highest government circles. Only approval by the Academy of Sciences could give their work more prestige. Kirov leaned back in his chair, eyes closed, to consider the consequences. If he and Baranov could find support in the Committee for Science and Technology, he might be close to leaving Directorate T. Then the KGB's dirty side might haunt him no longer, and his conscience might find some peace. For in these last few months, the cruelties of the secret police had disturbed him more and more.

He thought of the old Ukrainian woman, her square, defiant face in pain, her threadbare dress in shreds. In Prague the day before, the guardians of the State had mistaken her for a Ukrainian dissident. Two Russian advisers of the Czech police had supervised her interrogation, while a Czech bully read accusations against her. The woman was defiant, Kirov had told them, because she was protecting a relative. But the bullies had not believed him, in spite of his status and fame, and had beaten her while he watched.

Silently pleading for help, her square-jawed face resembled the faces of so many police victims in its combination of strength and fragility. The police had tortured thousands like her. Remembering the incident, he turned to the men in back. None, he thought, could succeed in a line of work that required human sympathy. Not one would he choose as a friend. He studied a thin, wiry figure who would not join the general conversation—the cruelest in the group, probably, and the most conscientious. Next to him sat the inevitable playboy, ostentatious in a blue tailored suit with a turtleneck sweater. Kirov visualized his unctuous approach to women, accompanied by hints of his KGB influence. Playboy and Puritan, two familiar types in the Secret Police—even in this passing glance he could see that they hated each other. And behind them, two squat figures gazed from their aisle seats at the military men in front: were they keeping track of the army, even on this transport plane? That was possible. He had known surveillance people, both men and women, who were incapable of any human exchange other than watching for hints of disobedience, people whose emotional range was reduced to a bare silent witness. In a two-second scan of the group, Kirov saw all this and remembered the Ukrainian woman. Had she sensed that he could help her?

He leaned back to compose himself. It would take all his strength to ward off these memories and feelings, for his conscience had grown relentless. Yet he must keep it in perspective. If angels were in crisis, a more profound conscience might be calling, one that saw past this moment in history, one finally that would redeem his paradoxical work.

Then he thought of his friends in the mosque. An image of the Well of Light renewed him. He could smell the desert and hear the names of God. The holy chant, sung there for a thousand years, was ringing in his ears. Knowing that he could protect the ancient center consoled him for the uncertainties that tormented him now.

Two hours later, Kirov crossed a narrow landing strip at an airport outside Moscow. In Prague the day had been brilliant, but here it was overcast. Swirls of dust blew up between the planes, and the hills to the west were covered with leafless birch trees. Pulling up his coat collar, he bent into the wind. The place looked uglier than ever, its hangars and maintenance shops sagging, its runways littered with junk. It was a startling contrast to the airports of Europe.

A man stood by the runway, waiting with a car. In a moment Kirov would be under permanent watch by the men of the KGB Center. Coming into Moscow like this, he thought, was like a soul's descent to the ordinary earth from the world of Hurqalya. Now he was bound by a smaller horizon. But the thought did not upset him. His decision was permanent, his course set. He would live this circumscribed life with the fullness he had learned from his teachers.

11 The State Committee for Science and Technology works with the Soviet Academy of Sciences to guide scientific research and development in the Soviet Union. Its analysts and translators track foreign science with a thoroughness few other countries can match. Its planners help guide the government and Party in nearly all their science spending. Its departments and advisory groups deliver opinions to its ruling Collegium that help shape the nation's five-year plans. No other group save the Academy of Sciences has more influence on scientific opinion within the USSR.

Within this influential body worked Georgi Baranov, Kirov's closest friend and ally in the government. The son of a Russian father and Uzbek mother, Baranov had been raised in Tashkent and trained to the Way of Hurqalya before Kirov was born by Kirov's grandfather, Ali Shirazi. Believing that the insights of their school had significance for evolutionary theory, he had studied biology, earning a doctorate at Moscow University in 1933. From 1934 until the war, he translated papers in embryology and genetics from English and French into Russian, gaining a reputation as an able interpreter of scientific developments abroad. During the war he helped administer a medical-supply factory, but resumed his studies of foreign work in 1946. In 1962 he joined the Committee for Science and Technology, where his knowledge of developments around the world informed the government's thinking about its scientific priorities. In all these positions, Baranov had worked patiently to promote the synthesis of science and spiritual illumination he had inherited from Ali Shirazi.

Except for the war years, Baranov had gone to Tashkent every spring to renew his spiritual practice. For more than forty years, he had returned to the desert mosque, performed the *zikhr*, and practiced silence in the Well of Light. During one of his retreats before the war, Ali Shirazi had made him the formal guardian of his grandson. The charge had been sealed with a vow: Baranov would bring young Volodya into the Soviet elite to promote the

Way of Hurqalya and protect their secret school. When Kirov came to Moscow in 1955, Baranov provided the connections that led to his present position in the Scientific and Technical Directorate of the KGB.

Sixty-four years old now, Baranov was well regarded by his government colleagues. His portly physique, the slight stoop of his shoulders, the heavily dimpled face with its kind and curious expression fit a Russian stereotype of the learned and well-loved professor. He sat behind his desk, his eyes magnified by thick horn-rimmed glasses.

"Your grandfather predicted it, Volodya," he said with a husky voice. "We have become the two leading experts, and the Academy has turned to us. Its operating chief, Ivan Strelnikov himself, will name you chairman of this unprecedented commission. It is the opening we have worked for all these years, the greatest chance we've had to win acceptance of our ideas."

He pushed a folder toward Kirov. "This describes the government mandate for the Academy study you will head. Last August, the two cosmonauts pictured here saw an apparition during a Soyuz flight and lost control of their capsule. The event has alarmed certain members of the Committee for Science and Technology, because their investigation cannot account for the cosmonauts' breakdown or the panic that happened in ground control, a panic that led to the capsule's crash. There are features of this, Volodya, that defy all ordinary explanations. As the government's leading expert in parapsychology and altered states of mind, you will be asked to provide new explanations for the behavior of everyone involved."

Kirov studied the cosmonauts' faces. Both were muscular, impassive-looking men in their thirties. "Boris Marichuk, the dark-complexioned one, was part Uzbek," Baranov continued. "He saw the apparitions first. According to mission control, he saw them almost continuously, until his struggle caused their crash. The other man, Doroshenko, could not calm him down."

"How long did the episode last?" Kirov asked, holding the photos to the light.

"About three hours, off and on. The summary gives the times exactly."

"And we have tapes?"

Baranov switched on a tape recorder. After a moment of static, a voice came on. "It is trying to tell me something!" Marichuk's falsetto crackled through the static. "Listen—it is trying to speak!" Then a second voice could be heard, trying to reassure him.

"This happened about an hour after Marichuk first saw the thing." Baranov stopped the tape. "Ground control begins to question him for more details."

"What color is it?" an angry voice shouted. "Marichuk, can you hear me? Tell us what *color* it is?"

After some static and metallic banging, Marichuk's voice was audible in the distance, sounding like a scolded child. "Green, emerald-green . . ." His words trailed off. "Now it has no color."

"Marichuk, do you hear us? Now, listen! Tell us what color it is. Or what it looks like. Does it have a shape?" Ground control was pleading. "Please describe its shape. Tell us what it looks like!"

"It doesn't have a color now." Marichuk was in pain.

"And its shape, what is its shape?"

"Now I am inside it . . ."

"This is Doroshenko." The second cosmonaut's voice came on. "He has gotten sick again. When he tries to describe it, he gets dizzy."

"This sequence is repeated several times." Baranov switched off the tape. "Ground control asks him about its shape, color, size, position, and he gets sick."

"Let it play some more." Kirov closed his eyes. "How long did the questioning last?"

"You'll have to the read the summaries, but I think they questioned him for over an hour. He never gave them a consistent description."

The tape was filled with electronic whining. "It has more than three dimensions," Marichuk's voice was barely audible. "Sometimes it is very close. *Very close*. Then far away. But I know we are inside it."

"He is in agony!" Kirov whispered.

"It is close and far," Marichuk's voice crackled. "But it has more than three dimensions . . ."

"That was all he ever said about it." Baranov stopped the tape. "That sometimes it was emerald-green, but usually had no color. That it had more than three dimensions, and that it seemed both far and near."

"And he always got sick when he tried to describe it."

"Until there was nothing to vomit. The space-agency people say he was throwing up blood."

"The Earth of Hurqalya." Kirov wrote the phrase on an envelope and passed it across Baranov's desk. "I think he saw something that lived there," he whispered. "You said angels were involved."

Baranov nodded, turning by reflex to see that his office door was closed.

"And Doroshenko?" Kirov asked. "How did he describe it?"

"He said it was a silver saucer, and gave its location precisely. One can see that he read science fiction."

"Familiar categories help prevent vertigo," Kirov said with a nod. "It is amazing that Marichuk held out for his perceptions so bravely."

"The ground control people were relieved by Doroshenko's description, even though it sounded like a flying saucer! The idea of an emerald labyrinth that seemed both far and near upset them." Baranov turned on the tape, and they listened to the second cosmonaut trying to soothe his comrade. In the background something like a hammer was banging.

Kirov imagined the cosmonaut floating in zero gravity as he struggled with his vision. Then shouts came from mission control. Terror was breaking loose at both ends of the radio transmission. Baranov stopped the tape and replayed the shouting between capsule and ground. "We have not taught our people that the planet is incomplete," he said. "Or that a larger earth contains it. Now everyone begins to panic. This sounds like madness! There is an investigation to discover why mission headquarters lost control like this. It has never happened before."

"It wants us to fly through that hole!" Marichuk was screaming. "Can't you see it? It wants us to fly through that hole!"

There were sounds of the two men struggling.

"That hole in front of us!" Marichuk's distant voice cried. "Just ahead. The thing is talking now, embracing me! It wants to take us through that hole!"

"We are going down," Doroshenko shouted to the ground. "Can't you control it? He turned on our retrograde rockets..."

His voice trailed off into static, and Baranov turned off the tape. "Here they began an uncontrolled descent," he said. "There were no more voices after this. The capsule exploded a minute later when it hit the atmosphere."

They sat in silence, shaken by the horror of it. Kirov picked up the space pilots' pictures. Neither seemed a likely candidate for encounters with extranormal entities. "He called it a 'a gate.' He wanted to fly through 'a gate,'" he whispered. "They seemed like simple men. Marichuk especially. He never tried to fake a description of it. What do you think, Georgi? Can you remember anything like this? In all our studies of UFOs, no one has stayed so close to one so long without describing it in ordinary language."

In the spell of the tape Kirov had glimpsed the apparition. Its opening to extra dimensions, the sense that it would embrace you, its command to fly through an opening into some other space, were all things he had encountered during his initiation to the Way of Hurqalya. "But why? Why?" he whispered, studying the cosmonauts' faces. "How long had they been in orbit?"

"Seven days, but others have been up longer. We are certain they weren't poisoned or drugged. Neither had a history of mental instability. Marichuk, in fact, had been up before."

"Has either one had hallucinogens?"

"Neither of them. I checked that carefully. The Committee has made certain that no one in mission headquarters is covering up. *Neither of them took any drug.* Both of them, however, had some training in meditation from our Indian doctor. Just like Tereshkova."

Valentina Tereshkova, the first woman in space, had suffered a nervous breakdown after the flight of *Vostok 6* in 1963. Like her, Marichuk and Doroshenko had trained with an Indian yogi. "The panic in ground control is amazing," Kirov said. "I will enjoy our doctors' attempts to explain it."

"Strelnikov is looking for other explanations," Baranov said, glancing at a picture of the famous scientist hanging by his desk. "And that is where our assignment begins. You and I have asked for this, my friend. We are the first ones he has turned to. Already he is trying to explain it away. He even asked me if the Americans could have done it! He asked me to ask you: could the Americans trigger such a panic?"

"Impossible. Not one chance in a million. No one could harness such forces."

"But your network, your Texas millionaire and his German friends? You think there is nothing there?"

"They are dabbling. Not one of them has made the kind of breakthroughs we hear rumors about. I have met them face to face. We have looked at their work from every angle. No one in the West could deliberately cause an episode like this—in Boone's Red Lab or anywhere else."

"But Boone's experiment with his Witch's Cradles and our satellites? Directorate T believes they had two successes."

"Because our two satellites broke down when Boone tried his experiments doesn't prove that his people caused it. Even if they did, the phenomena involved in this incident are of another order entirely. There is no comparison. Psychokinesis can only disrupt *extremely* delicate instruments—in satellites, perhaps, in certain computers, on a few radar screens. And perhaps you can have an effect telepathically on some people at a distance. But it is absurd to think that Lester Boone or anyone else could produce an apparition like Marichuk's or a panic in ground control."

Baranov settled back in his chair. Kirov's judgment confirmed his own intuition that psychic warfare was mainly the stuff of science fiction. "Then it must come from the fishermen," he said, pointing toward the sky. "And our cosmonauts went for the bait."

"They *saw* the bait, but couldn't be hooked." Kirov felt a sudden guilt. "Georgi, I have a confession. In Prague, when your note arrived, I thought of defection."

"I sensed it, as you know." Baranov's face filled with sadness. "This is a tenuous effort. But we are summoned to it—how many times has it been? And now we are called through our cosmonauts. If they did not take the bait, we must."

Realizing that Kirov might defect, Baranov had prepared himself. But his friend's admission pained him deeply. Losing his closest ally would jeopardize his lifelong work to educate the Soviet leadership to these mysteries. "You must never defect," he whispered, holding the younger Russian's gaze. "It would betray every friend of our work, and all our efforts through these twenty years. You know what damage it would do." He pointed to the ceiling. "The fact that all this has happened shows us that forces are helping. Something is calling you back, Volodya, *calling you back to your vows*."

Kirov returned his friend's look, letting him see the shame he felt. The opening these events in space represented deepened the horror of his near-defection. Too many of his fellows lost heart, forgetting their country's resilience. Too many of them could not see that their dreams could be realized here, in spite of all the difficulties, if only they worked to achieve them. When things were most hopeless, it seemed something always appeared to support him—in this case, a power greater than any difficulty. After a long silence, he looked down at the cosmonauts' pictures. "I take it there is more than this crash."

"The capsule crash is only half of the story," said Baranov. "Alexander Rozhnov has had a vision too! That is why the Committee of Science and Technology has asked the Academy for an investigative commission. Only Rozhnov, as Committee chairman, has enough influence to cause such an amazing request. Only he could involve Strelnikov in this."

Baranov opened a folder. "This report," he said, "contains a summary of Rozhnov's background. He described the experience to me. As you will see, it happened here in Moscow, in his apartment on Alexei Tolstoi Street. And it has happened more than once."

"Is he interested in esoteric matters?"

"He has flirted with methods of self-regulation. Techniques to control his heartbeat and breathing, but nothing more exotic than that. I wouldn't call him an adept."

Kirov scanned Baranov's report. "May I talk to him?" he asked.

"I am trying to arrange it before our meeting with Strelnikov tomorrow. He's desperate to understand what happened. His doctors have been no help. Again, no poisoning, no drugs, no instability. Just, poof! The thing appears, in the middle of Moscow this time!"

"He is an anthropologist and has studied the mountain people of Georgia. He must have studied their shamanism."

"Perhaps. But there is no evidence that he ever practiced their rituals. His most famous work was in linguistics. He has discovered ten or fifteen languages among the people of the Caucasus."

"And you are sure he is the one who called for the commission."

"I am absolutely certain. The Academy of Sciences has never been called upon like this to study the apparitions of cosmonauts and their connection to the mind's further reaches. And to think that Strelnikov himself will supervise it! The investigation could cause a sensation."

"It could lead to the openings we want," Kirov whispered. "Or to their ridicule. Strelnikov and his colleagues could use this to debunk all the things we seek. This is the greatest challenge we've faced."

Baranov nodded gravely. "But I think we are prepared." He paused, studying Kirov's face. "Volodya, let me ask you one more time. Are you absolutely certain that the Americans and Europeans have nothing to do with this? If they don't, we can be more certain of our course."

"Georgi, you must believe me. There is no special insight in Europe or America about such episodes. Our own backward country leads the world in its alertness to them. Nowhere else have UFO accounts been so carefully studied. Nowhere else is there a circle like ours. My grandfather knew more about these spaces than all the experts I have met in the West."

"And you are absolutely certain that nothing like this has happened to any of the American astronauts?"

"A few have glimpsed strange objects, technically UFOs. And a few have had mystical feelings. But nothing like this has happened. If it had, we would have heard about it. I cannot remember an incident like this in any Western report. To stay in contact for almost three hours as Marichuk did without reducing it to ordinary perceptions, or without blacking out, is amazing. It may be that a signal has reached us."

12 Since January 1964, the month of his release by the French police, Kirov had maintained a Moscow apartment in a three-story building on Udjinsky Pereulok, four blocks from the Kremlin. The yellow-brick building had been the home of Russian aristocrats in the nineteenth century and had been preserved for its historic interest, but was slated for demolition in 1980 by the Municipality of Moscow's city planners. Kirov's apartment was on the second floor, with an outside staircase that helped him keep his distance from the other occupants, most of whom were artists and widows of government bureaucrats. Its rooms faced a yard behind the building filled with maple trees that were losing their leaves this day in mid-October.

The apartment had a small kitchen, a bedroom with a single cot, and a spacious book-lined study. All three rooms were painted buttercup yellow like the building's exterior, but stains from leaking pipes ran down every wall. The place had a musty smell and seemed on the verge of losing its plaster to the joint erosion of water and age, but Kirov was grateful for its sanctuary. It was the one place besides his ancestral house in Tashkent and the mosque near Samarkand that felt like home, the one place in Moscow that carried something of the Light that gathered through his mystical practice. As he arranged the documents he had brought from Baranov on tables by his desk, he felt a gratitude. The stillness that had grown in these rooms through the years of his occupancy was as strong as ever. It would give him the peace and strength he needed in these next few weeks.

He unpacked his suitcase and opened the windows of all three rooms. Only the distant laughter of children playing in the yard behind the building broke the silence. It was fortunate, he thought, that this assignment permitted him to work here. The concentration he needed would be impossible in the offices of Directorate T.

He looked around his study. Two of the walls were lined with books from floor to ceiling, and on a table near his desk were arranged some twenty volumes that contained his reports to the KGB on the esoteric matters his new assignment would investigate. This room would be more useful than all the libraries in Moscow, for it contained the largest collection of material on the paranormal outside of his friend Umarov's library in Tashkent.

Kirov opened a study of UFOs sponsored by the Scientific and Technical Directorate of the KGB. It was the most elaborate and sophisticated study of its kind, including several hundred interviews with Soviets who claimed they had encountered entities from outer space. He reviewed its contents, looking for sections that would strengthen his report. In the clumsy language of parapsychology, several passages described the ancient teaching of his school about the ways of "crossing over." The subtle language of Ali Shirazi had been translated into engineering terms and phrases from Soviet psychology in a manner that made Kirov smile.

> There is a belief [one read] among certain Sufi, Zoroastrian, and Iranian mystery schools that the body of the believer may transport itself through space, change its shape and size, pass through solid objects, and enter a larger sphere of life around our planet. This superstitious belief can be seen as a prefiguration of certain psychotronic effects in which mental contents are attached to the microwave portion of the electromagnetic spectrum. The belief of certain Sufis that one can cross a boundary (*barzakh*) into other planes of life anticipates modern research with "virtual-state engineering"...

Kirov marked the page, then turned to another:

> Soviet citizens Boris Ivanovich Silver and Mikhail Georgivich Lumm, in the city of Bratsk, reported their sudden "lifting off" from the oil drum on which they worked and their hurtling through two "emerald cities." The two unfortunates claim that the Chinese people are secretly held in thrall by emanations from these enormous green structures, one of which "hovers some thousand meters from the ground like a giant spaceship!"

He thought of his grandfather's stories about Jabarsa and Jabalqa, the emerald cities of Persian mysticism that appeared to initiates in their ecstatic transports. Similar visions had appeared to these ignorant workers, as they had to Marichuk. This study revealed other accounts of glowing green cities embedded in UFO stories. The similarities between ancient and contemporary visions were sometimes amazing. He turned on the Marichuk tape. "The sky is all green," cried the cosmonaut. "But look! A giant ship! Coming down to take us on it!" For a moment there were cries from the ground, then Marichuk again, his voice more distant. "My head is going through it, Doroshenko! I am being swallowed!"

Kirov turned off the tape. There was no doubt about it: Marichuk had seen a labyrinth like the mystic Jabarsa. The cosmonaut's tortured vision was almost identical to traditional accounts. In an emerald city from the larger Earth you were swallowed up. Kirov shook his head with wonder...

On the day of the Tashkent earthquake in 1966, some of the survivors had seen the same kind of thing. A green light the size of a transport plane had hovered in the sky, and he had watched while some tried to explain it. It was a meteor, they said, or a Russian space device, or an angel from Allah Himself. Kirov had moved through the ruined streets, grateful for the fantastic luck that placed him in the neighborhood where the entity was most apparent. Despite the chaos and excitement, he knew that this might be the chance of his life to observe the responses of ordinary people to an encounter with supraphysical forces.

Some decided in the hours that followed that it had been a reflection of the sun. Many persisted in calling it a spaceship, and others a messenger from God. A few claimed it had spoken to them, telling them a new ship was coming soon to lift them from the city.

He remembered the light's disappearance. Like the folding of space in certain ecstasies the thing made a tunnel in the sky. If you fastened your attention on it you felt yourself sucked into its wake. Then the cry had gone up: *"The sky is turning green. Look at the emerald city!"*

The event left its marks on some. Two Uzbek farmers and their wives had shown him bruises on their faces, and a child had welts on his chest that resembled the Star and Crescent. He had been amazed to see how quickly bodies translated such a contact. It would be marvelous, he thought, if some Party worker had been imprinted with the Hammer and Sickle.

But for all its confusing effects, the visitation had prompted one coherent move toward understanding. This famous incident following the Tashkent earthquake had helped trigger the massive report before him. He slowly leafed through its pages, looking for other visions that resembled Marichuk's. Then he copied the items he had marked into a special folder.

When he was done, he turned to the file describing Alexander Rozhnov. Rozhnov was seventy-two and had suffered from stomach ulcers. He looked haggard in recent photographs, and Kirov guessed he had problems holding his own among the power brokers on the Committee for Science and Technology. Though he had turned to self-suggestion for help with his failing health, there was no evidence that he was interested in religious matters. According to the official biographical sketch that Baranov had placed in the folder, Rozhnov had not studied shamanism while working with the mountain people of Georgia.

According to Rozhnov's own account, the apparition had appeared in his dacha at Zukovka during a moment of deep fatigue as "a point of light dancing through the room." The thing had seemed enchanting in the twilight of an early autumn day, a diversion from his weariness, until it vanished. But two days later it had reappeared in his apartment on Alexei Tolstoi Street. Alarmed, he had drunk a glass of vodka—only to see it grow larger. For ten minutes he had watched "a humanoid shape made of pale fire" move around the room. Then, to Rozhnov's dismay, it appeared on the following day, lasting more than an hour, until a doctor came to his place with a bottle of tranquilizers. The episode had shaken him badly.

Kirov took two books from his shelves. One was a history of Islamic esotericism, with a section on the forms and powers of angels. The second was an unpublished study of his own, in which he had compared Islamic, Buddhist, and Christian angelic lore with UFO sightings, the hallucinations of psychotics, the visions of artists and prisoners, and a fantastic collection of other visitations. The Soviet Union ws a treasure trove of such experience. Most peoples of the USSR had mysticism in their blood, and religious suppression had not destroyed it. What was repressed would return, he had seen, even to cosmonauts and prominent bureaucrats. When he found passages that described visions like Rozhnov's, he copied them for his report. The ease with which he could find these correspondences showed how fertile this subject was, he planned to argue. The richness of these documents— some of which were sponsored by the KGB—showed that more research was needed. He and Baranov would try to convince Strelnikov that the Soviet Union led the world in its openness to the powers these visions suggested.

By four o'clock that afternoon, Kirov had finished his preliminary report. But his growing excitement needed tempering. It would be wise to review his course of action from another perspective.

Crossing to his bedroom, he found the Bukhara prayer rug his grandfather had given him. He unrolled it on his study floor and placed his meditation pillow on it. Sitting cross-legged, he gathered his attention in a long-practiced focus. A moment later he entered a trance. His physical surroundings disappeared. His excitement broadened to a peace that was filled with energy. Like his surroundings, his boundaries vanished . . .

Kirov didn't return to normal consciousness until it was six o'clock. In the depths of his trance, a year of anguished conflict had been lifted into healing perspective. When he opened his eyes his apartment shone as if he had been on a long retreat.

The esoteric adage said it best: all momentous programs had to seem right when you were both sober and drunk. His trance had been a form of drunkenness by this tested wisdom, and in it his new assignment seemed given by God. All his life had prepared him for these next few weeks.

Suddenly he felt an urge to see the Kremlin. He needed a walk after these seven hours of study and meditation, and it was a brilliant evening. Taking a jacket from his closet, he locked the apartment and went out to the street. Ten minutes later, he walked the tree-lined paths of the Alexander Garden below the Kremlin's high brick walls. A small crowd had gathered around the stone memorial that marked the tomb of the unknown soldier, and he hurried past it to the Troitsky Gate. Showing his KGB pass to the militia men on duty, he turned onto a walk that passed the modernistic façade of the Palace of Congresses. Down a path he could see tiny figures coming in for a Bolshoi performance. There was gaiety in the laughter of the crowd, a buoyancy in the air all around him. Lights sparkled in the buildings above, as if from a fairy castle. Suddenly he realized how much he loved this place.

For a moment it seemed that the world's physical and spiritual centers fused. The magic circle of the Kremlin mirrored the boundless center in his trance. The two centers were timelessly fixed, yet they reached everywhere. Did the men who lived and worked here ever sense it?

For half an hour he walked through the courts and gardens of the Kremlin, showing his pass to the occasional militiaman who questioned him. Gradually his exaltation gave way to a painful melancholy. For along with the promise here, there came a sense of cruelties beyond comprehension. This ancient monument was the receptacle of murderous dreams, of brutality and heroism, of a curse and an invincible blessing. Its stillness grew deeper as the sounds of nighttime traffic died, and he thought of the immensities in his nation's future. Its chances for spiritual adventure were as vast as its reach across the continents. He looked up to the sky and asked for strength to help it in the difficult days that were coming.

At 8:30 that night, Baranov called Kirov to his office in the headquarters of the Committee for Science and Technology. "Rozhnov is happy for this talk," he said. "I think he will tell us things that no one else has heard." His dimpled face aglow, Baranov looked like an oversized troll from a book of Russian fairy tales. Rarely had he been so excited.

They walked up a staircase to the bureaucrat's suite on the fifth floor, Baranov adjusting his necktie and smoothing his silver hair. Rozhnov was alone in his sparsely furnished office. He shook their hands gravely, poured them each a cognac, and offered them seats around a tiny fireplace. "I hear you are the leading expert," he said, smiling with a charm that Kirov had not expected. "I am glad we can counsel in private."

Sensing the old man's dignity, Kirov waited for him to lead the conversation. After a silence, Rozhnov gave a deep sigh. "I have heard the cosmonaut tape," he said. "At least I am in good company." He shook his head sadly at the tragic incident, then turned to Kirov with a crooked, engaging smile. His slender hands and face suggested an ascetic nature. He might have been a priest, Kirov thought.

"I have heard them, too," Kirov said. "It appears we are exploring a terra incognita."

"My doctors have proven that," Rozhnov said, looking into the fire. "Every one has a different diagnosis. One says it's fatigue. Another, that an ulcer has depleted my red-cell count, making me prone to visual illusions. Another says it's epilepsy. I think they all want to call the psychiatrists!"

In spite of his frail health, Rozhnov was a sturdy character, Kirov saw. None of the doctors had shaken his certainty.

"The thing I saw was like poor Marichuk's angel. It had an identity, a personality, more than some people I know. Does that make sense? It had substance. It had density. It had shape. And it was present on three separate occasions. The lady who cleans my apartment was there the third time and will tell you I was perfectly normal. She has told the doctors I had no fever, that I wasn't drunk, that I wasn't drugged. And yet they won't believe us!"

"Their business is sickness," Kirov ventured. "I've read your account and believe it is something outside the province of the doctors."

Rozhnov's watery eyes reflected the firelight. "Let me tell you what I saw," he said. "Each time the thing appeared, I felt that it wanted to communicate something. And each time it was more distinct. The last time, in my apartment on Alexei Tolstoi Street, it was as big as a man, burning with a pale fire as it moved around the room. I felt hypnotized by it, but had enough self-control to ask my cleaning lady if she saw it. She didn't, but said she felt something alien in the room. Then she broke down and sobbed. The incident frightened her so badly, poor woman, that she almost quit working for me."

"Was she upset by your reaction," Kirov asked, "or by the thing she felt?"

"Oh, the thing itself. She's grown used to my complaints! She kept crossing herself and asking it to leave the room, and yet she couldn't see it! If it happens again, I will lose her. Now she thinks my apartment is haunted!"

Rozhnov turned back to the fire, and the three men sat in silence. A presence had grown in the room, a concentrated stillness that made Kirov wonder if the old bureaucrat practiced meditation. "Yes," Rozhnov murmured, "the thing had personality and wanted to communicate. I would swear it was alive."

"Did you feel known by it?" Kirov asked. "Were you recognized?"

"Why, yes!" the old man exclaimed. "I sensed it was calling my name."

"And afterward, when the horror was gone, did the feeling of recognition persist?"

"Did it persist? I wouldn't put it quite that way. You see, I felt as if I recognized *myself* more deeply afterwards. The experience left me with a sense of something—of something more pervasive. Something deeper. As if there were more stuff here. More *being*. Do you see what I mean?"

Kirov nodded.

"Yes—more *dukh* or *dushe* or *bytiyo*. But those are poor words for it. There was more *being* here." Rozhnov gestured to suggest it pervaded the room. "It helped show me that. But why do you ask such a question?"

"Two old sayings from my grandfather. 'Angels are mirrors.' And 'What we are looking for is the thing that is looking.'"

"Where did your grandfather come from?" Rozhnov asked, gazing into his glass.

"From a village in Azerbaijan. He learned the first saying from *his* grandfather, who came from Persia. These things are very old."

"My family comes from country in Georgia near Iran. But I never heard those sayings."

"People only whisper them now. They are afraid of the doctors!"

Rozhnov glanced at Baranov, then looked back at Kirov as if they were suddenly old friends. "What else is there to know about these visitations?" he asked.

"There are Christian sects," Kirov said, "that speak in tongues, imitating the Pentecost, and Islamic saints who 'find the tongues of angels.' There are Siberian shamans who speak to the gods. Many of these people say that a world outside our normal understanding is trying to contact us, trying to communicate. And now all sorts of people who have seen apparitions are saying the same kind of thing. I have studied this for many years. It happened to Marichuk and it happened to you. Was there anything tangible that the apparition was trying to say?"

"There was something, but I will have to think about it. There was a sense of words, of language, but also of something deeper. Something did arise . . ." Rozhnov paused. "Something difficult. There were upsetting things, some too personal to tell you. I will try to sort them out."

"All three of us know how difficult it is to decipher jargons," Baranov interrupted. "I have that problem every day reading our scientific papers!"

"Ah, yes." Rozhnov smiled crookedly, his ascetic face relaxing. "How I know! We spend so much energy protecting ourselves from the unexpected."

The idea seemed to strike a vein of humor. He and Baranov laughed out loud.

"I am willing to talk whenever you want," Kirov said. "There is nothing more fascinating to me, yet few people of intelligence are willing to explore these things. You must sense that in our academics."

"That is why the investigation you will head is important," Rozhnov said. "I am sure you realize that. No man in the Soviet Union influences scientific opinion more than Ivan Strelnikov. He will review every word of your report. He will study every incident, every argument. And everyone in the Praesidium of the Academy of Sciences will study his reaction. This is the most controversial commission to be formed in years. You have a delicate mission, my friends. If you make a convincing case, the Academy will have to study these mysteries in depth."

For an instant, Baranov's eyes grew larger behind their heavy lenses. "But one commission's report will not change many minds," he protested. "Strelnikov will not be enthusiastic about our proposals."

"Even his mild approval will sway the Academy," Rozhnov said quietly. "The questions the capsule crash raises are already burning in our people. Our nation, I think, has come to a turning point. People everywhere are asking the kinds of questions the Committee for Science and Technology put to the Academy. We did not make our request on a whim."

"How many members of the Committee are concerned?" Kirov asked.

"I cannot give you the exact count." The old man closed his eyes. "But many of them wonder about the military's flirtation with psychotronics and suggestion at a distance. They know about Project Elefant. They see the spread of spiritual healing to clinics everywhere, the yoga training for athletes and cosmonauts, the esoteric groups that practice meditation. Certain members of the Committee want to know whether these things are healthy or dangerous, whether they indicate social breakdown or an advance our people are making." He paused. "Let me put it this way. There are enough government people concerned to warrant this call for a full investigation of the crash and its implications for our nation. More ministers than you think are involved. But perhaps that's enough for tonight. You have to see the formidable doctor Strelnikov tomorrow."

The three men stood and walked to the door. "Kirov, I want to see you again." Rozhnov smiled warmly. "You might have to save me from my doctors."

Kirov did not speak until they reached the building's entranceway. "Do you know much about his background?" he asked. "There is something about him I can't place, something he's holding back."

A cold wind was blowing. Baranov pulled up his overcoat collar. "What do you mean?" he asked, his voice barely audible over the passing traffic. "I felt he was completely straightforward."

"He was straightforward about his experience and the commission's importance." Kirov took his friend's arm. "But there is a presence about him I hadn't expected, something priestlike. I wonder what he learned in the mountains of Georgia."

"You are imagining things, Volodya. He is a fine scientist and a very good person, someone we are lucky to have as Chairman of our Committee, but an initiate of the Mysteries he is not. Are you nervous about your meeting tomorrow?"

"Not yet, but I will be." They stopped at the curbside to park. "Tonight, let us call on our guardian angels. We will need all the help we can get."

13 Ivan Strelnikov's Moscow laboratory had created more than half the original designs for industrial lasers in the Soviet Union, and Strelnikov's theoretical work on lasers was known worldwide. But his influence on Soviet science was based as much upon his personality and his position as Chief Scientific Secretary of the Academy of Sciences as it was upon his scientific reputation. He was a student of many sciences, with degrees in chemistry and geology as well as physics, and his opinions on developing trends in science had been sought by journalists, scientists, and government officials for more than twenty years. He was a forceful speaker, a brilliant master of ceremonies—having memorized hundreds of Georgian toasts and the jokes of ethnic groups from all parts of the Soviet Union—and a prolific writer. As one of his colleagues had said in a famous remark, to combat Strelnikov in scientific debate was to fight against an army of opinion. Most people who knew him believed that he would have risen to the Politburo by now if he had chosen politics as his vocation.

It seemed inevitable to the Russian scientific community that he would be elected Chief Scientific Secretary, for the job had come to demand someone with his many skills. The centralized structure of Soviet science required the Academy to scout the frontiers of knowledge, to keep all science in review, and to work with the government's Committee on Science and Technology in assigning priorities. The Chief Scientific Secretary was a chief coordinator of the Academy's massive apparatus, the man through whom the lines of communication ran between the Academy's ruling Praesidium and the thousands of institutes, committees, and commissions that constituted the scientific bureaucracy. Until

Strelnikov was elected, many academicians had thought that the job was too big for one man. Now it was said that he was the only one who could do it.

At sixty-four, Strelnikov still had a muscular frame, conditioned by swimming and wrestling. Six feet tall, he was a formidable wrestling partner for the men in his sports club: some called him Ivan the Terrible. Among his fellow scientists, his imposing physical presence increased his dominance. It wasn't fair, some said, that he had so much brawn to go with his learning and wit. Yet most academicians were secretly proud of their Scientific Secretary. Like most Russians, they liked to identify with a genuine hero.

But Strelnikov did not feel like a hero this morning. The commission he would soon discuss had been proposed in spite of his objections. Once again, he would listen to arguments that parapsychology and the study of mysticism had a place in the Academy, that they were crucial to the future of science. But the form in which the arguments had arisen this time was stranger than usual. That he must supervise an investigation of two cosmonauts' hallucinations and their connection to paranormal phenomena in general dismayed him. What pressures in the government had caused this project to be born? Had Alexander Rozhnov, able scientist though he was, secretly fomented the discussions that had led to this extraordinary mandate? The old man had been ailing, and there were rumors that he suffered from hallucinations not unlike those of the men in space.

But there was a more basic reason for the mandate, Strelnikov thought. The repeated call for a new appreciation of the paranormal was an unfortunate legacy of the nation's religious past, a result of Russia's failure to pass through the Enlightenment of the seventeenth and eighteenth centuries. It was conceivable that the peoples of the Soviet Union hadn't sufficiently developed the disciplined habits of mind to support a scientific culture. As he sat in his spacious office on the Praesidium's second floor, he remembered an American Nobel laureate's remark that Soviet science had a looseness about it that permitted new beginnings, a remark made with good-natured mockery. The remark still nettled him. In response he had been forced to admit that Soviet science still didn't have the West's pervasive discipline. It was fortunate, he thought, that he hadn't been called upon to defend this commission on disembodied spirits!

Suddenly agitated, he started pacing. This commission just might cause a scandal like Project Elefant. He shuddered at the thought of the sagging barracks in Novosibirsk filled with military rejects trying to influence unsuspecting enemies through telepathy and microwave bombardments. Project Elefant was a national disgrace, a spectacle he had worked against for years. He would see that this commission didn't lead to anything remotely like it.

Crossing to his desk, he opened the file Rozhnov had sent him. At least Georgi Baranov had been assigned to the project. Having observed his work for several years, Strelnikov respected his intelligence. But Kirov was another story. Though Rozhnov had recommended him as the Soviet Union's leading specialist in the subjects the commission would study, it was disturbing to think that the man worked for the Secret Police. Commissions headed by KGB men wouldn't promote the Academy's reputation for scientific integrity.

Lost in these reflections, Strelnikov did not see his secretary come through the door. He started back in alarm when she spoke.

"Georgi Baranov and Vladimir Kirov are here," she said. "It's about the commission on the space capsule crash."

"Let them in," he said, buttoning the jacket of his dark gray suit. "No messages when they're in here."

When his two visitors entered, Strelnikov did not rise at once to greet them. Only after they had crossed the room did he stand to shake their hands.

Sensing Strelnikov's distaste for this meeting as soon as he came through the door, Baranov felt intimidated. Kirov, however, was inspirited by this first glimpse of the famous man. Up close, Strelnikov seemed younger than on television. His prominent cheekbones and glowing skin showed that he was in excellent shape, and his blue-gray eyes had a penetration and clarity Kirov had not expected. But most impressive and challenging to Kirov was the man's complexity. In this first instant of greeting he could see that it would be impossible to influence Strelnikov through debate. Only arguments or images that reached around his certainties would sway him. For in him Kirov saw two selves, one of which was ripe for an awareness wider, subtler and more complex than Strelnikov's practiced arguments. This emerging intelligence was not fully connected to the great man's public self.

"It seems a long way from the Praesidium to the problems we are here to discuss," Kirov began. "A long way from lasers to angels."

"Too long, perhaps," Strelnikov said evenly. "It seems late in the history of science to study disembodied entities."

Baranov checked an impulse to apologize for the proposed commission. "We don't understand the mandate completely," he said. "It seems the government is worried about the panic in mission headquarters during the incident. Their concern has spilled over to this proposal."

"And their concern had caused a worry here," said the Scientific Secretary. "Some members of the Praesidium are wondering about the government ministers who support this commission. Are they cracking under the pressures of their jobs?" A first hint of good humor softened his expression. "Has either of you sensed that?"

Baranov rolled his eyes as if to say yes, some of the ministers might indeed be cracking. "It wouldn't be the first time I sensed it," Kirov said, smiling with irony.

"Baranov," said the Scientific Secretary, "you and I have discussed parapsychology before. But what does your colleague think about it? Rozhnov says he is the leading expert."

"In such a tiny field," Kirov said, "it is easy to be the leading expert. I have studied the subject, though, for more than twenty years."

"But you are only thirty-eight, according to Rozhnov's account. You must have started early."

"In Tashkent and Samarkand, where I was raised, there are people who preserve the traditional wisdom about these things. I was lucky to study with them."

This Kirov, Strelnikov thought, had a remarkable self-possession. But there was something about the man he couldn't place, something veiled. It must come from his KGB work. "What things did you study?" he asked. "I am ignorant about parapsychology."

"The qualities of light and their relation to consciousness, a subject that goes back to the Zoroastrian faith. It is a subject that bears on our proposed commission."

Strelnikov was struck by Kirov's blue eyes. For one uncomfortable instant, it seemed that the man read his thoughts. "Which qualities of light?" he asked. "I don't understand what you mean."

"Think of laser light," Kirov said. "It is coherent, and doesn't disperse. Tradition says there is an inner light you can make through your own concentration that will cohere to penetrate stone. If it were directed toward certain images, it would create a replica of all existence, a mirror of the world, something like a hologram made with lasers. It is interesting to find such correspondences with our modern discoveries."

"Are you and Rozhnov in league?" Strelnikov raised an eyebrow. "He gave me a book—something Indian, I think—that described the same idea. Have you formed a cabal?"

"A cabal?" Kirov was surprised. "I didn't know he read such things. I met him for the first time last night."

"This had better not be a plot to influence me," Strelnikov said, looking at Baranov with mock suspicion. "That would not sit well in the Praesidium."

"Rozhnov is not involved," Kirov smiled. "But we think that the Academy should study the old traditions. That much we will warn you about in advance!"

"And I should warn you that I am skeptical about the old traditions," Strelnikov replied, leaning back in his chair. "I hope you will not propose another parapsychology institute. Every year we get such a proposal."

"Our proposals will come when the investigation of the capsule crash is done," Kirov said. "We may propose much more than a parapsychology institute if it turns out that the cosmonauts' apparitions were angels!"

Kirov was tougher than he looked, Strelnikov thought, remembering he had survived torture by the French police. "It says in your KGB file," he said, "that you have studied apparitions. Did you do it for Directorate T? I was surprised to learn that the Committee for State Security was interested in such matters."

"We have interviewed several hundred people who claimed to have seen apparitions, to find what features they shared. We found some striking similarities between their reports. You might want to look at the study. I have never been able to interest the Academy in it."

"What similarities did you find?" Strelnikov asked with amusement. "Can you give me some examples?"

"Many of these people said their apparitions wanted to communicate with them. Sometimes the things they saw embraced them. Nearly always there was reference to an extraordinary light, a light that brought joy and healing, and a few said it left marks on their bodies. Many said the experience had profoundly affected their lives. Reading their remarks, one feels the intensity and authenticity of these peoples' experience. In reviewing it yesterday, I was struck by similarities with the two cosmonauts' experience. There were similarities all the way through."

"Yes," Strelnikov murmured, taking off his glasses. "I would like to review your study. I have listened to the cosmonaut tapes."

"And there are other studies you should see." Baranov leaned toward the desk as if he were sharing a secret. "Kirov has worked on this subject for years."

The Scientific Secretary rubbed the bridge of his nose. "Do either of you know about Project Elefant?" he asked. "It deals with some of these questions."

"But it is not the kind of enterprise that leads to knowledge," Kirov said without hesitation. "It has nothing to do with science."

"How do you know about it?"

"In my work for Directorate T, Project Elefant falls within my field of intelligence gathering."

"Ah, yes. Of course." The Scientific Secretary sighed. "I keep forgetting that the Committee for State Security has an interest in these matters."

"Project Elefant is the military's work," Kirov said. "My superiors in Directorate T are skeptical about it, though they think it is useful as disinformation."

"But how does that help the Soviet Union?"

"Some people think it diverts American resources from more effective weapons."

"Do you believe that?" Strelnikov frowned. "Their military isn't so stupid!"

"You're right," Kirov said. "But some of our people look for rationalizations. The American military has never mounted a significant project in parapsychology, and there have never been more than ten or fifteen full-time parapsychologists in the entire United States. Project Elefant is not even useful as disinformation."

"I am relieved to hear your assessment. Most academicians think Project Elefant is a national disgrace, both morally and scientifically." Strelnikov paused. "But what do you think about the possibilities of psychic weapons? Can clairvoyance be harnessed for warfare?"

"It will never replace our reconnaissance satellites," Kirov said quietly. "Nor will psychokinesis take the place of bullets. Besides, nearly every study shows that hexing shortens your life. You may not know this, but the people at Project Elefant have an alarming rate of alcoholism and cancer. That should teach us something."

"So you feel that the paranormal can be used in healthier ways?" Strelnikov asked with a skeptical look.

"We think it deserves more study," Baranov said. "I think the government's call for this commission was a good decision."

"There shall be a commission, all right," Strelnikov said with a sigh. "The Academy couldn't refuse such a forceful mandate. But I must tell you both how sad I am about it. The cosmonauts' hallucinations, I believe, can be explained as a product of stress or poisoning. We haven't explored all the circumstances surrounding their mission. And in regard to the larger questions of the paranormal, well, I don't see how one commission can tell us anything fundamentally new. But I bow to the Committee for Science and Technology. It is staffed by able people and they want us to sponsor this. Kirov, you seem qualified for the job. Your position in the KGB will not help your cause among our academicians, but your work in the field and your Order of Lenin won't hurt." He took a file from his desk. "Here is a short description of the procedures you will follow. Four weeks from now, in mid-November, we will hold a first review. My staff will choose a committee that will look at your discoveries and proposals, and if it recommends further study, we will circulate your entire report in the Academy's Praesidium for its consideration. You can ask for no higher court of scientific appeal."

He stood. "Good luck, comrades. I hope to see you in good spirits four weeks from now. By then, perhaps, I too will have something to say about lasers and the inner light. I promise to read Rozhnov's book."

After his visitors had left, Strelnikov sat at his desk reflecting upon the exchange with Kirov. This was a complex character, he thought—a strange combination of modesty and self-assurance, of honesty and something concealed, who seemed to combine good sense with his interest in these fantastic subjects. But the commitment he felt in the man to the things they had just discussed disturbed him. Kirov was clearly an advocate of mystical studies and would make the best case he could for their inclusion in the Praesidium's agenda. In the weeks ahead, he would track Kirov's moves with care to make sure that his advocacy didn't embarrass the Academy.

After leaving Strelnikov's office, Baranov and Kirov parted, but at nine o'clock they met again for a walk along the Moscow River to discuss their meeting with the Scientific Secretary. A crescent moon cast a pale light on the water below, and the red-brick walls of the Kremlin rose above them.

"He has given us freedom for a month," Baranov said in a voice that other strollers could not hear. "But his review will be difficult. He will not favor our proposals."

"But I don't think he will actively oppose us," Kirov said. "He might be intrigued by our reports."

"You took a risk with your remarks about the inner light and lasers." Baranov turned toward Kirov, his heavy glasses reflecting the moonlight. "I thought you were rushing things."

"I knew we would not see him again for a while, and I wanted to leave something for his meditation. His work on lasers has prepared him for such thoughts."

They walked in silence, passing the golden domes of the Kremlin cathedrals. Most of the other strollers had turned off the promenade. "So what is our first step?" Baranov asked.

"I am taking a new ally to see Umarov and the Well of Light," Kirov said. "His name is Darwin Fall, and he has written a book he will contribute to our commission. Then I will visit Project Elefant and the Baikonur Cosmodrome. There are people in both places who will help us. Meanwhile, Georgi, I want you to assemble all the material we have gathered during these last twenty years—my studies, our summaries of European and American parapsychology, the studies of altered states and work on the biofield, the movies of Kulagina that show her telekinesis. When I get back from Central Asia, we will outline our proposals for an institute to study much more than parapsychology. And one more thing. Why did Rozhnov give Strelnikov that book? What's the old man up to?"

"Yes!" Baranov exclaimed. "That amazed me. Rozhnov didn't tell us he knew about such esoteric matters. Is he hiding something from us?"

"Try to find out." Kirov looked down at the moonlit river. "And let it be known discreetly that our project is under way. The study of the mind's further reaches will gain a new prestige when people hear about it. Never has the Academy given the subject such an imprimatur."

"It is a remarkable opportunity," Baranov whispered. "But there will be dangers. The stakes are higher now."

14 Two days after his last meeting with Kirov in Prague, Fall arrived at the National Hotel to occupy the room reserved in his name. It was on the third floor, facing Red Square and the Kremlin. Through swinging French doors he could see Lenin's tomb and St. Basil's Cathedral beyond it.

That night Fall walked around Red Square. On this moonlit

night the Kremlin buildings rose splendidly above their high brick walls. The city seemed more beautiful than ever. On Marx Prospekt down to the Kremlin Promenade, hundreds of people were strolling. Fall walked to the river, then around the Kremlin to St. Basil's. It gave him special satisfaction to make this perambulation of the whole Kremlin expanse. Because the beauty of this autumn night filled him with energy, he turned into Marx Prospekt and went down to the river again.

The promenade above the river was deserted, but as he stopped to admire the moonlit water, two men approached. One of them seemed familiar. Though his face was hidden between a large fur cap and an upturned overcoat collar, he walked with a gait Fall recognized.

"Sergei?" Fall ventured. "Aitmatov! It's me, Darwin Fall!"

Kirov turned to see him. "Why, Fall!" he said. "When did you get here?"

"Just a few hours ago. Isn't this amazing!"

"I will phone you," Kirov said. "Will you be at the hotel in the morning?"

"Yes." Fall hesitated. "I'll wait for your call. I talked to Atabet and he said that he had never heard of that mosque. I'll tell you about it tomorrow."

"Good. I will phone. Enjoy our magnificent city!" Kirov gestured toward the Kremlin, then walked off rapidly with Baranov.

Fall watched him walk away with a chilling recognition. This Aitmatov was not the same man he had met in Prague. His carriage, his accent, his manner had changed.

In the foreign currency bar, three Germans were talking quietly with two Japanese businessmen. They did not look at Fall when he sat near them. A blond waitress in her thirties came up, and he pointed toward a beer sign. "Heineken?" she asked, and he nodded. The barman, a dark, athletic-looking Georgian, looked at Fall with curiosity, then told the waitress he was an American.

Fall thought of Aitmatov. In spite of his friendly greeting, the Russian had been guarded. Had he changed his mind about their meeting here? Would he disappear like Magyar and his friends in Prague? A melancholy French song was playing on a phonograph, something he had heard here before. The record was worn out, its static more prominent than the music. Was the hotel too poor to replace it? He signaled his displeasure, but the barman only shrugged and pointed toward the ceiling as if the matter were in the hands of higher-ups.

As he finished the beer, he felt a sadness forming. Even here there was a sense of deprivation. That a leading hotel would hang on to worn, old records was a telltale sign of the country's poverty. Or else the barman was too timid to change it. So many Russians were afraid of their bosses! Things hadn't changed since 1969. There were reminders everywhere of Russia's social cowardice.

Absorbed in his thoughts, Fall did not see a redheaded man come up behind him. "What were you thinking?" the intruder asked. Grinning down at him was Nikolai Gorski. "What was it?" the large face insisted. "What was your thought!" Then he picked Fall up and hugged him.

They kissed on both cheeks. "What a surprise!" the Russian said with a laugh. "I came as soon as I got your message."

During Fall's visit three years before, Gorski had often tried to surprise a thought like this. It was part of his telepathy training. "You look different!" Fall exclaimed. "You've lost some weight."

"I get in shape for my new part. I play a very old man." As Gorski sat at the table, he drew in his cheeks to suggest an aged figure. "But what are you doing here?"

Fall described his meetings with Aitmatov, making sure the waitress could not overhear them.

"I've never heard of him," Gorski whispered, "in all my telepathy experiments, here or in Leningrad. His behavior sounds very strange."

Fall told him what Aitmatov had said about Project Elefant. "That is crazy!" Gorski rolled his eyes toward the ceiling. "He thought we were signaling Soviet dissidents? Maybe the man is not all right."

"I saw him tonight by accident, walking with another man along the river, and he seemed different than he was in Prague. But I'm sure he's not a kook. He knows Stefan Magyar. I met them together there. And he must have pull to get me a suite so easily. Maybe he's connected to some government ministry that deals with parapsychology."

"Maybe." Gorski shrugged. "But I've never heard of him or Project Elefant. I don't know who he is." He signaled the waitress for a glass of wine. "But tell me more about yourself. Your Atabet has fired my imagination!"

"You got my letters?"

"Both of them." Gorski nodded. "They are printed on my brain. But I must ask you, are they true? This Atabet has lived out your theories!"

"Our friendship is the greatest confirmation of my life. To have worked so long on these ideas, then find someone who embodies them . . ." Fall lowered his voice. "More has happened, Nikolai, than I said in my letters. I have seen him manifest the things we talked about! You remember our talks in '69 and all the theories I had. One year later I met a living proof."

"It is hard to believe," Gorski said, shaking his head with wonder. "How many know about him?"

"Just six of us. He refuses to bring in others."

Gorski glanced around the room. "But if he is so gifted and showing you so much," he whispered, "why are you over here? What makes you search for spiritual guidance in Russia?"

"Nikolai, don't ask me to be rational about this. I've had this obsession with Russia for years. Lately it's focused on Vladimir Kirov. You remember the rumors about him here in '69, the stories about his powers." Fall glanced at the German businessmen. "But there's more I'll tell you when we can talk more freely. Rumor has it that Kirov's in trouble now with the KGB bosses."

"I don't understand," Gorski said with a shrug. "We've tried to trace the rumors about him for the last three years with no success. We haven't found a thing. Darwin, Kirov may be a ghost."

"But now I'm glad I came!" Fall said to change the subject. "Now I get to see you! I'm eager to hear about your work. What've you been doing?"

"Very little lately." Gorski frowned. "For an amateur parapsychologist things are getting tighter. It is hard to experiment freely. Naumov too is having trouble. I feel a tightening all around, in our parapsychology group, in my theater. Vozneshensky and Yevtushenko are restricted, and the underground music groups. They're closing down, step by step. It is a reaction to the freedom of the sixties."

They were silent. "But you know," the Russian said at last, "my telepathy experiments never made an impression. The universities and Academy ignored them. Only a few government bureaucrats got interested, and our friends. There is nothing, really." His face filled with disgust. "It is all politics and technology, like we said before. Our two nations have put their faith in Fords and Volgas."

"But we shall keep the faith!" Fall raised his glass. "We proved that Moscow and America are closer than they think. You read my mind like a master!"

Gorski laughed, his expression brightening.

"You described the elephant," Fall said. "Its grainy texture, its rump. And the trunk—you called it a movable nose dropper.

That was best of all! And you described the chair I was sitting in exactly. We were all impressed."

"You see, the planet *is* a single consciousness!" Gorski raised his hands with delight. "Distance disappears like that!" He reached across the table to touch Fall's shoulder. "But someone's coming I want you to meet—a friend of mine, Avram Berg. I told him to come here."

Following Gorski's look, Fall turned to see a short, stocky, bearded figure rapidly crossing the room. He wore a brown leather jacket and jeans. "Nikolai! They would not let me in downstairs," he said in English. "You did not leave a message. The fool at the door tried to call the police!" His words had a throaty sound, as if they came directly from his chest. "The idiots! I had to flatten them!" With a mischievous smile he sat down between them and shook Fall's hand. "That is what we do to these idiots, Fall. We flatten them!"

"What do you expect?" Gorski remonstrated. "They do not let hippies in here. You must wear a necktie, or at least a shirt." He pointed to the bit of dirty undershirt that showed at the neck of Berg's jacket.

Berg glanced around the bar as if deciding how loud he could talk. His startling appearance was heightened, Fall thought, by a beard shaved away from his broad, high cheeks in a manner both devilish and cherubic.

"I told him about our experiment," Gorski said to Fall. "Avram is a TV producer and is interested in the field of hidden human reserves."

"But listen!" Berg touched Fall's arm. "These telepathic experiments should be shown on our television. I would like to film you and Nikolai this week. We can improve your results, and show it on TV to millions. Are you willing to do that?"

"Willing to go on Russian TV!" Fall felt himself leaning away. "Doing experiments in telepathy? Nikolai, is this on the level?"

"On the level?" Berg asked. "What is 'on the level'?"

"Are you serious?" Gorski frowned. "He wants to know if you mean what you say."

"*On the level*." Berg savored the words, passing his hand across the table. "Yes, I am on the level. Absolutely flat!" He giggled. "As level as the floor. Nothing is going to roll off me!"

"But I don't know how long I'll be here," Fall said cautiously. "When would this program happen?"

"I go to the authorities tomorrow." Berg was urgent now. "Nikolai, we have no time to spare. My chief wants an American on his show to demonstrate detente. I told him about your experiment with San Francisco, and he was *flattened*." He turned toward Fall with twinkling eyes. "You have to move when the bosses are interested, or you lose your chance. Can you do it?"

"Do what, exactly?" Fall was unconvinced. "Repeat our experiment?"

"Yes. But I will add Lozanov's methods. We will speed up Nikolai's responses with suggestology. I will do that part myself. Now look." He started to whisper. "Every bloody Russian has his version of the American Dream, and my chief's is to coproduce TV specials with your networks. I told him this would help. First we get you, then other Americans on programs here to talk about hidden reserves. We will do five or six of them—one on telepathy, one on spiritual healing, one on peak performance. . . ."

"Telepathy and spiritual healing!" Fall exclaimed. "They'd let you do that? Nikolai just told me things were tightening up."

"In some places." Berg tapped the table impatiently. "But loosening up in others. There are more Sufi, Gurdjieff, Zen, Cabala, Yoga groups than ever. Not to mention UFOs, lost continents, biofields, Kirlian photography, reincarnation, survival of bodily death." He waved his arms expansively. "Russia is a great ashram, but still without a vision. Who said it—'we live in the time between the old gods and the new'? Underneath what you see, Russia is like your California!"

Fall looked to Gorski. "Is that right?" he whispered. "That's what I thought in '69."

Gorski shrugged, showing both weariness and wonder. "If Russia is a great ashram," he said, "it is the strangest one the world has ever seen. It is buried deep, very deep, under the factories and five-year plans."

"But Kola," Berg whispered. "Every one of your friends is a Cabalist! Or a student of hidden reserves. Or he believes in the continent of Atlantis. If we have these TV shows, that will help! When American scholars get interested in something, that influences our academics, then more and more people with pull. We are all in this together." He pulled a worn paperback from a jacket pocket. "See this? Ken Kesey's book *One Flew Over the Cuckoo's Nest*. It is a bible for most of my friends. And why? Because our country—like yours—is an insane asylum! My friends all think they are McMurphy." With a huge sigh, he pulled a package of postcards from another pocket. "These are scenes of San Francisco. Your city is my American Dream." He looked at them one by one, then passed them along to Fall. "I have come to love your city. And to think that our missiles are pointed at it."

Berg's mobile emotions had turned to sadness. "I know a guy

who worked on one that was aimed at the Golden Gate Bridge. When I showed him this, he cried. He said that in a war *he could not destroy heaven*."

Fall watched him with amazement. Rarely had he seen so many moods cross a face so swiftly.

"To prevent this," Berg said, shaking the pictures, "we need more cooperative ventures. *Beginning with this TV show*. Will you do it?"

Gorski shook his head sadly. "Avram," he sighed, "we will do it when your chief calls. Until then, the thought of it will lift our hearts." He winked at Fall, as if to say he had heard other such proposals from his friend, then signaled the waitress for drinks.

"You doubt me," Berg said. "But why? I can make my own specials now! I can't get into trouble. I am not a dissident, not a criminal, not a spy. Fall, I am a neutrino—invisible to the hacks, weightless as far as they can see, with the ability to pass through walls. There are several of us, a whole cloud of neutrinos, carrying the same kind of message. You must have people like that in the States."

"There are thousands interested in things like this," Fall said. "But we don't have to hide it there, if that's what you mean by being invisible."

"Yes, you don't have to hide there." Berg seemed chastened by the thought. "You don't have to be neutrinos." There was silence as he stared at his postcards.

"Every Russian I know has an image of your country," he said. "Though we know it is an insane asylum, it seems like the best one on earth. For each of us it takes a different form. Misha wants an American wife, Vadim an American guitar for his band—and a big muff amplifier. Another wants a U.S. jeep because he saw one in a movie. Your country fills our fantasy."

"And now a series of TV specials?" Gorski frowned. "Do you think that will help detente?"

"Look!" Berg said with anger. "Both countries face their own crises. Here it is our demand for more freedoms and material things. Over there it is violence, drugs, and crime. But at the center is what? A lack of vision! A set of old-fashioned ideas! A spiritual hunger! Look. The old religions aren't filling the void. Not the churches, the synagogues, or mosques. We need a vision for the modern age." He pointed toward the ceiling. "A vision that includes both this world and *that*."

"You mean the bosses?" Gorski whispered, thinking Berg's finger pointed toward the omnipresent bug.

"Not the bosses," Berg said loudly. "I mean the worlds our

97

esoteric groups are looking for. The worlds that Socialism and science don't show us!"

The German businessmen had turned to see the source of this harangue, and the waitress approached with displeasure. "Shut up!" Gorski whispered. "You will get us into trouble."

"Give me glass of water, darling," Berg said to the waitress. "I entertain my American friend."

She studied his face for a moment, then smiled. He had won her instantly. "See how I flatten them?" Berg grinned. "Do not worry, Kola. Every Russian agrees with this, right up to Brezhnev himself!"

"Where do you get this term 'flatten'?" Fall asked. "I've never heard a Russian use it."

"From Scientology. I studied to be a Clear."

"Scientology!" Fall exclaimed. "Here in Russia! But that's not the way they use the term. To 'flatten' an emotion means to reduce its negative charge. You don't flatten a *person* like that waitress."

"*I* flatten them." Berg pounded his chest. "No matter what the Scientologists do. That waitress is *absolutely* flattened."

Fall and Gorski stared at one another, aware that they were getting drunk. But their intoxication came from more than alcohol. Fall had felt the same mood here before, the same exhilaration and fear. All things seemed possible when Russians and Americans conspired like this about their nations' futures. Suddenly the world lit up. But there were forces everywhere to thwart a man like Berg. "You have an audacious dream," Fall said at last. "I would like to help you fulfill it."

"Good!" Berg whispered as if they were sealing a pact. "I will call in the next few days. We have no extra time." He rose from the table, squeezed Gorski's shoulder, then crossed the bar as if bouncing on springs.

"Is he always like that?" Fall asked.

"Always," Gorski whispered. "Ever since I have known him. A new idea every day, and sometimes one actually happens. You will hear from him, though. No doubt about it."

"He's right about the American Dream," Fall said. "My friends in the U.S. Embassy said it was more alive here than it is in the States."

"Every human emotion invites its opposite," Gorski said, looking into his glass. "Enantiodromia—as an actor I know it well. If I play a murderer long enough, I want to be a saint. If I play a hard man, I want to be soft. If I play a soft man, I want to be hard. It is the same with nations, perhaps. Underneath the warheads, our peoples could love one another."

"Maybe detente will lead us there." Fall lifted his glass. "Let us drink to that."

For another hour they talked about the people Fall had met in 1969. Vladimir Raikov, a psychiatrist, continued his work on hypnotic regression to develop the powers of artists. Gennady Sergeyev studied psychokinesis. And Edward Naumov continued to proselytize for parapsychology and hidden reserves. But all were careful not to offend the authorities. Their caution inhibited their creativity, Gorski said wearily. Project Elefant and projects like it existed in another world, screened off from them by the military and the KGB.

Reluctantly they parted, Fall waving as Gorski descended the broad carpeted stairs to the lobby. The Russian turned and waved, then went out to the street, exhilarated. Seeing his American friend had filled him with the excitement of three years before. But as he walked toward the subway, hunched against the wind, he felt a vague disquiet. If Jacob Atabet was the force Fall described, if he and Fall were discovering so much about the body's powers, why would they chase rumors about a Soviet spy? What was missing in their experience? The discoveries Fall had described in his letters were not enough for them, it appeared, but Gorski didn't see how they would further them in Russia.

15 The following morning, Fall awoke to the sound of a woman's voice at his door, calling out, "Good morning! A message here!" Before he could answer, a uniformed maid came in, placed an envelope at his feet, and left. The manners of hotel personnel hadn't changed in these last three years, Fall thought. You were never safe from these intrusions.

Inside the envelope was a handwritten message:

Forgive my rudeness last night. I could not believe it was you! Will you let me buy you lunch? Can we meet at two o'clock, at the entrance to St. Basil's Cathedral? I have a surprise for you! Sergei Aitmatov.

Unlike the written English of most other Russians Fall knew, this note had no Cyrillic letters or inverted phrases. Such command of the language was added evidence that the man was no ordinary engineer. Fall wondered if he should talk to Gorski about the invitation, but his eagerness to see Aitmatov overcame his hesitation.

When they met near St. Basil's, Kirov's guarded manner of the night before was gone. Dressed in a khaki bush jacket and faded blue jeans, he looked more robust then he had in Prague. Visibly, his spirits were restored.

"Moscow is beautiful today!" Kirov said, gesturing toward the sunlit towers of the Kremlin. "On a day like this it is great to be a Russian!"

"Thanks for the California weather! Are you trying to convert me?"

"I am warming you up for a big surprise." Kirov slapped his arm. "But come! I have a restaurant where we can talk."

They walked rapidly across the cobblestone expanse of Red Square, past the GUM department store and onto Chernshevskogo Street, Kirov pointing out places of historic interest. After a few hundred yards, they turned up a narrow alley. Opening an unmarked door, Kirov led Fall inside. A man in a seedy blue suit led them to an alcove in an empty dining room.

"What kind of place is this?" Fall asked. "There wasn't any sign on the door."

"There are restaurants like this without signs. You have to know your way around." Kirov's slightly Oriental eyes filled with merriment. "But here is my surprise. We will go to Tashkent tomorrow. I have some business there, but time enough to see that mosque!"

"Can you get a ticket just like that?"

Kirov passed his palm across the table. "*Blat,*" he winked. "You must know the right people. We will fly there tomorrow and meet some members of that school I described. Then we will go out to the desert and see that mosaic."

A waiter laid out plates of sliced cucumbers, brown bread, and butter. "You eat what he gives you," Kirov said, "and be thankful there is something green. Vegetables are rare in Moscow this time of year."

"Who eats here?" Fall asked. "Is this some kind of club?"

"The clientele is part Tatar, you see." Kirov nodded toward a massive figure moving past their table. "Does he scare you?"

The man sat at a table nearby. His large, dark face with its high cheekbones and slanting eyes conveyed a sense of menace. "The last of the Golden Horde," Kirov said, pretending to study his plate. "Don't look now, but he's smiling at you."

"Should I smile back?"

"Not if you can help it. If you do, he will come to our table. He seems to like you very much."

Facing away from the large smiling face, Kirov feigned a look of terror. Fall smiled in spite of himself, and the Tatar grinned in response.

"Please don't smile anymore," Kirov said with a deadpan look, "or he will buy us dinner."

They sat in silence, buttering slices of bread, and the man finally turned back to his companions. "Are you ready for Central Asia?" Kirov asked. "You will need some sweaters and hiking shoes, and a warm overcoat. If you don't have them, I can get them for you in Tashkent."

"I'll need hiking shoes," Fall said, "but otherwise I'm ready. Since Prague I haven't stopped thinking about that secret school. There are a thousand questions I want to ask you about it."

"Not now," Kirov said expansively. "I hope we don't have to talk metaphysics on this glorious day!"

"I can't stop thinking," Fall persisted, "about your Earth of Hurqalya. Is it simply a metaphor? Or is it a state of mind, or an extension of physical space . . ."

"That is unfair!" Kirov threw up his hands. "To answer it will take a week!"

"We have a week. You can finish in the desert."

"All right, I will begin to give you an answer. But for this you will owe me a dinner and a very good bottle of wine." Kirov wiped his hands with a napkin and leaned closer to Fall. "I will answer with a story that took place in Moscow some years ago. It will take a few minutes to tell." He paused as Fall put down his fork to listen. "There was a man from that secret school who came to work here in 1955. Life in Tashkent, where he had grown up, was blessed with teachers and friends, and he had a garden where his meditation always brought him close to God. But in Moscow everything changed. It was cold and hard and lonely. His work was difficult, and he asked his chiefs to send him home. When they refused he prayed with all his heart and soul, until he had a vision. In a blazing revelation, he saw Moscow swallowed in an earthquake, and he cried to God for help. The vision was so intense, its imagery so vivid and present, that he thought his room was sinking into the earth. But God spoke to him, saying that he should look for a ray of light coming down from heaven and climb it toward the sky. At that very moment such a ray appeared, and he climbed hand over hand out of his room and out of the crumbling city."

Kirov paused. "Now I know this man. You must believe me

when I tell you that he climbed into a city with buildings and rooms like ours, with streets and parks and people. But the space that contained it was a marvelous elixir! To breathe was to taste delight—to move was to dance. Instead of a sinking room and crumbling city, there was a world more beautiful than any he had seen before."

Kirov sat back and folded his napkin carefully. "And now for the best part," he said. "When the man opened his eyes, he saw that his vision had actually delivered him into that radiant world. His room, his building, the rug on which he sat were the same as the ones in his trance. The heavenly city was Moscow! In the words of his teachers, he had gone through the 'first gate' of the larger Earth. And he saw at once that this was permanent. Though he might forget sometimes, he would never forget completely. A trace of this blessedness would stay for the rest of his life.

"But there was more. In time he would enter a 'second gate.' When his work in Moscow was done, he would return to the desert for a deeper kind of meditation, to enter this Hurqalya more fully, with his body as well as his mind, winning a more glorious life within the larger Earth. In this second transformation, his elements would become the luminous form we are meant to enjoy." Kirov touched Fall's arm. "The 'first gate' is what the saints have shown us; it is the way to God, the way to our true Orient. The 'second gate' is the way toward making our union with God more complete, the path that you and your friends have begun to explore. Does this story help you?"

Fall sat without answering, studying the Russian's complex expression. He did not understand the story completely, but decided to save his questions. Its meaning might be clearer in the desert. "There's an old teaching," he said, "that matter is the densest form of spirit and spirit the subtlest form of matter. It goes back to the Platonists and beyond. Your story reminds me of it."

"Many traditions point toward that understanding, and many of them are still alive in the Soviet Union. They are alive among some of my friends. In the next few days, if all goes well, you will learn about them."

16 On weekends Tashkent's open market was especially busy, Kirov said, because farmers had free time to sell the produce from their private plots. Some of them came from state farms and collectives more than fifty miles away to make the extra profit permitted by the government, while others sold herbs and vegetables they had grown in the middle of the city. Everywhere the booths and pavilions were crowded.

"You can see twenty or thirty ethnic groups," Kirov said, "most of them living in harmony." He nodded toward a handsome Tatar woman dressed in Western slacks and blouse, carrying melons and corn toward a Volga sedan driven by her blond Russian husband. Behind her walked a barefoot Uzbek boy wearing short pants and a white cotton shirt, his brown Turkish features alive with curiosity about the stately woman. As she got into the car, he watched her wistfully, then produced a yo-yo to show her some tricks. She smiled radiantly, drawing looks from the men on the street. As the car drove off, the boy waved good-bye as if he had been smitten. After watching the car a moment, he skipped down the sidewalk to follow a bearded patriarch wearing the traditional *khalat*, or long coat, and conical hat from Kazakhstan. The old man was a mullah, Kirov said. A boy carried bundles for him, and two passing women bowed respectfully.

Melons, corn, red and green peppers, pistachio nuts, herbs, flour, and long rows of cheeses were arrayed on wooden tables inside the pavilions. The bargaining over prices was incessant. Kirov nodded toward three Uzbek women wrapped in bright flowered shawls who were arguing with a blond, blue-eyed man wearing jeans and a Levi shirt. He was a German from the Volga region, Kirov said, but spoke little Uzbek. The women would get their price. Two rough Kazakh men who looked Japanese to Fall watched the argument with amusement, grinning to reveal magnificent rows of gold teeth.

As they crossed the teeming market Fall marveled at the variety of faces: aquiline profiles from Tajikistan, Chinese features from Kirghizia, and the dark good looks of Georgia. There were Ukrainians whose families had settled in Uzbekistan during the nineteenth century, and Azerbaijanis and Turkmen and Jews. This was the hub of Asia, Kirov boasted—one of the world's richest meeting places for traditional and modern cultures. He pointed to new office buildings near the market. "Old and new, East and West, Muhammad, Christ, and Lenin," he said with pride. "Soviet Central Asia seems to work. Most of these people are satisfied. And some are more independent than you think. But come."

Kirov signaled a muscular Uzbek who stood by a dented sedan. The man opened the back door for them, and a moment later they hurtled down a narrow street onto a boulevard. Careening from lane to lane, they accelerated to fifty miles an hour. "Where are we going?" Fall asked with alarm. "Does he want to kill us!"

"He goes slower than most," Kirov said, grabbing the seat as they skidded to a stop. "But brace yourself, anyway!"

They turned at an intersection, swaying dangerously. Fall held the front seat for safety.

"He is showing us his skills," Kirov said. "He sees you appreciate them."

Another car careened down the street ahead, and their driver gunned the motor. A race was on. Fall covered his eyes as they swerved past two motorbikes. But their driver had more to show off. Accelerating again up a rise in the street, he leaned forward and slapped the dashboard. As they hit the top of the rise they sailed—all four wheels off the ground—onto a dirt road that ran between rows of mud huts.

"Old Tashkent!" Kirov shouted. "We don't give everyone this special tour!"

Donkeys and cows trotted away from their taxi as they bumped along the rutted road. Kirov looked through the dust that swirled behind them. No one had followed them.

They reached a stand of trees and stopped. Squeezing the driver's shoulder like an old friend, Kirov told Fall to get out. "Follow me," he said. "I know a shortcut."

Walking rapidly, they went through a wooden gate in a high brick wall. A moment later, they stepped out onto a tree-lined street with two-story stuccoed houses. Most of the windows were barred, in the traditional style of old Tashkent. "A little adventure," Kirov said casually. "Intourist wouldn't take you this way."

After the wild ride, the quiet neighborhood was startling. The houses looked solid and prosperous, and the paved street was well maintained. Two middle-aged Russian women standing by a door were the only people in sight.

"This is my neighborhood," Kirov said. "I was born and raised here. Hardly anyone recognizes me, though, I've lived in Moscow so long. But here! Before we go to see my friends, let's look at this museum." He pointed to a garden fronting a tall, arched entranceway into a building with domes and tile ornaments of Islamic design. "The Museum of Applied Arts," he said. "My friend Umarov will send someone here to meet us."

In the garden stood a pepper tree with branches that hung to the ground. An Uzbek woman in her thirties who sat on a bench by the tree nodded politely as they passed.

Inside was an ornate entrance hall with an arching ceiling some thirty feet high. In its turquoise shadows, tiles with Persian arabesques and angular Uzbek designs lined the eaves and casements. The artistic synthesis here, Kirov said, was typical of mosques and mausoleums in Khiva, Samarkand, and Bukhara. Rooms like these were described in countless tales of the Silk Road and its great oases.

Galleries with white stuccoed walls adjoined the entrance hall. In long glass cases were displayed Uzbek pottery, Bukhara rugs, brocaded dresses from Samarkand, and Kazakh jewelry of turquoise, gold, and silver. For half an hour, as they enjoyed the exhibits, Kirov described their history with the same pride he had shown in the market. To Fall, the noise and dust of Tashkent seemed miles away. There was a stillness in this part of the city that would support contemplation and study, a silence surprising to find after the noisy, smog-filled boulevards Kirov had shown him that day. It seemed a perfect place for Umarov's circle.

As they admired a great Bukhara rug hanging on a wall above them, the woman Fall had seen outside entered the gallery. She nodded at Kirov, and he gestured for Fall to follow. As they left by an unmarked exit, Fall asked if they might be followed.

Kirov shook his head, then led Fall quickly down a deserted alleyway. A moment later they turned abruptly through an open doorway and stepped into a garden enclosed by two-story houses. An Uzbek man in his twenties bolted the gate behind them.

"All is well," Kirov said, taking off his jacket. "No one followed us here."

His heart pounding, Fall followed Kirov to a rug-covered bench that stood in the shade of a porch. Kirov gestured toward the garden. "I learned to meditate here," he said. "The place was my grandfather's home."

The garden was enclosed by three houses and the high brick wall that faced the street. Beds of carnations and roses were bordered by trellises some three feet high covered with peppers and grapevines. The arrangement of the wooden screens formed a maze Fall recognized—a Persian design he had seen in a book on Iranian mysticism.

"Who lives in these houses?" he asked.

"Umarov and his students," Kirov said. "It is a school of philosophy."

Kirov faced away from Fall to hide his emotion. The ambiguities of his work struck him here with dramatic clarity. It would not help to have Fall see his change of mood.

To compose himself, Kirov imagined his grandfather's face. He saw the old man again, cutting flowers, moving stones, readjusting these screens for his students. A garden like this could lead the heart toward God: Shirazi had brought the secret from Persia. These vines and flowers formed a mystical diagram in which you could walk for days in meditation. Kirov remembered his first illumination here when he was only fourteen.

Then he heard the old man's musical voice saying that this friend of his, this young, handsome Umarov, would someday be a man of the *baraka*. Volodya must remember: *Umarov was his brother in the Way*. Only they could carry the teaching through the dark times to come.

It had been in 1945 when Misha came home from the war—Kirov remembered clearly. Umarov had worn the medals he had won for bravery as a fighter pilot pinned conspicuously on the shirt an American pilot had given him as a token of their friendship. Shirazi had seated them both on this porch to describe the troubles ahead. And then the old man had said it. He, Volodya, would have to suffer as Misha had done in the war. This garden, the *zikhr*, the Well of Light would depend upon the friends he would win in Moscow and abroad. Even then, Shirazi had seen into his future. Even then, he had seen that foreigners would find a Way like theirs, strangers with vision, people like Atabet and Fall . . .

Footsteps on the balcony interrupted Kirov's thought. "Sergei," Umarov shouted, honoring Kirov's alias. "Sergei Mironovich!" On the stairs above appeared a tall, athletic figure dressed in a yellow shirt and jeans. Kirov stood as he came down the stairs, and the two men embraced with gusto.

Umarov's dark face looked Spanish to Fall. In this first instant of greeting, the man resembled a Mexican rancher he had known in Arizona. The impression was strengthened by the almost identical scar that ran along the edge of his jaw.

Umarov gestured for his visitors to sit down on the benches beside him. Then he turned to Kirov, his dark, handsome face filled with irony. "Isn't it good," he said in heavily accented English, "that an American brings us together? In spite of our friends in uniform."

"Do they still watch?" Kirov asked, nodding toward the wall.

"*Nyet*," Umarov smiled. "They have given up. But still we must be careful. A new General for Uzbekistan is trying to win promotion by finding Islamic subversives. You will have to watch him from your window in Moscow. But what about these Americans? I have their catalogue."

Fall glanced nervously toward the garden wall. The others smiled. "You think they are listening?" asked Umarov, his dark eyes filled with energy. "Please! They are not that good. Police microphones here do not work. You can ask our friend." He nodded toward the young Uzbek, who sat on the ground near his feet. "He used to work for them."

The young man smiled shyly. Umarov lifted his arm in a gesture of nonchalance. "We seem harmless to them. I am a retired hero teaching meaningless philosophy to unemployed boys. And Volodya comes here because he owns these houses."

"Officially, one leases the ground from the State," Kirov explained. "My grandfather built this compound, then gave it to Misha and me. Friends gather here to learn about the Earth of Hurqalya."

"The State will not reclaim it unless they want to build another boulevard," Umarov sighed. "By the grace of Allah and our friends in Moscow, we are protected. Protected from *what*, I am not sure. Our bosses grow more confused—about Islam, economics, and progress. You must have seen that."

"No, I haven't," Fall answered. "When I was here in 1969, the people I met only talked about parapsychology."

"You shall see," said Umarov wickedly. "They all have ten thumbs. Take a look at the plumbing in your guest house. It is an Intourist place, so you will be lucky to have hot water. But enough about them. This is more disturbing!" From a shelf behind him he pulled out the Greenwich Press catalogue. "Sergei has told you about our mosque near Samarkand and its famous mosaic. How did your Atabet paint it? Does he work for your CIA?"

Fall smiled. "He is clairvoyant. He has been watching you."

"I thought so!" Umarov slapped his thigh. "The police are everywhere. But this painting is remarkable."

"It is pure coincidence. He told me so by phone this week."

Umarov studied Fall's face as if to appraise his depth. "You are a conscientious fellow," he said at last. "A real bulldog! Sergei tells me you have collected an encyclopedia about the mysteries of the body. Why in the name of Allah have you done that?"

"It keeps me busy. It was a hobby, and now it's an obsession. It gets more interesting all the time."

"Is he always so modest?" Umarov asked Kirov with mock surprise. "And your Atabet?" he asked Fall. "It would be hard to believe Sergei's stories about him if we had not experienced these mysteries ourselves. Sergei, I think, has told you something about us."

During their flight from Moscow the night before, Fall and Kirov had compared the similarities between Atabet's bodily changes and the traditional marks of a seer who entered the Earth of Hurqalya. "But there are differences in our understandings," Fall said. "We have no tradition like yours to guide us."

"Sergei told me on the phone today about your conversations. His account was so fantastic that I want to hear it from you. Please do not be modest. This is an extravagant subject."

Seeing that Fall was reluctant to discuss his friend with a stranger, Kirov turned to Umarov. "Atabet was only sixteen," he said, "when his mind was swept into God. They put him in a mental institution." Umarov closed his eyes and nodded, and their voices hushed. "Since then," Kirov went on, "the vision has never left him. He says it sustains all his work. What is his saying, Darwin? 'The One is our base for all further adventure.'"

Fall nodded, but did not answer. The Russian's feeling for Atabet was more powerful than he had guessed.

"And this painting?" Umarov asked, placing the catalogue before him. "Does it come from his visions too?"

"Yes," Fall said. "Nearly all his paintings do. He says they're a place to practice the body's transformations at a distance."

"But he did not choose the path," Kirov said. "He did not start with an abstract idea. I say this, Darwin, because Umarov distrusts philosophers."

"From this painting," Umarov said, "I can see that the man does not live in abstractions. You can feel his closeness to the Light."

"And you should know about Atabet's visions," Kirov said. "From his boyhood, Misha, Atabet has had an interior sight with which he can see the structures of the body, down to its cells and atoms."

Umarov and his Uzbek attendant listened carefully. "Yes," Fall said. "He's always had this gift—or affliction—in which images of bodily organs flood his consciousness. He couldn't control it at first. It's obsessed him for twenty years."

"And it leads to this painting?" Umarov slapped the catalogue. "There is more to his vision than bodily organs!"

"I think it is best," Kirov said to Fall, "for you to tell us step by step how Atabet reached his present understanding. I will try to keep Misha from interrupting."

Umarov leaned forward to catch every word.

"It's a complex story," Fall said. "From the beginning his visions have led him in two directions. His first realizations were of the timeless One, of the Godhead in its essence unlimited by time and space. But then, a few months later, his visions of the body started. At first they were a torment, driving him to find out 'Why? What is it they're trying to tell me?' When he found in the yoga sutras that there was a power called the *animan siddhi* that could focus the mind at will on the smallest thing in the universe, he saw that his hallucinations might be powers in disguise. Maybe it was his destiny to use them. So he started to welcome them. When he was twenty-one he started painting. He tried to turn them into art, practicing his inner sight in a way that seemed less frightening. Then, spontaneously, he started to paint luminous flesh, portraits of new living tissue. That led him to his vision of the body's secret destiny, *because the transformations he was painting began to appear in him.* More and more it seemed that his body was incorporating the luminous states he put in his art.

"But he had nothing to support him in this, no spiritual tradition, no textbooks, no guide. That's where his friends were important. There's a Tibetan lama, a *rimpoche*, who's helped him. And a friend from his teens, Corinne Wilde, who's been with him through all his changes. And then my book. My scholarly work gave him the conceptual framework he needed. Our friendship's an incredible thing, giving me his discipline and inspiration and bringing me my intellectual support. Our work together—along with the rimpoche's knowledge of Tibetan yoga—finally led to an experiment I told Sergei about. Atabet called it a 'descent into matter.' It alarmed the rest of us; in fact we tried to stop it. But he said 'the Lord' was forcing him to it."

"Forcing him to what?" Kirov asked.

"Something was forcing him deeper into his cells and molecules, into his atoms it seemed, until he got control of the body's most fundamental energies. The moments of luminosity he had felt for so many years could become more stable that way, he thought. Then he could master the process more deeply. To do it, though, he would have to go back layer by layer into the past. In trance he would contact his cells directly. Because the molecular and atomic patterns in our body are like the ones that existed in our primordial history, he called his adventure a 'return to the First Day.' It was a little fanciful, we thought, but he kept calling it that: 'A descent to the First Day when matter first rises from Mind!'

"So his adventure began. He didn't leave his apartment for

weeks, and there were some unmistakable changes in him. But after three months, he simply burned out—came close to death, I think. For the last year he's been recuperating and assimilating the changes he passed through."

As Fall detailed this strange account, Umarov grew more troubled. There was silence when he finished, broken only by the rustling of leaves in the garden.

"Who saw these changes?" Umarov finally asked. "How many of you were with him?"

"Five or six of us, off and on, through the whole three months. But we can't agree about what happened! It seems you have to change yourself to perceive those transformations."

"Well, then, how confident are you about the things you saw? You are still new to disciplines like these."

"I'm not certain. The experiment lasted through the autumn—morning, noon and night—and for most of that time he was focused intensely, often in a trance that charged his place in San Francisco with amazing energy. As time went on, I found myself changing my mind about the things I saw, because sometimes his presence made me feel drunk. Twice, for example, he seemed to disappear, and I thought, well, he's changing the spin of his molecules, or the quantum action of his quarks! Maybe my eyeballs were failing. Yet the impression was overwhelming. *He seemed to vanish* for a minute or more. I was alone with him both times it happened. But there were more certain things. He took on a subtle luminescence that we all saw. After a while his skin looked softer, more alive, yet its boundaries seemed less definite . . ."

"As if it were disappearing?" Umarov asked.

"Yes. It gave that impression. But certain parts of his body seemed more volatile than others, more prone to change—his eyes and face, for example. It seemed to me at times that parts of him were moving to another world or vibrancy, while the rest would not go along. But you could sense his survival instincts stuggling to maintain balance, holding onto the body's ordinary structure. Twice marks appeared on his chest like religious stigmata. We thought they might be a kind of circuit breaker to keep him from burning up, but that was pure speculation. Toward the end of the experiment, sometime in late November, the atmosphere around him became too intense for me. Twice I felt he was pulling me into another world completely. Once, in fact, I thought I'd landed on another planet!"

"When these things happened," Umarov asked, "what happened to the building? Did he break any doors or windows?"

"How did you know? Yes—some fuses blew and there were rattlings like poltergeists. But his apartment doesn't seem the worse for wear. If anything, it seems well preserved. That comes from his other moods. Usually it feels like this garden—still and ordered and peaceful. I felt the similarity as soon as I got here."

Umarov sent his student for tea, then leaned back against the wall. "Let me understand this better," he said. "You say he could see his own insides by a direct interior sight, down to his cells and atoms. But how do you know he really saw them? We don't have that in our tradition."

"He saw them first in his adolescence. Then he began to paint them. We have a friend, a hematologist, who's taken pictures of Atabet's blood cells under an electron microscope. Atabet says the photographs are identical to some of the images he's seen in trance. And in medical books there are dozens of pictures like the ones he sees. He's taken to calling some of his trances cellular or molecular or atomic *samadhis*, states of oneness with these various structures. But his perceptions are still more complex. Not only can he see different levels, he can see every structure of the body through different lenses of the mind—that's how he puts it—not just the way they look under the microscope. Sometimes his seeing takes symbolic forms. Organs might look like fish, cells like cities, atoms like dancing lights."

"This is strange to us," Umarov murmured. "But there is a saying in our school that this *jasad*, the body of ordinary elements, is 'an earth and an ocean and a light.' Is that like his descent into matter, in which he perceives his organs, then the 'sea of cells' you describe, then the brilliance of atomic patterns?"

"If it is our destiny," Fall said, "to uncover what is unconscious in us, then a descent like his makes sense. You can see it as a kind of remembering, or anamnesis in the Platonic sense, of the patterns and ideas in the body. If this 'earth and ocean and light' reflect the ancient layers of the universe, then a developing perception of them might bring a more intimate knowledge of our past. And since awareness aids self-mastery, insight like this could help us win new powers in the body. You might see it as an extension of our modern project of self-discovery, making the unconscious conscious, down to the oldest and most basic levels. That idea is a powerful guide for Atabet. He has even taken to saying that the body's resistance to change, its homeostasis, its very stubbornness, makes it a marvelous prison from which to win new freedoms in the universe."

Umarov sat cross-legged on the bench, his dark features almost invisible in the growing shadows. "Sergei," he said, using Kirov's alias, "they have not heard about the Earth of Hurqalya, and yet they enter it step by step, telling themselves all the while that they are voyaging into the past. What a strange interpretation they give it!" He traced a line in the soil at his feet. "If this is ordinary time, or the line of biological evolution, our way to God runs like this." He drew another line perpendicular to the first. "The resurrection of the human form will happen in a larger Earth than the one we ordinarily inhabit, in the 'eighth climate' of the Persian mystics, in the Earth of Hurqalya. For us, history is not before or after. History is under our feet. In our practice we don't go back, down to the cells and atoms. We grow *out* of this limited space, this prison of the senses, this heavy atmosphere, so that the power and love and light we contain can expand to their rightful stature."

History is under our feet–Kirov silently repeated the sentence. His grandfather had often used it in disagreeing with his father. The schism that divided his family, the wound that separated his father from the wonders of Shirazi's school, had begun with a difference in vision like the one that was unfolding now . . .

"I do not know your teaching," Fall said. "But maybe we are talking about completely different things. Atabet knows we can realize God without changing our worldly lives at all. He and I know that from the vantage point of spirit all history can look like *samsara*, a wheel of death and rebirth. But we think there must be more to the universe than that. This stupendous evolution is an unfolding of God. Part of our present crisis on earth comes from our failure to see it. But to see it the body must become a more conscious vehicle."

"Ah, yes!" Umarov's dark eyes were shining. "The body will become the luminous face of the soul. It will be immortal. That is our school's ancient witness. But for that do we need this psychic hemorrhaging? These eruptions of cells and organs that torment your Atabet? Perhaps he is blind to his gifts. Maybe the body he seeks could develop more easily if he entered Hurqalya directly."

"And how would he do that?"

"Tomorrow Sergei will take you to the Well of Light. That is the best answer I can give you. Have you heard about the 'black light' of God's abyss? It is an illumination that blinds our earthly eyes so that the soul may inhabit this body without causing the difficulties your Atabet suffers from. When the mind of the aspirant is lost in this holy darkness, there is a *transformation from above*—that is the phrase in our school—a transfiguration in which his flesh and bones are flooded with God's *baraka*, His highest alchemy. Then this *jasad*, this body of ordinary elements, can fuse with its highest light, its original person, the *jism-al-asli*. Here it can last for a moment, but only in the Earth of Hurqalya can it be completed. Only there can the light of this union be held with certainty. Only Hurqalya is large and free enough." Umarov paused. "Perhaps it is the world you felt during Atabet's trances, that opening you called another planet."

Fall paused before answering, turning to Kirov for guidance.

"Misha," Kirov smiled. "You are swift tonight. Perhaps they have another way to the body's resurrection."

Umarov cocked his head to the side, forming a wicked smile. "You like this American, Sergei," he said. "What has he done to you? I am testing his understanding."

Kirov answered with a disbelieving look. "Darwin," he said, "do not be intimidated."

"Aha!" Umarov slapped his thigh. "Sergei, Sergei, always reconciling. Will you deny us the pleasures of combat? In spite of Sergei, Fall, I think you should ask if your friend misperceives his gifts. Perhaps it isn't necessary to take his body apart. Maybe these cellular, these atomic *samadhis* are nothing but circuses—blocking the soul's ascent."

"Atabet would say he hasn't had a choice," Fall said. "These images and trances—these *samadhis*—began when he was only sixteen. He had to face them or go crazy. His genes, his destiny, his soul, or God aimed him in that direction. We are all explorers, with an opportunity to follow many leadings. But some paths are peculiar to our temperaments. Ali Shirazi, it seems, found a powerful way. Atabet has one that few will choose. But the changes he has gone through are unmistakable. If you knew him, you would recognize its *baraka*."

"Ah, yes!" Umarov threw up his hands with mock disgust. "Each soul is unique. We have that too. There is a saying of the Persian sheiks that each soul is a world in itself. And each *jasad*, when joined to its soul, becomes a galaxy! Maybe your Atabet is a god of the sea or of the underworld! Maybe he is Poseidon or Hades!"

"But Misha," Kirov said, "we must remember Ali Shirazi's use of terms. 'Every spiritual state should have ten names,' he told us—a name for every facet of its splendor. Hurqalya is also Eran-Vej, the Zoroastrian Place of Visions at the center. It is also Jabarsa and Jabalqa, the emerald cities—or the 'true Orient.' Our poor conceptions only capture slivers of reality. We need many names to remind us. And it is the same with our practice. This Atabet will teach us, I think."

Umarov's attendant came onto the porch with a silver samovar.

They were silent while he poured their tea. Vines rustling in the first evening breeze made the only sound in the garden. The smell of roses was intense.

"Misha," Kirov said, "because we are going to the *mechet* tomorrow, it will be good for our guest to hear about our teacher."

In this fragrant silence, Umarov described Kirov's grandfather, their teacher Ali Shirazi.

Descended from Persians and Azerbaijanis who lived near the Caspian Sea, he came to Samarkand in 1891 to find the Well of Light. His teachers, followers of Iranian sheiks in the line of Suhrawardi, believed that the human form would rise at the end of history. They had used the ancient name, Hurqalya, to designate the world of resurrection, but they believed it to be completely separate from our earth—cut off from ordinary matter by an impassable river of forgetfulness. The school near Samarkand, however, held a different teaching—that a way was kept into that complex space in which the human form would rise. Bodies could go back and forth, once they learned the Way between this planet and the larger Earth in which it turned.

The Uzbek master of the school near Samarkand saw in the young Shirazi those gifts of bodily rebirth that marked an adept of the Way. Before he died he made him his successor.

Shirazi brought to the school the language of Neoplatonic Iranian seers descended from Suhrawardi, a language especially informed by the belief of Ahmad Ahsai that each body's subtle counterpart would rise at the end of the cosmic cycle to join its soul in Hurqalya. But Shirazi changed Sheik Ahmad's esoteric physiology to accord with his own experience in the Well of Light. For he had learned the secret of ascent: he could move at will beyond the formations of ordinary matter.

In the years that followed, Shirazi's radiance and power attracted students who were neither Muslim nor Zoroastrian. For the first time, the Way of Hurqalya was joined by agnostics, Marxists, and others who did not follow traditional religions. Beginning in 1924, Muslims and Bolsheviks sat side by side in this garden, listening to his lectures and practicing his meditation. Materialists and idealists alike could find in Shirazi's teaching ideas compatible with their own. For in the Well of Light, he said, it made no difference whether you regarded matter as the densest form of spirit or spirit as the subtlest form of matter.

As Umarov described Shirazi's Marxist students, Kirov thought of his father. By 1940 the Bolshevik had come to hate the patriarch. Like other Party leaders in Central Asia he saw all esoteri-cism as an obstacle to Socialist progress. The only real progress came in *this* world, not another one. Shirazi's repetition of the saying "all history is under our feet" determined him all the more to separate his son from the old man's teaching.

The final confrontation had happened on this very porch in 1949, after the Soviet Union's first atomic explosion. Each man saw the event as a great beginning—for his father, the beginning of Soviet status as a superpower; for Shirazi, the opening blast of Seraphiel's trumpet before the earth's resurrection in the World of Hurqalya. On that day, Kirov had resolved to integrate their separate visions. The transformations of body and soul that Shirazi taught must be compatible with his father's social pro-gress. He would work all his life to join them.

Umarov ended his account with a description of Shirazi's car-riage and looks. He was descended, it was said, from Alexander's Macedonian soldiers—that accounted for his startling blue eyes. And he was tall for an Azerbaijani. Until he died, he dressed in the traditional manner of the Uzbeks, wearing a long cotton robe in the heat and a *khalat* when the weather turned cold. He died in 1953, two months after Stalin's death, leaving the school's protec-tion and guidance to Kirov and Umarov, who were then nineteen and thirty-three.

"We were young," Umarov murmured. "Too young. We are still too young, perhaps." A gentle mood had filled him as he talked, softening the lines of his face. The patriarch seemed a presence in the garden. Fall wondered if he were attracted by their reminis-cences from the Earth of Hurqalya.

"Can souls in Hurqalya return?" Kirov asked, as if reading Fall's mind. "What are we to think of these tales? Will they vanish in the morning light? Sometimes I ask that question. That is why I have collected the reports I told you about, all the studies of conscious-ness and special powers of the body. Someday, perhaps, we will compare our evidence."

Umarov studied Kirov's face, wondering if he would tell Fall his true identity. But this was not the time, Kirov had decided. In the days ahead, innocence would be Fall's best protection.

17 It had been two hours since they left the paved road from Tashkent, and their driver, a middle-aged Uzbek who knew each turn of the trail, had parked their Russian jeep to let the motor cool. Fall climbed a rock to survey the valley below. He could see no sign of life between this ridge and the distant horizon. The dry yellow hills stretched some twenty miles to the west, turning red as the sun set behind them.

"We are on the edge of the desert," Kirov said. "Nobody lives within a hundred miles, except for a few sheepherders."

Fall stamped his feet for warmth. "How do you get up this trail when it's raining?" he asked.

"You don't. In the winter, our people go for months without supplies. That is a time for fasts and vigils."

Kirov and the driver got back in the jeep, Fall taking a seat behind them. With a lurch they started up the hill.

"He has driven this road for twenty years," Kirov shouted. "You have nothing to fear."

They climbed a narrow gorge in the jeep's lowest gear, the wheels spinning at times in loose sand. Looking back, Fall watched the valley darken. Not a single light marked a human dwelling. After ascending for fifteen minutes, they reached a sandy plateau. "There it is!" Kirov said, pointing to a hill some two miles distant. "You can see its minaret."

The ancient retreat stood silhouetted against the dark blue sky, a tower, and parapets. Kirov reached across the driver and blinked the headlights twice. He repeated the signal and a light from the tower answered.

The driver found a trail along the plateau's western edge. Looking up, Fall saw a vulture high above them, its wings ablaze in the last rays of the sun. They were a thousand feet above the valley. Sandy wastes stretched in darkness toward the red horizon.

After this treacherous drive, Fall's excitement had given way to fatigue. He gripped his seat as they negotiated another incline, hoping they would soon reach the mosque. Kirov, though, felt a growing peace. Despite the wind and the roar of the engine, he sensed the presence he had known since his boyhood, the stillness in which this wild country seemed to hang suspended.

They passed between two boulders and stopped. Directly above stood the fortress walls. Then, to Fall's amazement, a wooden gate swung open, revealing a Soviet flag illuminated by the light of two torches. The bearded man who held it waved them on, lowering the Hammer and Sickle toward them as they passed. "We are still Soviets," Kirov said. "Please bow in return."

Though the man could not see him, Fall bowed as the gate closed behind them. Four bearded figures dressed in Uzbek robes greeted Kirov with embraces. Bowing toward Fall and the driver, they began to unload the supplies that Kirov had brought from Tashkent.

The courtyard they had entered was sixty yards long and forty yards wide, and was enclosed by walls that rose some thirty feet above them. The air was heavy and still, though the wind outside was howling.

"Follow me," Kirov said. "The driver will bring our bags." He led Fall into a pitch-black corridor. Their footsteps echoed from invisible walls as they went down a curving stairwell. Two men dressed in long, dark robes and the traditional Uzbek skullcaps stood at the bottom. They embraced Kirov and bowed toward Fall, then gestured to rugs on the floor.

"They speak the Tajik language," Kirov said. "They have been caretakers here for years." The men looked like the Tajiks Fall had seen in Tashkent. Their strong, aquiline faces reminded him of profiles carved into an old Persian frieze.

A fire burned in a hearth with a chimney. "We will eat now," Kirov said. "It is the custom here to feed guests at once after their trip through the desert."

The man near the hearth filled bowls with carrots and cabbage floating in a thick lamb broth. As they ate, Kirov closed his eyes to conceal his joy. It took several moments to regain his composure. Respecting his mood, the caretakers ate in silence.

After their noisy ride, Fall welcomed the silence. Leaning back against a wall, he felt his attention coming to a steady focus. A presence had formed in this place, he thought, that made meditation easier. Softening his gaze, he saw flecks of light in his bowl. Then an image of Atabet, his skin swimming in a strange luminescence. Closing his eyes, he felt an odd elasticity . . .

"Darwin," Kirov whispered. "I am sorry to hurry you, but we have a long night ahead."

Startled, Fall looked up. The two caretakers had cleared away the bowls.

Kirov's blue eyes sparkled. "It is easy to fall into reverie here," he said. "The *baraka* is strong. But come. I will show you a place to sleep."

They went down another stairwell, Kirov holding a torch. Parts of the building were built of stone, while others were hollowed through unsupported earth.

"Are we *under* the mosque now?" Fall whispered.

"The building upstairs is built on this one," Kirov answered, his voice echoing in the narrow passage. "This part of the place was built in the days of Tamerlane, in the fourteenth or fifteenth century."

The passage turned left into a long stone vault. Kirov held the lamp to the walls. "You see these inscriptions?" He pointed to rows of Arabic letters. "They are the names and dates of people buried here. This place is called a *mazar*, a burial vault for members of our school. Some of these tombs were built in the eleventh century."

The inscriptions ran along the wall for several hundred feet. Kirov pointed to the ceiling. "They are buried all the way to the top, some of them the bones of saints. Their presence reminds us that we have many helpers on the Way."

They walked in silence along the catacomb, then stopped beside a beautifully carved inscription. "Ali Shirazi," Kirov whispered. "I carved this nineteen years ago."

The headstone was smaller than the others. Under Shirazi's name were three lines of Arabic letters. "What does it say?" Fall asked as Kirov touched the carving.

"*Nur wujudi dha ib. Nur wujudi jamid. Tajdid al-khalq*. Sayings he liked to use. 'Both souls and bodies are made of the same holy light, and they will become one in the New Creation.'" Kirov pressed his forehead to the rock, whispering a sentence in Russian. Then he turned abruptly and led Fall out of the vault.

They went down another stairwell. By now, Fall guessed, they were eighty or ninety feet below the courtyard. They entered a room with a small wooden cot. "You will sleep here," Kirov said, lighting a second lamp. "I will show you where to wash tomorrow. The driver brought your bag and blankets, but don't go to bed. There is more to see."

Fall looked around the cell. Its stone walls had a subtle iridescence. He opened his suitcase and found a fur cap, then sat to enjoy the silence. There was a second depth within this earthen cellar, a presence even more profound than the one he had felt before . . .

When he looked up, Kirov stood at the entrance. "We will give you a tour," he said. "Free of charge. Our guide is waiting."

Fall felt reluctant to leave this pleasurable stillness. He rose slowly, trying to preserve it. "Watch your step," Kirov said. "The passage will get steeper."

They were moving down an incline, past more doors and

arches. "This place must have been enormous!" Fall exclaimed.

"Not in circumference," Kirov answered, "but in depth. It goes down, as you can see, into places even older." Their guide's lamp cast twisting shadows on the wall and brightened the glistening surface of the stones.

The passage now turned left, and before them stood a huge stone door. Two megaliths some eight feet tall supported a massive lintel, a structure that might have come from Stonehenge, Fall thought. It looked like the entrance to a temple. "The second mosque, the one from Tamerlane's time, was built on this," Kirov said. "The Bureau of Antiquities knows nothing about it. Watch the ground when you enter. There are holes you might fall into."

The guide led them into a cavern. "Wait," Kirov whispered. "I want you to gather your senses. He is going to show us something."

Kirov waited for Fall's breathing to subside. "Now," he said. "Turn around and see it."

In the first shock of surprise, Fall saw a light more vivid than the lamp. A sun was embedded in the earth, rising through a city. There was no doubt it was Atabet's painting. One detail stood out at once—a thin, gray line bisecting the picture diagonally to form an X with the city's slope. The X seemed to cancel the scene, just as in Atabet's version. Fall stepped closer. The parapets and towers of the city in the mosaic differed in detail from the buildings on San Francisco's Russian Hill, but their contours and textures were the same. "I see why you brought me," he whispered.

Fall gazed at the throbbing sun, deadly in its pale splendor. What was it meant to suggest?

"There are several stories about it," Kirov said, replying to the unspoken question. "One says it is a place for human souls to pass between the worlds. Near it, the elements reconstitute themselves more freely, and a few have gotten powers of the jinn. But another legend says that this is the sun that will rise in the west. The sun at the end of our age. It will rise as the earth is setting in the world of Hurqalya. As you will see, there was a school here older than Islam. I think the legend comes from that. It could be Zoroastrian, or Vedic, or older still. It might come from the Stone Age."

"Did the Vedic *rishis* come here?"

"One legend says so, but we know so little about them. But what is that sun about to do? Is it rising through the city?" Kirov's face had an ageless quality in the flickering light. "And what is that city? Do you see it might be made of living cells?"

"You're right," Fall said. "It's just like Atabet's painting. That city, he says, is like a thing he sees in trance, the body as it might be."

Kirov whistled to set up an echo. "This cavern is immense," he said. "When I was a boy I came here to chant. My grandfather was a master of the *zikhr* and taught us to use the place like a musical instrument. He called it Seraphiel's trumpet. But come, I have another thing to show you."

Their guide led them out of the cavern and down another incline. "These caves," Kirov said, "were escape tunnels for the buildings above. As the surrounding valley filled with desert sand, new floors were added continually. The place is a tower in the ground." They heard trickling water. "There are springs down here. And an underground river. But here is what we came to see."

They had come to the edge of an abyss some twenty feet wide. It dropped away beyond the lamplight. "This is the Well of Light," Kirov said. "Initiates have practiced here for thousands of years."

"How far down does it go?"

"No one has reached the bottom. The walls are too slippery, and there is no place from which to lower a rope safely more than forty or fifty meters. Tomorrow we will test its depth with our minds."

Walking up the incline, Fall began to tremble. The intensity he felt in these caves was no longer pleasurable. Their immensity was becoming oppressive. Inside his cell, he tried to control himself. The crucial thing was to remember the quiet surrender he had learned from Atabet. If anxiety threatened to overwhelm him, eventually it would pass. If his boundaries vanished in this darkness, his essential identity would not. He let his fears present themselves as familiar voices: he might fall, he might faint, he might suffocate, he might panic. His body might fly apart. With a shudder, he remembered a vision of a huge black bird plucking his organs out, a vision from the month he had begun meditation. And the memory of his fall from a cliff near San Francisco, to survive with just scratches and bruises. Images of disaster came and went until he was almost asleep.

It was midnight. Blowing out the lamp, he lay on the cot and pulled the blankets around him. For the next five hours he slept fitfully, with odd dreams: scenes of Prague and Moscow, of airport inspectors taking his bags away, of Aitmatov leading him into a Kremlin hall. Was Leonid Brezhnev trying to show them the secret of the Hammer and Sickle?

"Time to get up." Kirov was gently shaking him.

Rising stiffly, he followed Kirov up the narrow stairs. In a damp room off the courtyard, he washed his face until he was fully awake. Then they went down to the room with a stove, where the men who had made them dinner brewed a strong green tea. "Drink two cups," Kirov said. "We will stay down there for about three hours."

Though his body felt heavy and stiff, Fall sensed energy gathering—a force that could turn into fear. He drank the bitter tea and stamped his feet nervously. All would be well, he told himself, if he remembered that anxiety would pass. Kirov smiled encouragement, but said nothing as they started down toward the well.

Descending slowly, they reached the megalithic gate. As they passed it, Fall saw a feature he had missed before: a shining star between two animal horns carved on the massive lintel. It looked like Islam's Star and Crescent but might have been a Bronze Age symbol of the sun and bull. Did the glowing mosaic inside reveal this ancient joining of earth and heaven?

They went in single file now, the two caretakers walking in front.

"I'll go first," Kirov whispered when they reached the precipice. "There is a ledge about four feet below us." He went down nimbly, as if he knew each edge of rock, then Fall inched down behind him. Kirov knelt on a rock outcropping and waited for Fall to sit. Then he blew out the lamp and whistled loudly. It was an eerie sound, high-pitched and wavering, like a muezzin's call to prayer. A long echo came from the well. "We will sit in silence," Kirov said. "Our friends will come back in three hours. Try to sense how deep this cavern drops."

A grotto like this might drop a thousand feet, Fall thought, but there was a smell of fresh air and water. It occurred to him that this abyss might open to a sky below. Were there stars in all directions? As he had the thought, he felt himself floating . . .

Without effort, without fear, he was suspended.

There was no sense of weight, no pressure from the rock—only emptiness. His sense of boundaries vanished. Then, like the first light of dawn, a subtle land appeared. A shimmering latticework, small dancing forms like crystals.

Floating in zero gravity, cohering gently, glowing filaments stretched in every direction. This was a body in the making, he could see, a dazzling net of light and music. He let it float around him. There was no telling now how far it reached, for through the glowing fibers a million stars were shining.

It all pulsed to a secret beat, and though it was completely stable, Fall knew it could explode. A long, still moment passed. Then the thing transformed itself into a pattern more intricate than before.

A presence was entering step by step to bring him strength and courage. For in this dazzling net there were faces too radiant to look at. Faces and a power that could kill. Fall repeated his name for support, seeing that every change like this came from a place inside him. It would be his task to befriend this power and that would take him the rest of his life.

"We must go now." Kirov's blue eyes were sparkling in the lamplight. "They are waiting."

Two bearded faces looked down from the ledge above.

"Was that three hours?" Fall whispered in amazement. "We just sat down!"

"I've been trying to rouse you for over ten minutes," Kirov said. "You're sure you weren't asleep?"

The two bearded figures smiled as they helped him off the ledge. Their kindness was a tangible energy, it seemed, a part of the presence in this grotto. And it occurred to Fall that Kirov was an angel. But as they started up the incline from the well, he sensed the Russian's dark complexity. He had an image of him being tortured, then one of him hiding in an alley sobbing. The man's life, Fall realized, was filled with splendors and horrors he could only guess at.

"Are your legs all right?" Kirov asked. "You sat there without moving."

"Like rubber springs," Fall answered. "I think my cells got changed!" His body seemed light as air, and with the slightest shift of focus he could sink again into that brilliant latticework his heavy frame was made of. Walking slowly up the slippery rock, he held back tears of joy. His early intuitions about the body's secret, his years of scholarship, his meeting Atabet, his trips to Russia— all led to the vision he had just been granted.

Kirov led him to the grotto. With one glance at the mosaic, Fall recognized Atabet's intent. The latticework of shimmering stone was like his vision in the Well of Light. It showed a version of our human flesh in its coming splendor: the city might be subtle cells, the hills a body's contour. The rising sun, however, showed a fatal turn the earth might take. The X across it spelled disaster.

Two cities burned like running sores. As he stood transfixed, Fall saw that this backward sun would have to find a better birth than Hiroshima or Nagasaki.

18 As Darwin Fall sat in the Well of Light, Jacob Atabet hurried across the hill above Olema on his way to the Vedanta retreat three miles from the farm house. It was five o'clock, and the sun was setting. It would be a half-hour's hike from here, he thought, and allowing time to visit with students at the retreat, it might be 6:30 before he got back to the farm. Tomorrow would be soon enough to get the painting.

But as he hesitated, an image of Russian Hill appeared in the shadows at his feet. He knew that if he did not see the painting soon, the hallucination would torment him. Buttoning his jacket against the cold, he jogged through the grass toward the highway.

The two thousand acres of the Vedanta retreat stretched from Highway 1 near Olema to the ocean at Point Reyes. As Atabet crossed its grounds through a stand of redwoods, an image of his painting danced in the shadows before him. At a turn in the trail, he stopped. In the woods ahead stood a snow-white deer, part of a herd imported from Asia. Motionless, the animal sniffed the air for danger, then bounded ahead through the trees. Thankful for this distraction, Atabet jogged behind the deer to the big frame house that served as the retreat's guest quarters. One of the Vedanta students had driven a tractor from the fields. He got off, leaving the motor running, and came up to Atabet. They went inside together.

In the meditation hall, another student was drawing blinds against the setting sun. In the darkened room the painting glowed with preternatural brightness. "Has anyone touched it?" Atabet asked with displeasure. "It looks like someone tried to clean it."

Only the regulars had seen it, they protested, and none of them would do something like that. Atabet checked both their faces, then sat on the floor to study the odd effect. Obediently, the young men knelt beside him.

Later, this meeting would seem strange to them all: after a few words of greeting, they had fallen into sudden concentration. The student's tractor would run out of gas before the spell was broken.

Atabet's concentration deepened, and the aura that preceded his trances appeared. It felt as if he were entering a long, dark well . . .

Living things were moving in the dark. Urchins and anemones, octopi and squid slithered past. Then tiny sacs like plankton swarmed in a warm, rocking sea. With a shift of attention, Atabet knew he could turn these glistening beads to human cells, and if he focused deliberately, they would coalesce to living tissue.

But the tunnel drew him on. Passing through the sea, he fell into a starry night. All around him dazzling lace was spun to the beat of his heart. A new body formed while he watched, a body of shimmering patterns that rose from his own insight. From this deeper station of his consciousness, he could spin this suit of lights at will . . .

"Hey! One of you guys left the tractor running." A red-faced man in overalls stood above them, frowning. "Now it's out of gas!"

One of the students jumped up. "What time is it?" he asked.

"It's after six," the frowning figure answered. "You've been here almost an hour. Get that tractor in the barn, damnit!"

The two students went to the door, then stopped for Atabet. He had always been an enigma, a disconcerting combination of generosity and unspiritual manners. Now he sat before the painting, giving no sign that he heard them. "Should we leave him here?" one whispered. "I don't think the Swami would like it."

"Jacob?" he ventured. "We're leaving."

"Then leave," the answer came back. "And tell the foreman I'm taking the painting with me."

"Come on, leave him!" said the man in overalls. "And get that goddamn tractor in the barn before it's dark. Tell the Swami he's gone into trance."

The three men left, slamming doors behind them. Alone in the house, Atabet focused on the painting. It might be possible, he thought, to drop through the floor, descending ghostlike into the room below. Holding back an impulse to laugh, he shifted from his cross-legged position. Suddenly and without effort, he was standing.

Had his earthly body died?

He looked around the room to see. Now he felt like rising. He might sail up into the Swami's bedroom or reach through the wall at his side. Yet empty space had a subtle density. He walked back and forth to test it. His body had changed and objects seemed transparent.

But would this state collapse, even as he glimpsed it? He moved to the window with care, balancing carefully. He touched the wall and felt his hand bounce back. The repulsion felt as if it came from something magnetic. He reached toward the windowpane. Like the wall, it seemed to develop an opposite charge as he tried to penetrate it. He turned and walked toward the door, his sense of lightness growing. Were these changes here to stay?

It had happened invisibly through this year of recuperation. His cells had altered while his ordinary will relaxed. He went to a lamp and lit it. Like the window, it gently repelled him as he pressed its metal stalk. Though forms retained integrity, their edges were less resistant. It was as if he could play with shapes at will, sharpening or softening their textures. He looked at his wristwatch and laughed. This change of atomic relations had persisted for three minutes. He walked back and forth like a child, swinging his arms in circles. What would running be like? Or working with a brush?

Turning left, he saw the picture glowing: and there was Hiroshima in the sun. Agonized faces were melting, while a cry of horror filled the room. The whole vista was throbbing to tell him that the new body he wore was an alternative to this devastated world.

He stood for several minutes, letting the meaning sink in. Could he maintain this state in light of the horror he saw? He shuddered and tested his steps. The freedom and joy remained, even in this shadow, but it was inextricably joined to the potential disaster his painting revealed.

Walking back to the farm that night, he felt pleasure streaming through him. Looking up, he saw Polaris in the northern sky. And the shadows of the blue wood were rolling, billowing gently into an abyss he would soon explore. His form changed constantly. Even now, hurrying down the path through rocks and branches, he could sense the nets of light around him, weaving incessantly, spinning a new nervous system. This body was inexhaustible, a meeting place of quicksilver and music . . .

19 The Praesidium of the Soviet Union's Academy of Sciences is housed in a former palace of Catherine the Great facing Leninskii Prospekt and the Moscow River. Inside its entranceway, two stairways curve up the sides of a large foyer. On a Monday morning, six days after his meeting with Kirov, Ivan Strelnikov slowly climbed the left-hand stairway to his second-floor office.

Strelnikov had spent the weekend reading materials submitted to Kirov's commission, and the issues they raised preoccupied him. Dismissing the State Committee's mandate to study these esoteric matters would be more difficult than he had thought. The issues surrounding the capsule crash had begun to bother him deeply.

The KGB parapsychology studies that Kirov had given him were carefully organized, each of them drawing on the judgment of physicists and social scientists who did not believe in ESP. To his surprise, every study concluded that parapsychology had little military or intelligence value. Strelnikov was glad for that, yet he felt sympathy for the dissenting opinions attached to each report. For all his prejudice against the field, each of these studies contained more compelling evidence than he had ever seen. Over the weekend he had felt his contempt for the subject decreasing.

In one study that especially impressed him, two prominent engineers had studied telekinesis. With several colleagues, they had observed people move objects by an invisible power, working in laboratories where fraud was impossible. Strelnikov knew and trusted both experimenters, and had decided to question them about their observations. He was also surprised to learn from the file that an American weapon maker named Lester Boone was trying to use psychokinesis against Soviet satellites. Though he concealed the fact from the U.S. government, Boone spent a million dollars a year on experiments that resembled those of Project Elefant. The Committee for Science and Technology had cited the fact in calling for the Academy investigation of the capsule crash.

But what preoccupied Strelnikov most was not in these KGB studies. He was obsessed instead with Rozhnov's book. All morning he had thought about two of its passages, occasionally rereading the chapters in which they appeared. The mind was a torch, one read, emitting images like particles of light. Meditation ordered the mind's emanation into a coherent stream, a pure beam of inner fire free from turbulence. Strelnikov was struck by the image because he had often felt a remarkable clarity while thinking about coherent light, and he had sometimes felt states of unity like the one the passage described.

Another section of the book contained a second startling image: when the inner fire produced by meditation was turned toward a human body, the seer could perceive its living elements in "their prismatic splendor." The phrase astonished Strelnikov, for in a reverie years before, an image of coherent light forming rainbows as it passed through human tissue had led him to see the potential of lasers for the spectroscopic analysis of living cells. These striking parallels between his own insights and the passages in Rozhnov's book had made him curious about mystical illumination for the first time in his life.

Lost in thought, Strelnikov ignored the greetings of two colleagues. Only his secretary's announcement broke into his reverie. "Yakov Kozin will be here to see you at nine o'clock," she said.

Thanking her, he went into his office and hid Rozhnov's book. It was good, he thought, that Kozin was coming The surveillance man's critical judgment would balance his unexpected fascination with Kirov's project.

Yakov Kozin had built and adapted the instruments in Strelnikov's physics lab until 1955, when the Secret Police recruited him for surveillance work. Since then, he had designed cameras and listening devices for almost every branch of Soviet intelligence, and during the last few years, he had supervised the KGB's best surveillance people.

In the course of his police career, Kozin had developed a lasting suspicion of Kirov and his friends. An admirer of Stalin, he knew that Sergei Kirov, the dictator's rival in the 1930s, was Kirov's second cousin. He also knew about Ali Shirazi and his secret school. Sensing Kirov's revisionist dreams for the Soviet State, he resented his good standing in the intelligence *apparat*, his Order of Lenin, and the glamour that surrounded his name. To Kozin, Kirov promised the deviation from authority that his cousin had been famous for. Entering Strelnikov's office, Kozin did not hide his feelings.

"I am sorry to bring bad news," he said, "but there are things you should know about this Kirov commission. People in Directorate T have asked me to warn you."

Kozin was dark and wiry, brimming with intensity. As if to contain himself, he gripped the arms of his chair.

Strelnikov sighed at Kozin's impatience. "Yakov, we have plenty of time," he said. "What is bothering Directorate T?"

"Two problems," Kozin said with a glance toward the door. "The first is Kirov, and the second is the commission itself. You know that if this project gains prominence, the Academy will be ridiculed everywhere. It will be the joke of scientists around the world."

"But it will not be given prominence." Strelnikov raised his hand as if taking an oath. "Do you think we are fools?"

"*You* will not give it prominence, but Kirov might."

"He can't. We will not let him."

"But this space-capsule crash is causing rumors. You know how people talk—there are stories now about unidentified flying objects!"

"Don't be silly." Kozin's alarm amused the Scientific Secretary.

"Yakov, I hope your superiors aren't concerned about that!"

"I'm afraid they are." Kozin leaned toward the desk. "They are worried that the subject was discussed by the State Committee for Science and Technology."

"But the West has its UFO craze. Eisenhower had to set up a committee like ours to reassure the American public, and chose a man more prominent than Kirov to lead it. I think he was the head of their Bureau of Standards."

"Yes," Kozin whispered. "But they never sounded an alarm like this. No president would make an inquiry of this scope. The newspapers would ridicule it. Can you imagine the headlines? 'American government to investigate angels!' It could never happen."

"Then what should we do? Merely humor the Committee for Science and Technology?"

"No," Kozin said. "But their concerns will disappear in two weeks if no one stirs them up. You must put a timetable on the project. If you don't, Kirov will find something to embarrass you. An Uzbek woman who saw a spaceship in her melon patch, or a mullah who heard angels singing, or a Moscow student who deciphered the Cabala through quantum theory. You know—the sort of thing he has made a career of."

There was a stilted silence, then Strelnikov laughed. "What else might he turn up? There *is* evidence for clairvoyance, after all. Your KGB research shows that."

"How much evidence?" Kozin held a thumb and index finger half an inch apart. "About *that* much. It is one of our embarrassing projects, this psychoenergetics, or whatever they call it now. Few academicians like it. Most Western intelligence people think it's absurd. Our Washington Residency says the CIA thinks we do it as disinformation. Sadly, it is part of our superstitious heritage, along with our Cabalists and mullahs and shamans. Of course, Kirov believes it points the way toward the future. Poor Kirov. His report will show that an Uzbek lady was taken aboard a spaceship and sexually examined. She will say her examiners wore silver suits, had pointed ears and penetrating eyes, except for one who looked like her neighbor's handsome son! It is an embarrassment, I tell you! Kirov is a poor version of Rasputin."

Strelnikov's feelings were mixed. It was reassuring to hear his own doubts stated so forcefully, but there was an extra charge in Kozin's manner that he did not trust. "You must admit," he said, "that Kirov is qualified for this investigation. The Committee for State Security has sponsored his work for years. He is your leading expert in these fields."

Having expected the Scientific Secretary to be perplexed and angry about the government mandate to study the capsule incident, Kozin had revealed his disgust without inhibition. Strelnikov's even manner surprised him. "Yes," he said with deliberate calm. "Kirov is our leading man, but that presents other problems. Can we keep a confidence?"

Strelnikov remembered Kozin's habit of collecting secrets about people he disliked, a habit he had already developed when they worked together twenty years before. "Please, Yakov," he said. "Don't tell me about his religious beliefs or his sex life. I don't care if he has a mistress."

"Unfortunately, this does concern his religious beliefs," Kozin said. "His superiors in Directorate T are worried. You may check on this yourself."

"And why are they worried?" Strelnikov asked, remembering similar conversations with Kozin in the 1950's.

"He has traveled alone in Europe for over a year without gathering anything useful. Some people in Directorate T suspect he might be plotting something. You know he dreams of a new Soviet nation."

"I didn't know that." Strelnikov sighed. "What does his dream consist of?"

"No one is certain." Kozin leaned close to the desk. "But his religious sect would join Socialism and mystic disciplines in some kind of religious state. Its members have secret passwords and a plan to win sympathy in Moscow. We must see what effect they have on Kirov's study. This commission gives him great prestige, a scientific standing he hasn't enjoyed before. You should realize that."

"Do you think I'm stupid? I know that perfectly well. But I doubt he will propose that the Academy of Sciences recommend the formation of a religious state! He's not a lunatic. Yakov, what are you saying?"

"There's no telling what he will recommend. His superiors in Directorate T only say he should be watched. They know he belongs to a sect with social ambitions."

Strelnikov suppressed his growing irritation. "Thank you for the warning," he said, "but I think you worry too much about subversive plots. Yakov, remember that this is 1972, not 1932. The cabals and conspiracies you fear are mainly a thing of the past. Do you actually believe that a man of Kirov's intelligence would think he could overthrow the state?"

Kozin stared at the wall behind Strelnikov's desk. "I remember you said something like that in 1953," he said quietly, "when I uncovered a plot against Stalin. Even then, you said I imagined too many cabals. Events soon proved I was right."

"But things have changed. You should give our nation credit for progress! The kinds of conspiracies that existed then, the kind you helped uncover, simply don't exist now. Our intellectuals and government leaders may disagree, but they don't try to kill one another. Kirov might entertain strange ideas about progress or science or some government policy, but he can't possibly plan to overthrow the state. You must see that, Yakov. Your kind of suspicion does not help our country. It only forces legitimate discussion underground—where it might become dangerous, indeed!"

Strelnikov had always been naive about these matters, Kozin decided. He would report the man's blindspot to his KGB bosses. "Arguments are futile," he said softly. "Are you giving Kirov's study a deadline?"

"He has four weeks to finish his report."

"And will he be monitored?"

"This is an Academy study. We are not the police."

"Then you are taking a risk." Kozin paused, shaking his head with regret. "You should know that Kirov has taken an American with him to a mosque near Samarkand where his secret school is located. We are watching them because the American has discovered Project Elefant. We have evidence that he works for the CIA."

"Are you sure?" Strelnikov asked with disbelief. "Did they send you here to tell me this?"

"Yes. They think we should have him followed, and they want me to supervise the job. Here is a letter from his chief."

Strelnikov read the letter. It recommended that Kozin monitor Kirov's activities, and asked for the Academy's consent. "My people will follow his activities closely," Kozin said, "and monitor the American's rooms."

Strelnikov knew he could not refuse this police request. Attempting to conceal his anger, he granted the permission.

"None of this will reflect upon the Academy," Kozin said. "We have watched Kirov for three days already, but with discretion. We will continue to be discreet." With a grave expression, he rose to leave, but Strelnikov didn't look up. Ignoring the insult, Kozin left the room.

Strelnikov sat cursing his predicament. He had known that Kirov's commission might embarrass the Academy; its subject matter alone would cause controversy. But now that the police were involved, its problems would be compounded. Yakov Kozin had a genius for making trouble.

Strelnikov leaned on his desk, covering his face with his powerful hands. Over the weekend, he had thought of Kirov more and more, finally deciding to work with him closely in the weeks ahead. Kirov's intelligence and subtlety, so apparent in all his reports, would serve the Academy well in responding to the State Committee's mandate. No one else had so much experience in studying these controversial matters. And yet, Kirov might want to use his new position to further some extravagant program. His KGB bosses must know something about his aims. Strelnikov shook his head sadly. In spite of his attraction to the man, he would have to view his work with distrust. If Kirov used the Academy's prestige to further some hidden agenda, he might cause a scandal.

20 From a platform on the courtyard's southern wall Fall and Kirov could see the rocky plateau some three hundred feet below. Beyond its western edge, the plateau dropped sharply to the valley a thousand feet lower. "North of the valley," said Kirov, "you come to the Kyzyl Kum. There is desert in that direction for two thousand kilometers or more. And there is wilderness all around us." He pointed south. "Those ridges run to the Pamirs and the Himalayas. So you see, no one comes to this place unless they want its secret badly."

Fall held the rail for support. Every movement seemed dangerous now, for his body had uncertain boundaries. With the slightest shift of focus, he could see the shimmering filaments he had discovered in the Well of Light.

Then, as the first edge of gold appeared above the eastern hills, a call came from the minaret: *Allah, Allah* . . . The cry cut the air like a sword. "Allah is great," Kirov murmured in English, kneeling on the platform. Fall watched him face Mecca and bow. Voices were chanting beneath them now, praising God and His eternal splendor. The glistening desert seemed a sea of music.

When the chanting stopped, Kirov knelt in silence. No one moved in the courtyard, no sound came from the wilderness beyond the fortress walls. Fall watched the sun appear above the mountains. Finally Kirov rose. Fall followed him down to the courtyard, holding the wall for security. He felt he could step out in midair, light as a bubble, carried by the light around him.

Fire burned in a rough stone hearth outside the courtyard gate. Nearby, loaves of bread and a huge bronze urn filled with tea were propped against a rock. One of the old caretakers unwrapped a bundle of dates and cheese. Fall sat down beside him. Six caretakers ate—one an Uzbek boy in his teens, the others men in their sixties, all wearing Western-style work shirts and trousers with the traditional skullcaps of Uzbekistan. All but the boy, Kirov said, had studied with Ali Shirazi.

The distant valley shimmered in a light-blue haze. Along a river some ten miles distant, mist rose like a long velvet snake.

The caretakers studied Fall shyly. "This has always been a secret place," Kirov said. "None of them has seen an American here before."

"Does it have a name?" Fall asked.

"The school has never taken a name. Only a location. It is sometimes called the Gate to Hurqalya."

"Hurqalya . . . " Fall savored the word. "Isn't it a Persian word for heaven?"

"It meant 'the celestial earth' to some of the sheiks in Iran, or 'the world of the illumined.' The term goes back to Suhrawardi and beyond, perhaps to the old Persian religions. But our school has widened its meaning." Kirov patted the ground at his side. "A larger Earth holds this one. The skies may open, and the ground give way into the vistas you saw inside the Well of Light. But for that a new body is needed. The body you saw in the dark. Have you heard the old prediction, that humans would make three great migrations?"

Fall looked around. Though they were not looking at him, the others were listening carefully, as if through his inflections they could follow his words. No, he said, he hadn't heard the prophecy.

"The first migration was across the continents, until we went round the globe. The second was to other heavenly bodies." Kirov paused. "And the third will be to the space of Hurqalya. We have finished the first and have just begun the second. No one is certain when the third will start. But here, in this crumbling *mechet*, we keep an opening to it."

Kirov wrapped some bread around a piece of cheese. Everyone waited for the American stranger to respond, but he did not. With the slightest wrong turn of his mind, the marvelous suspension he felt could turn to vertigo.

"Chasing other planets will not get us there," Kirov continued. "In outer space we are still underwater. Spaceships are only superfish. There are skies beyond our earth sky, but spaceships will not fly there. And a new range of elements. Our bodies, though, when they become vehicles of light, can make the journey. Some UFOs, we think, can do it. Some, in fact, would like us to be their companions. Like fishermen, they try to hook us! But we must leap through the sky to take the bait and breathe their air, as you did today.

"If you want to use Indian language, we can call the larger Earth the World of the Gods. There, the *devas* are the shining ones in a high *samsara*. But that is forcing our language. The idea of *samsara*, that the universe is only a cycle of death and rebirth, can obscure our vision that matter might open this way."

"That is what I argue in my book," Fall said. "The asceticism of the mystical traditions has helped hide the body's secret."

Kirov produced his battered copy of the Greenwich Press catalogue. Holding it up for the others to see, he told them in Russian that without knowing it, Fall was a member of their school. The six men grinned, and one said something in Russian that made them all laugh.

"He asked if this makes you a Soviet citizen," Kirov said. "He wonders if you would like that."

"Tell them yes," Fall answered. "But it makes them American, too!"

Kirov translated his remark, and all six nodded in agreement. Though the old man's question had been asked with irony, Fall's straightforward answer touched a truth they recognized.

The boy said something in Uzbek. "He wonders," Kirov said, "if you see that the Hammer and Sickle, the Star and Crescent, and the symbol on the grotto entrance are alike."

"Yes!" Fall nodded. "Last night I had a dream that Brezhnev was showing me the secret!"

Kirov translated the words, and the six men seemed delighted. "Brezhnev is our friend," one said in English.

"But we didn't think he knew the secret," someone said in Russian, causing another round of laughter.

For a long while the group drank tea and enjoyed the warmth of the sun. But Kirov was in a mood to talk. "You know, Ali Shirazi understood the other traditions. He was a learned man. But he never accepted the idea that the world was some kind of illusion. For him, every particle of matter contained the power of God. That is why the human body is filled with miracles. That is why it can mutate like yours did today inside the Well of Light."

Fall still felt too precarious to answer. It would be better to listen and see. Better to follow Aitmatov into the next perception. For as the Russian nodded at him, Fall saw the skies grow dark. Through the sun another sun was shining.

He leaned on a rock for support. With the slightest permission, he might drop through the ground at his feet. Everything cohered through some playful and tenuous agreement. Kirov made a cradle with his hands. "We must find a body for the larger Earth," he said, "as if we were an amphibious species. To come into this Hurqalya we need the new form you sense. Your Atabet has been doing this all his life, I think, through all his troubles and adventures."

Fall looked past his wistful eyes. The sky, it seemed, was opening to another light. Were there faces watching? And figures moving with the sun? Blinking the impression away, he looked at Kirov for support. He would fasten on his remarkable face until he got his bearings.

21 Fall's state had persisted for nearly eight hours, and even now in this wind-whipped distraction, his boundaries seemed uncertain. He could not shake the impression that a hand or a foot might pass through the walls of the bouncing jeep.

"How far to Samarkand?" he shouted.

"Not far!" Kirov said over his shoulder.

A precipitous drop had appeared, and as they started down it, the last edge of the sun dropped below the western horizon. The hills ahead were filled with blazing light.

Fall still heard the *zikhr*, its powerful beat echoing in the fortress walls. First the six caretakers, then Kirov, then a truckload of men from Bukhara had taken up the holy chant—*al-Allah, al-Allah*, it is up to Allah—as they moved in a circle to the sound of drums. While a guard stood watching for intruders, they had called the name of God all day until their departure at three o'clock. The ceremony, Kirov told him, was performed on the school's holy festivals, sometimes with thirty or forty people taking part.

"How long will the *zikhr* last?" Fall shouted.

"Until sundown," Kirov said. "About ten minutes from now. But look! There's Samarkand."

The city's silhouette appeared on the horizon. With its modern, high-rise buildings, it seemed another world from the one they had departed. Conversation being an effort, Fall sat back for the view. Caravans had approached this oasis at dusk for thousands of years, he thought. Marco Polo might have traveled this very road. Behind them, the barren hills were on fire in the sunset. The mosque, the *zikhr*, the Well of Light formed a surging tapestry around him. *Mechet*, *mazar* and Hurqalya—the names summoned memories of Sufi tales and Persian Mysteries. Half-closing his eyes, Fall sensed the light around him. It seemed a permanent presence now, like a second body . . .

The Earth of Hurqalya. Ali Shirazi had said that ordinary telescopes might discover its worlds someday. They might discover entire planets swallowed in their own Wells of Light. Some unexplained things in the sky might come from parts of the universe that were open to a new kind of matter. They might be beckoning, he had said, inviting our world to join their unimaginable adventure.

Suddenly the trail ended. The driver eased the jeep over a rise and onto pavement. They were on the main road to the city.

"Is the school part Sufi?" Fall asked.

"You saw the entrance to the grotto," Kirov shouted back. "That was there before Islam. And the Well of Light was there before that. My grandfather thought it might be as old as the caves of Lascaux."

A military truck shot past—the first vehicle they had seen since the previous day. As he turned to watch it, Fall felt his body growing more intact. The sense of uncertain boundaries was fading. But in its stead there was an effervescence, a subtle streaming near his heart. Another truck shot past. His body had changed, he thought. Never had it felt so elastic.

Fifteen minutes later they parked on a crowded street and went to their rooms in a guest house near the city's market. As he showered, Fall's whole body glowed as if it had been rubbed with alcohol. In the presence of Atabet's trances, he had sometimes felt a similar elation. As he toweled himself, he saw sparks fly off his skin. Half-closing his eyes, he watched the space around him fill with spores of light. Then a deep, familiar mood impelled him to remember . . .

A year before, Atabet sat on his Captain's Seat before the luminous painting. For twelve or thirteen hours he had occupied the same position, standing occasionally to walk across his studio or look out to the bay. All night he had sat there, building the membrane of oil paint he called his 'second body.' Fall remembered the joy and fatigue he had felt watching his mentor work, hour after hour, day after day, while the painting grew in power.

For three days they had sat there together, entering the atmosphere Atabet generated. He was building a passageway, he said, an altered time and space through which they could travel to other places . . .

As Fall watched the spores of light around him now, Atabet was vividly present. Their project of the last two years, their search for the secret of matter, had broken open in this unexpected way. They had found allies and traditions that would strengthen and illumine their work—allies where they had suspected enemies.

Kirov sat in the guest-house dining room studying three men near the door. Their backgrounds and personal idiosyncrasies, their strengths and weaknesses seemed obvious to him, and he tried to guess their business in Samarkand. In the clarity he felt, everyone he looked at seemed transparent.

"Who are they?" Fall asked, leaning across the table. "Do you recognize them?"

"They are engineers. Probably here to work on restorations of Tamerlane's mosques. The one in jeans is Jewish and will go to the West someday. He hates life in Uzbekistan." Kirov smiled. "The desert, the *zikhr*—they clear my eyes. The Earth of Hurqalya is more apparent."

Kirov decided to lighten the conversation to save Fall from embarrassment. For he could read him now with startling clarity. "Samarkand," he sighed. "Its charm is ruined by progress. They are planning a new hotel that will look like the Samarkand Hilton."

Fall smiled at the image, and for a moment they talked about the city's becoming a tourist center. As they talked, Fall's past became present to Kirov in detail. He could see his mother, hear her voice, feel her presence. Kirov could see her in Fall's awkward physique, in his widely set blue eyes, in his stubbornness and honesty. And he could see the father, too—irritable, brilliant, quick to begin new businesses and quick to end them, always ready to see the absurdity in men's great works. Kirov could see him in Fall's skeptical smile, in his restlessness, in his hint of nervous instability. Fall's rough, choleric complexion seemed a battlefield where his mother's refined and persistent will took on his father's untamed energies.

Kirov signaled the waiter, veiling his emotion. For in Fall he saw a reflection of his own torments. Fall's religious calling and doubts, his passion to reconcile contradictory truths were like his own. His path was as difficult, as alien to others, as uncertain finally . . . "Darwin," he said, "what would you like tonight? They have a good wine from Tashkent, almost as good as the Austrian spring wines. Let's see how it compares to your California Chardonnays!"

"It can't compare," Fall said. "Ours are as good as the French."

"We shall see! Do not be so confident." They both laughed when their waiter, an Uzbek boy in his teens, said that Samarkand made the best wine in the world.

"The only way to settle this," Fall said, "is for you to come to the States. In the California vineyards there is a secret gate to Hurqalya!"

"I cannot travel to the West," Kirov replied, glancing away. "Maybe someday, though."

The waiter poured wine for them both. They drank in silence. "Not bad!" Fall exclaimed. "I wouldn't have believed it!"

Forcing a smile, Kirov looked into his glass. To hide his full identity now seemed a betrayal. Someday perhaps Fall would understand. "Yes, the wine is pretty good," he said impassively. "They work hard on it."

"You are troubled, Sergei," Fall said. "There is sadness in your face."

Kirov looked at the table. "My name is Volodya," he said. "That is the more personal form of Vladimir."

"So Sergei's your middle name?"

Kirov did not respond. He wanted to share everything now, bring all his secrets into the witness they shared. In the Well of Light they had formed a bond that could not be broken. "I am the man you came looking for," he said. "My name is Vladimir Kirov."

Fall had trouble answering, for with each sentence he formed there came a new sense of shock. Why hadn't he recognized something so obvious? "You've been trying to reach us for more than a year," he whispered. "Why couldn't you do it directly?"

"The nature of my work," Kirov said. "There were dangers in your knowing."

Fall tried to compose himself. "Do you deal in military secrets?"

"Only in subjects like those we've discussed—parapsychology, altered states, apparitions. Their military value is doubtful. Does this news upset you?"

Fall was pulled in two directions. He felt an unbreakable bond to this man, a bond that had begun forming the day he first heard his name. But their friendship presented incalculable dangers.

"Does it put me in collusion with you," he asked, "knowing you work for the KGB?"

Kirov shook his head. "KGB people," he said, "inhabit most of the institutes you visited here before. They know about your work already. As long as you don't give me military secrets or work against American interests, you won't break any laws. But you can't tell anyone my name. We will get into trouble if the authorities learn I have told you."

They sat in silence while Fall gathered his thoughts. "You might think I made a mistake," Kirov said at last, "working for Soviet intelligence. But a destiny led me to it. The mosque, the *zikhr*, the Well of Light might have been taken from us if I had not had my KGB position."

"I heard rumors in Prague about you," Fall said with hesitation. "The CIA people there told me you were in trouble with the KGB bosses."

"It was only a rumor," Kirov said quietly, "a rumor the KGB started to take Western intelligence off my trail. Because I was traveling in Europe so much they were afraid I might be captured."

"And I've heard other stories. Someone told me you won the Order of Lenin for espionage against our military."

"Where did you hear that?"

As Fall described the stories he had heard, his shock began to pass. Meeting this man seemed destined. Their immediate interest in one another, the surveillance in Olema, their meeting in Prague, and their hours together in the Well of Light had joined them step by step.

"Only once," Kirov said, "have I done military espionage. I was in Paris in 1963 studying parapsychology. A Frenchman was guiding my studies, a scholar of Iranian mysticism and friend of Henry Corbin, who was an expert on Suhrawardi. By coincidence he knew the head of French Intelligence and learned that the French were watching some people of ours who were taking military documents from the American Courier Center at Orly Field. I helped our people escape a trap—the details are not important—and I was caught. In prison I was tortured, but managed to convince them that our espionage people were involved in another project. It took the French police off a course that might have led them to the Courier Center. Some of it has been reported in your press." He looked sadly at Fall. "I hope this doesn't separate us. There is much I hate about our system. And much I love. I am working to make the Soviet Union the best nation it can be."

"I believe you," Fall said. "In the Well of Light today I felt the pain you live with. You were close to defection in Prague."

Fall appeared to understand, Kirov saw, but it would take him time to decide about their friendship. "We must be open with each other," he said. "For there is a work we seem destined to do together."

Fall looked down at the table, veiling a sudden guilt. Did Kirov think he was involved with American intelligence? Had someone told him about his knowing Lester Boone? As he sipped his wine, he felt a new anxiety. Maybe Boone's support, coming as it did indirectly from the CIA, would compromise their friendship.

The young Uzbek stood waiting for their orders. "They have a *plof*," Kirov said. "A kind of pilaf. Does that sound good to you?"

Fall nodded, then looked down to conceal his face. His connection with Boone felt like a betrayal.

"Don't be worried," Kirov said, guessing that Fall was concerned about the dangers involved in knowing a KGB man. "We won't get into trouble." He sipped his wine, then rearranged his table setting. Half-closing his eyes, he tried to recapture his mood before this exchange had started.

"But look," he said. "Since yesterday I have wanted to ask you about Umarov. Were you upset by his challenge?"

"Umarov?" Fall was surprised. "I liked his openness."

"You weren't disturbed by his remarks?"

"No!" Fall said. "It's good to see our work from another perspective. And more than that—you offer us more understanding, Volodya, than anyone I've met." He reached out to touch Kirov's arm. "There's no other group that can help us like yours. After these two days, I see that clearly."

Kirov felt a rush of gratitude. Despite the questions his revelation had caused, Fall understood and forgave him. "Both our groups," Fall said, "seek a new understanding. But we need your experience, your patience, your faith in God's grace. Today I could see that something's been growing inside me—and in Atabet since our experiments last autumn—in something like Umarov's 'dark cocoon.' Nature's grace must work in secret when you've taken your body apart. That's one of the things your school can teach us."

"Angels work in ignorance," Kirov whispered. "That is still the way our world works. But we need your bold spirit. That has been my intuition since I heard about the Greenwich Press. It is important that you know this. Our tradition is *not fixed*. It survives because its vision grows." He leaned across the table. "The earth must grow or die. A mutation of our world wants to happen. But

139

the understanding it needs for that does not exist yet. Our school doesn't have all the answers. You could see that in my people today. You saw them, most of them working men with little education. Only Umarov's students care about the connections of our Way with science and evolution, the relations of nations and cultures—the kinds of issues you explore in your book. We need your openness, your willingness to explore new directions."

"But you have a tradition," Fall said. "We're almost starting from zero. Maybe that's led us to look for roots in evolution and Atabet's 'return to the First Day.' Maybe these stories we tell ourselves come from our rootlessness."

"*Nyet*!" Kirov said with passion. "Your path was given to you! Atabet did not want his psychic eruptions, those visions of organs and cells. He did not ask for a mental asylum. He had to understand his demons or go crazy. And the same for you. Your obsessions were a curse until he showed you a practice. Your work comes from a passion you don't understand. Angels work in ignorance in the lives of you and your friends. You do not have a visible tradition, but a secret one is working in you."

"Our two visions," Kirov said, "come from different cultures, are expressed in different languages, and lead to different kinds of practice. And yet they have amazing similarities. I see that clearly now. Atabet's trances drew you toward a world like the Well of Light. As he goes back in time, toward the 'First Day of the Universe,' he opens to the Earth of Hurqalya."

"You know," Fall interrupted, "my great-grandfather had an idea like yours. 'We carry the larvae of the next human forms'— that's a line from one of his books. This thinking runs in both our families."

"Your great-grandfather!" Kirov said with surprise. "Was he a philosopher?"

"His name was Charles Fall. He was a friend of Henry James, Senior. They worked on a synthesis of socialist and mystical thought."

"Even our families draw us together!" Kirov said. "I want to read their books. A synthesis like that was the dream that took me to Moscow."

"Their books are out of print, but I will send you old copies from the States."

"Your great-grandfather was right to link social and mystical thought. Ultimately you can't separate them." Kirov leaned close to Fall. "The crises our two nations face make it even more important that they work together. Their collaboration must grow, otherwise the world is in danger. You know the problems in

America. Our nation is troubled too. You cannot see it as I do, but many of our people are losing their faith in themselves. Our morale is suffering as the old Marxist dreams and the slogans about progress lose their attraction. We need new visions, reasons to live when the old myths are dead. If our leadership were open to truths like the ones we've glimpsed, or if enough of our people were, what a mandate it would give them! What a mandate for both our peoples!"

Kirov paused, for a heavyset man with Kazakh looks had taken a seat by the door. Though he pretended indifference, the man was listening to their conversation intently. "But there is hope," Kirov said. "There are seeds of this vision in Marx, if you search his writings for them. He was inspired, after all, by Hegel."

"But how many Soviets know that? Is anyone trying to reconcile Marx with our kind of interest?"

"There are a few theorists working," Kirov said, studying the man by the door. "Someday they might be famous. Maybe Soviet thinking will embrace these ideas and give them a surprising new life. Marxism, after all, foresees an end to ordinary history in the withering away of the State. It lacks a psychology, though, to explain what the new age is like. To complete itself, Marxism needs something like our experience of this morning."

The stranger turned to see them, and Kirov remembered that he was a Kazakh agent of the KGB who kept track of Umarov's students. "Don't look back," he said, "but someone is watching us. The police have us under surveillance."

"Are we in trouble?" Fall asked with alarm.

"I don't think so. But they are putting me on notice about our trip today. This is their way of saying they didn't like it." A look of disappointment crossed his face. "Tomorrow I will have to go to Novosibirsk without you. That is what the police will say. You must go back to Moscow. Can you wait there for me?"

"How long will you be in Novosibirsk?" Fall asked with a sinking sensation.

"For three days, but do not be alarmed. No one will bother you, and I need to see you. I am directing a project that could help further our ideas, a study sponsored by our Academy of Sciences to explore the things we've discussed. I need your help with it."

"But my visa only lasts for another week."

"Good!" Kirov said. "We will meet there three days from now. If your morale begins to suffer, remember that the Well of Light is waiting. The power and freedom it holds cannot be denied forever. Someday, we will see an end to ordinary history."

141

22 For six years Project Elefant's two-story barracks had gone unlandscaped and unpainted. Some of the windows were broken and much of the plumbing leaked. By deliberate policy the building was left in decrepitude, to reassure the project's many critics that the army shared their low opinion of psychic research. Still, a small core of psychologists and army men were now committed to Project Elefant, and their work produced just enough inexplicable results to justify a staff of sixty. It was a convenient place, moreover, to dump members of the officer corps who suffered disabling depression. The old barracks had become a retirement home for them, in effect a kind of sanatorium.

As Kirov made the rounds, he felt the same combination of moods he had felt here since its founding. There was a subtle embarrassment everywhere—in the stoop of the project director, in the avoidance of eye contact, in the reports the staff delivered. And with the shame there was resentment. Kirov could feel it in the staff's response to him. Anticipating his negative report, they instantly perceived him as an enemy.

But something more disturbed him, another layer in the mood of the place. Most of the staff took pleasure from inflicting pain. Depressed and hostile to begin with, they had developed their own oblique malevolence through their experiments. Kirov wondered if their muffled energies helped cause the building's disrepair.

In a narrow room at one end of the building, a staff meeting was in progress. Every member of the group watched Kirov with distrust. Which of them, he thought, would observe him for the secret police? Though no regular agent had been assigned to him here, he suspected that every one of his conversations would be reported to the KGB Center in Moscow.

Boris Latchev, the project's director, introduced Kirov to the group, then took him into his office. Kirov guessed that their talk would be recorded.

Latchev gestured toward a chair, then slumped behind an old metal desk. "I am very discouraged," he said. "We hear more and more rumors of our termination. Do you hear them too?"

"There have always been rumors that parapsychology is finished," Kirov shrugged. "But it goes on decade after decade."

"Our field has a difficult history." Latchev's red-rimmed eyes rolled back with frustration. "For every positive result ten failures. For every success a hundred other explanations. An Academy of Sciences team explained our results away last month.

They are trying to have the project disbanded." Latchev threw up his hands. "They have even enlisted the Chairman of the State Committee for Science and Technology."

"Alexander Rozhnov?" Kirov masked his surprise. "Are you sure?"

"Yes. He was here to see the Argentine boy, Ramón. The one from Lester Boone." Latchev seemed embarrassed. "Rozhnov spent an entire day watching him perform."

"Rozhnov spent a day with Ramón?" Kirov held his amazement in check. "What kind of things were you doing?"

"His Umbanda hexing, with dancing and shouting. It was stormy, but Rozhnov insisted on seeing it all. We were fortunate, though. There was the kind of thing you told us Boone produced—a ball of light, a seeming apparition! Three of the staff and Rozhnov saw it."

"He has not told us about the incident," Kirov said casually. "That is curious."

"Not so curious," Latchev said with a sigh. "People close up after these incidents. The stronger the results, the more decisive the denial and forgetting. I am surprised he encouraged your study. Maybe his experience with Ramón had a delayed effect."

"You say that several people saw the apparition?"

"Three staff members. I wasn't there when it happened, but they said it was clearly visible."

"What did Ramón see?"

"He panicked and had a convulsion. The thing was a deity of the Umbanda cult, he said, an angel of death. When it embraces you, your body moves to another dimension."

"And Rozhnov saw it too?"

"Yes. He had to sit down when the thing was over. The laboratory was a bedlam."

"When did this happen?"

"In August, around the twentieth."

Kirov contained his excitement. August 20 was the date of the space-capsule crash. "You must check the date," he said. "Can we get your files?"

Latchev went through his file drawers, while Kirov carefully framed his next question. "Latchev?" he asked calmly. "Has Project Elefant tried experiments with the space agency, any work with telepathy? Rozhnov would be interested in that."

"Yes, we have," Latchev said, bringing two folders to his desk. "But first here is the date. August twentieth. You can look at our descriptions. But yes, we have done some things in space. We tried to duplicate the telepathy experiments on Apollo Twelve on the days before Ramón's fit. Unfortunately, the space agency has not given us their tapes to check the cosmonauts' responses."

"Your experiments took place on August eighteenth and nineteenth?" Kirov asked, pretending to study the file.

"And on the twentieth." Latchev said, "We were hopeful with Ramón as the sender. It was the first time we had used him in a long-range try like that. I hope he didn't cause some metal to bend in the capsule. These forces are so unpredictable." A look of mischief crossed his pale face, then he smiled despite himself. "He has broken pipes around here. It would be awful if he caused trouble in the capsule."

"How did Ramón feel during the experiment?" Kirov asked, still looking at the file. "Did anything happen to him?"

"On the twentieth came the apparition and Ramón had his fit, the kind you warned us about. We had to strap him down. Unfortunately, he couldn't remember what had happened when it was over."

"And you heard nothing from the space agency? Who authorized the experiment?"

"Zaitsev, the mission chief. We were surprised they cleared it, since they've turned down most of the others."

Kirov asked to see the target images, and Latchev took a set of files from his desk. There were six pictures: a photograph of Red Square, a portrait of Lenin, a drawing of a man stabbing a woman, a naked woman reclining on a couch, a mosque, and a drawing of a monstrous face. "This monster," said Latchev, "is something Ramón brought with him. He says it is a god from his religion. Since he was the sender, we let him use it."

"How long did the experiment last?"

"For an hour on the eighteenth and nineteenth. Then a half-hour on the twentieth before the fit began. Only three sessions were planned, so the experiment was almost completed."

Kirov closed the file and leaned back casually. "How many of your staff said they saw the apparition?" he asked.

"Three of the five who were present."

"And how did they describe it? How dense was it? Could you see through it?"

"All three thought it was three to four meters tall. They all agreed it was fiery-looking. But density? I don't remember."

"Did it make any noise?"

"Only for Ramón. He said it sang to him, like a high Umbanda god. He said it was beautiful . . ."

Latchev's words were interrupted by a short grotesque-looking man who came running into the room. "Latchev," he whined, "Ramón is having a fit!"

Latchev leaped up and motioned for Kirov to follow. Together, the three men jogged through empty corridors to the other end of the building. In a room padded from floor to ceiling they found the Argentine boy. Two men held him down on a cot.

Ramón turned to the door and sat up with a force that sent the attendants sprawling. He lunged toward Kirov with arms spread wide. "Kirov!" he cried. "You will save me!"

Before Kirov could step aside, the boy wrapped his arms around him and dragged him to the floor. Instinctively, Kirov relaxed and they rolled out the doorway into the corridor. Suffocated by Ramón's embrace, Kirov began to lose consciousness. He did not struggle though, but gathered concentration instead. While the shouting attendants tried to separate them, he fought to hold awareness, focusing deliberately on his heart. And then, like the sky behind parting clouds, there was a stillness like deep meditation. By surrendering to its vast serenity, he could allow the energies in Ramón to speak, could hear what they were saying . . .

A high melodious voice, more haunting than a muezzin's call to prayer, sounded in the distance. Out of the darkness a sun was rising. Then, at the edge of his mind, there appeared a slow band of fire. A flame like a hand wanted to plant something in him. Resisting the fear he felt, Kirov focused on it. It had urgency, and a voice, and it wanted to communicate. As it reached his heart, an ecstasy started. . . .

"Are you all right?" Latchev gasped as they stood him up. "Your nose is bleeding!"

Bending down to regain his composure, Kirov focused his attention on the seed that had just been planted inside him. It was trying to tell him something . . .

"Strap him down!" Latchev yelled, as the attendants dragged Ramón away. Pale and spent, the boy offered no resistance. They strapped him into the bedframe.

Latchev handed Kirov a towel. "I thought he would kill you!" he said. "He has broken steel bars in his fits."

Kirov sat on the floor with the towel. In the sweet afterglow of shock, he watched a vivid image form . . .

Two shadowy figures fringed with light circled around each other, and then began to embrace. Kirov wiped cold sweat from his face as another image formed. Two drops of water, vividly etched against an emerald wall, slid into one another. Again he wiped his forehead, bracing himself against unconsciousness. He had to face it, a voice said. He was being given a revelation.

Two men were dressed in uniforms, two cartoon figures of his father and Ali Shirazi. Side by side they stood, as if in a satirical drawing, looking at each other fiercely. Their pride, their rigidity, their blindness to each other's virtues were manifest in their scowls and gestures.

In a receding spiral, living cells flowed toward one another. Clouds of dust, and stars, and galaxies. Everywhere the universe joining . . .

"Can we get you anything?" Latchev asked, bending near his ear.

Kirov looked up at the four staring faces. They seemed pathetic now, the sadness of Project Elefant written in every twisted look. "Thank you," he said. "It's wearing off. I'll be all right in a minute."

"That was a sexual attack," Latchev said with a smirk. "Ramón still has an erection."

"He is possessed," Kirov whispered. "Treat him gently." Was this what the cosmonauts had feared, he wondered—the erotic element of the apparition?

"It was disgusting." Latchev's assistant smiled crookedly. "We must get Ramón a girl!"

The only way to receive an angel, Kirov thought, was to be undivided. For the least fear could turn into panic as you were drawn toward a pleasure like death.

An hour later, after Kirov had regained his strength, the group walked through the sagging building. "There is too much sickness here," Latchev complained. "This is not healthy work. Many of our people have skin disease—herpes, boils, acne—and some have diabetes. These afflictions are occupational hazards."

Kirov had heard this before. Every military project involving psychic powers had destructive side effects. And yet, certain people seemed to thrive on such activity. A group of four men and a woman described their work with pride.

"We are certain of it!" exclaimed a muscular blond man with Slavic features. "Our Anya has had shingles for a week. We have this report from Bratsk."

Latchev studied a photograph, then nodded with approval. "This group," he told Kirov, "is trying to produce skin diseases on a prisoner in a gulag near Bratsk. She has proven to be a good target for suggestion at a distance."

Kirov examined the picture. Scabs covered the woman's arms and neck, and her face showed extreme discomfort. A doctor's report was attached, describing her affliction and stating the time of its onset.

"We work best in groups like this," Latchev said wearily. "But our results are still hard to predict. Take Anya, this prisoner. She has responded to every one of our experiments, though she knows nothing about them. But others suffer nothing at all. Why some are susceptible and others not is still a mystery. It may have something to do with their physical health. The sicker you are to begin with, the more effect you are likely to feel. Outside of that, however—poof!" He threw up his arms with frustration.

"But you are too cautious, Boris," the blond man protested. "Look at Gulag Seven."

Gulag Seven, a prison near Novosibirsk, was a special target of their experiments. The same day this group had placed its hex— in this case a hex accompanied by microwave bombardments—an epidemic of diarrhea had broken out there.

"But to what end?" Latchev sighed. "The Academy of Sciences will not believe it. They say the disease is common there, and dismiss it as coincidence. They say that psychotronics is a farce. How can we impress them?"

Kirov pretended sympathy, but he formed a resolution. He would recommend the dismantling of Project Elefant. This hideous enterprise had nothing to do with the Soviet Union's rebirth. It cast a shadow over all his work.

But it had given him the opening he needed. The connections between Ramón's fits, Rozhnov's visit, and the apparitions of the cosmonauts would trouble many who studied his report. This information might bring decisive support for his proposals.

Fringed with dirty snow, the runway seemed to stretch forever into the frozen wastes beyond Novosibirsk. No trees or mountains relieved the desolation. Waiting for his plane to Moscow, Kirov thought of Anya. One photograph had shown her naked from the waist, her breasts and shoulders covered with scabs and rashes. Pain pulled at her eyes and mouth in a way that would haunt him for years, but it had brought only pleasure to the people who had lain down the hex. One had even produced a bottle of vodka to toast their success. Kirov felt a growing depression. Were all his aspirations doomed by such perversity? Would his proposals to the Academy be twisted like this? To control himself, he paced along the runway in the snow.

But something deeper pressed through his emotion, something left over from his struggle with Ramón. As he stopped to gaze at the bleak horizon, he remembered his father's fight with Ali Shirazi . . .

Young Volodya was forbidden to study with the traitor, his father had shouted, and their family must shun Islam. Kirov heard his grandfather's answer: "To the illumined, history is under our feet. Salvation has nothing to do with past and future." Then his father's fierce reply: "We have history under our Soviet feet! And history is our salvation!"

Kirov's father, born Miron Kostrikov, had changed his name in emulation of his cousin Sergei when he left home to adopt a new identity for the Revolution. He helped build the Party in Tashkent during the 1920s, married Shirazi's daughter there in 1931, and fathered Vladimir, his only child, three years later. In spite of his hatred for Stalin, he remained a believer in the communist ideal. Ali Shirazi and his school represented the superstition and feudalism he had fought so long against.

"History will be under *our* feet," he had shouted as he declared the old man a traitor to the state.

As he walked toward the courier plane, Kirov felt his family's shame at this denunciation. His mother had never recovered from it, given her allegiance to both father and husband. Like other Muslim women who married Russian Bolsheviks, she had never reconciled the two sides of her life. From that moment, she was a woman without a family she could count on.

But Kirov had quietly defied his father. Stealing away to the desert mosque, he had taken the vows that would shape his life. As a boy of fifteen, he swore that the mystic teachings would be joined to politics. The social justice his father worked for would converge with his grandfather's vision of a new heaven and earth. The vow led him from Tashkent to Paris and his Order of Lenin, and from there to this government study. At each step it seemed that an invisible power confirmed the way he had chosen. And now, the seed planted in his brain by a boy he had brought from the United States for a hideous project of psychic research was telling him something important about the entire process. His whole life, it seemed, was a project to find common ground. America and Russia had a common purpose—that was what this voice was saying. But there would only be room for them both in a larger Earth. *In a larger Earth.* Only there could the stupendous energies of the two nations find enough room for fulfillment.

As he took a seat in the empty army plane, Kirov wondered if his thought was too grand. Surely the two nations could cooperate without these impossible visions. There were more immediate tasks to do before such an enterprise could excite a significant interest. As he often did while having second thoughts about his work, Kirov thought of his father. He saw him at the market in Tashkent, his muscular frame unbent, proudly examining the fruits and vegetables as if they had come from his own garden. The old Bolshevik saw all of Soviet Central Asia now as his handiwork. For anyone who cared to listen he would compare the life of its peoples to the plight of other nations in the region. Look at the wars and banditry raging from Kurdistan to the Indian border—the poverty, the poor education! Subsidies and fifty years of peace had lifted the standard of living in the Soviet lands of the Silk Road to the highest levels in their history. The scars on his Volodya's feet and testicles, like his own wounds, had not been made in vain.

Looking out the window at the rows of new buildings carved from the frozen wastes below, Kirov filled with love for his father. The elder Kirov's witness had been crucial to his work. Without his father's faith that the Soviet State was capable of transformation, he wouldn't have arrived at his present position, a position from which he could help reveal the spiritual genius of the Soviet peoples. Kirov's depression began to lift. His father had endured setbacks for more than fifty years without losing faith in his vision. He would take courage from his example.

23 Yakov Kozin also had visions of success, for his agents had revealed the following facts about Boris Marichuk: his mother had once been hospitalized for "nervous fatigue"; he had been a dreamy adolescent, given to religious fantasies; he had "improvised" during border chases of Turkish and Iranian planes, disobeying his commanders' orders more than once; he had boasted about telepathic powers to fellow cosmonauts; he had suffered from insomnia and daylong depressions; and, most telling of all, he had once confessed to sexual feelings toward a fellow pilot. The profile was perfect. The man had hysteria in his genes—and homosexual tendencies. The angel that wanted to embrace him was a projection of his feelings for the other cosmonaut, and the surrealistic form it took was the result of his latent instability. Kozin was surprised that the space psychologists could have missed this explanation.

Tapes of the episode confirmed his judgment. With its embraces and beckoning to mysterious places, Marichuk's apparition clearly had an erotic aspect. Doroshenko's breakdown might have come from a similar panic. Both feared losing control, not only of their capsule, but of their sexual urges. Doroshenko had been chosen in part for his looks, Kozin remembered, because the space agencies had wanted an attractive hero. Their efforts had worked only too well.

And Rozhnov had a similar history. His mother, too, had been unstable; he suffered from insomnia and ulcers; he had been interested in esoteric creeds. There was enough in his background to show a secret instability. Kozin was satisfied that these discoveries would discredit any occult explanations of Rozhnov's or the cosmonauts' hallucinations.

But Kozin wanted to do more than debunk mystical theories. He wanted to permanently discredit Kirov, and his surveillance had shown him a way. His agents had learned that a secret Muslim group opposed to the school of Hurqalya would try to undermine the proposals of Kirov's commission. Kozin saw that he could link the group to Kirov's school, exposing them both at once. It didn't matter to him that the Muslim group disliked Kirov's promotion of ethnic harmony or the corrosive effect of his mystic vision on Islamic fundamentals. Their apparent similarities would make them seem fellow conspirators to the police authorities.

To help establish this connection, Kozin told his agents to find members of Kirov's school who might cooperate. If necessary, they could use bribery, blackmail, or torture. On the day Kirov toured Project Elefant, one of them entered the desert mosque pretending a pilgrimage. By sundown he had spotted someone he could turn against Kirov.

24 The Special Commission on Soviet Values of 1966 was a puzzle to many. Few stories about it had appeared in the Soviet press, and foreign intelligence agencies had never uncovered its agenda. Some who were there said it was called to review the changes in Soviet youth during the Khrushchev era—their interest in jazz and jeans and American customs, their new sexual freedoms, their revulsion at Stalin's atrocities, their unwillingness to serve in the army. Others claimed it had something to do with the response of the Soviet people to broadcasts from space: the rapturous language of certain cosmonauts had triggered a demand for religious books, and people everywhere had asked, "Is there a God after all? That is what our cosmonauts are saying!" And there were stranger stories. Some people said the meeting had dealt with UFOs and contact with extraterrestrials. The fact that the government had never tried to stop these rumors caused further speculation. Were they hiding something too dangerous to hint at?

Kirov shared the general ignorance, but he suspected that there were similarities between the 1966 meeting of the Special Commission and the committee sessions in which his study was proposed. Baranov confirmed his intuition when they met upon Kirov's return from Novosibirsk. He had gotten transcripts of the meeting from Rozhnov.

"The old man was amazed he'd forgotten so much about it," Baranov said as they walked near the Moscow River. "And he is surprised how poorly everyone remembers. Then he said a startling thing. *No one has made special efforts to keep the meetings secret.* There were about sixty-five people there, and the thing produced all sorts of rumors. But you should read the transcripts! They were faced with a dilemma like ours—cosmonauts' euphoria in space, groups inspired by their broadcasts to take up mystical disciplines, ordinary people getting interested in esoteric religion. The rumors tell part of the truth. The big difference from our situation, though, is that the commission's report in 1966 recommended that the government watch these things for their dangers. Then they would all be squelched. Rozhnov put it this way: the events they were alarmed about could act as *agents provocateurs*, flushing out the dangerous people. When the time was right, they would be arrested. So Volodya, we have come a long way. Now there is an assumption, among some of our leaders at least, that these events carry deeper connections, that there is something of value in them. We have a Committee for Science and Technology smart enough to see that. Rozhnov is sobered by it all. He told me he forgot how closely the 1966 meeting resembled the one this October."

"It gives us more ammunition, Georgi." Kirov lowered his voice. "And we will need it now. Kozin is on our case. Our friends in Directorate T say that he has gotten the Academy's consent to our surveillance."

"I know," Baranov nodded. "They told me yesterday."

"Strelnikov has learned about my trip to Samarkand with Darwin Fall, and must be wondering." Kirov stopped to see if anyone could hear them. "But Georgi, I have revelations!"

Kirov reviewed his discoveries about Rozhnov's trip to Project Elefant, Ramón's possessions, and the experiments with the cosmonauts. Baranov shook his head in amazement.

"No one has made the connection," Kirov said. "Or if they have, they aren't talking. The people who know that Marichuk and Doroshenko were doing telepathy experiments with Project Elefant haven't heard about Ramón's possessions. Only Rozhnov knows that Ramón saw an apparition like the cosmonauts', and no one at Project Elefant knows about Rozhnov's visions in Moscow. Communication between Project Elefant and the space agencies has broken down completely, it seems. The space-mission people are embarrassed about the telepathic experiments, and Latchev's people don't know about Marichuk's visions."

"It will seem far-fetched. And beyond belief for many. *Beyond belief!*" Baranov gave a low whistle. "How can we present these facts and have them still believe us?"

Kirov did not answer. A man was following them carrying a briefcase that contained a device through which their words could be heard at a distance. "It was beautiful in Samarkand," he said, signaling Baranov that it was time for disinformation. "Fall will tell us about U.S. secret work in parapsychology. He knows what the CIA is doing and will help us with Boone and the Germans."

"You were smart to show him the sights."

"He will tell us *everything*. But it is not money he is after, only leads to our people. A few old monasteries keep him happy."

"It is a silly field," Baranov said loudly enough to reach the device in the briefcase. "Does he believe in angels?"

"If they appear to the right people. So I will make sure he does not learn about our cosmonauts! That would get back to the CIA."

Their follower had dropped back among the passersby. "But to answer your original question," Kirov said, signaling their freedom to talk, "I don't know how we will convince the skeptics. We can only suggest the connection. I can put some scientific language on it, the engineering formulas will help. But all this raises another puzzle." He stopped and faced the river. "If Rozhnov saw Ramón and knew about his possessions, why didn't he tell us? Do you think he's told Strelnikov?"

The man with the briefcase was approaching, and Kirov indicated to Baranov that it was time to end their conversation. "We will discuss the matter further," he said, turning away abruptly. "I will see you tonight."

In Baranov's apartment that night, Kirov examined a report from the Special Commission on Soviet Values of 1966. Though the document was entitled 'A Review of Attitudes Among Soviet Youth,' its subject matter ranged beyond the interests of young Russians to reactions among the Soviet people in general to the excitement of the *Kosmicheskaya Epockha*, as journalists were calling the new age of space. Pervading the lengthy report was the government's worry about excitement engendered by space flight's mystic overtones. One section contained summaries of conversations among Soviet citizens on space and ecstasy, on stories their parents had told of the wonders in heaven, on the similarities between religious scriptures and things the cosmonauts were saying about the universe. Reading these firsthand accounts, Kirov recognized the government's alarm. Lined up like this, such sentiments and declarations seemed to show a turnaround in Soviet sensibilities, a religious awakening perhaps. But had the reactions to space flight been so profound? Did these files exaggerate it?

"Who was responsible for these studies?" he asked.

"I'm not sure," Baranov said. "The preparations for the meeting are still a well-guarded secret."

"We must find out. The people responsible might be our enemies."

"Perhaps. But there is something more." Baranov turned to the report's concluding section. "Here is a proposal for institutes to explore the greater mysteries of the mind. It is sympathetic to the spiritual sentiments the Commission studied. Reading it, I remembered the rumor that there is another group like ours at the highest levels of the government."

"That is hard to believe. If there were, they would have reached us by now."

"But perhaps they have. Don't you see? Maybe Rozhnov is one of them!"

"Yes—Rozhnov!" Kirov whispered. "I felt something about him from the moment we met."

"What do our friends in Tashkent say about such a circle?"

"Nothing. Nothing whatsoever. Umarov scoffs at the story. He says we are growing too suspicious. But what are you suggesting, Georgi? That Rozhnov made up the stories about his visions?"

"Perhaps. Or else he had them and decided to keep silent about Ramón's experiments."

"And leave it to us to make the connections! That might be how a highly placed circle would work. But he seemed so sincere when we talked. I saw no sign he was lying."

"One grows practiced in the art, especially when one rises so high." Baranov strummed his fingers on the table. "Yes, they could be testing you and me. But who else might be involved?"

Kirov thought a moment. "Sheik Muhammad Khan, vice-chairman of the Islamic Directorate in Tashkent," he said at last. "I met him by chance this morning at the Academy, and he said a curious thing, something about 'Tamerlane's Angels.' It sounded like a secret sign Umarov gives his students. He's on our review committee. Was he trying to tell me something? Could he be linked with Rozhnov?"

"I doubt it. The heads of the religious directorates are too tightly controlled."

"But a member of the Way has patience. Maybe the sheik has waited for years to make his move." Kirov closed his eyes. "My grandfather had a phrase—'Angels work in ignorance.' If there is a highly placed circle sympathetic to our aims, we should let them lead us. That, after all, is what our work requires—that we leave the results to God and his friends."

"Perhaps." Baranov sighed. "Though I have doubts about the sheik. Maybe a word will be passed."

"Perhaps it *was* passed," Kirov said. "And I did not understand. When he gave our secret sign, he said, 'Our people are increasing in number. One day the Lord will favor our fruitfulness.' Was he saying they have a long-range plan to establish an independent Moslem state in Central Asia? Tatars, Kazakhs, Uzbeks, Turkmen are filling the army now. Someday they will outnumber the Slavs."

"But a pan-Islamic movement would not be sympathetic to our aims. Some factions in Islam will oppose us as surely as Kozin will. Militant Muslims do not like the Way of Hurqalya, and they are growing in number now. They do not like our promoting ethnic harmony and the study of other faiths. If the sheik is part of their conspiracy, he will not be our ally. We are lonely steersmen, Volodya. Events will tell whether Muhammad Khan is our ally or not."

25 The KGB was still uncertain about Fall's purpose in coming to Russia, and they didn't know what Kirov had told him about his intelligence work. Because the police knew so little about their relationship, Kozin could fill the void with stories that would compromise them. In consequence, Kirov decided, they would have to put their collaboration in the KGB records. During a walk through Gorky Park, he and Fall rehearsed a talk they would have in Fall's hotel suite for Kozin's microphones.

When they met that night at the National Hotel, Fall pretended innocence. "But Sergei," he asked, using Kirov's alias, "what do you really do? It is hard to believe you're an ordinary engineer."

Kirov was pleased at Fall's acting ability. "You're right," he answered. "Engineering takes me into fields close to my religious interests, into paraphysics, psychoenergetics, parapsychology, psychotronics. That's how I'm involved in the study I described, the study we want your help in. But let me put it simply. We would like to enlist you in our cause, *to help our government*. I would like your book, your pamphlets, your knowledge of American parapsychology, to help us in our studies of the mind. I would like you to be an unpaid consultant to us. Consider it part of a scientific exchange."

"You want my book?" Fall asked. "How can you make use of something so technical?"

"It will help us with our investigations of supernormality," Kirov said. "It is a priceless document, of course, so I appreciate your reluctance to share it. The scriptures teach us, though, to throw our bread upon the waters. You will have the satisfaction of helping awaken our higher possibilities in the Soviet Union."

"What irony," Fall said. "To have my work read here first. The KGB will see it before I interest a single publisher in the States!"

"So you see," Kirov smiled, "the competition between our systems can facilitate exploration of the mind!"

Kirov winked at Fall. Even as Kozin cursed this gambit, he would have to admit how skilled he was at such recruitment. "And I would like you," Kirov said, "to discuss your visit here with Atabet. Talk it over with your friends, then see what you will bring us."

Fall was winning immunity with each passing moment, Kirov thought, for KGB people besides Kozin would review this episode. But he wanted to do more than protect his friend. He wanted to produce an exchange that would be instructive to Fall in the future. He would demonstrate the blindness of people like Kozin to the subtleties of the spiritual life.

For ten minutes they sat in silence. To Fall, the sounds of traffic in the streets below seemed like distant echoes of the *zikhr*. The bells of the Kremlin might have rung in the ancient mosque. It was amazing, he thought, how quickly this presence appeared when they practiced meditation together . . .

"There is an old Sufi saying," Kirov whispered, "that angels throng together on earth when they find this remembrance, wing against wing, until the highest are in heaven."

Fall nodded, then closed his eyes again to savor the richness he felt, the joy that attracted such angels.

He has him hypnotized. Kirov imagined Kozin's voice, its flat, contemptuous inflection filled with grudging admiration. *The poor American doesn't know what's happening. The man is a master at this.*

So intense was the stillness he felt, that Fall did not move when Kirov stood up. He opened his eyes with difficulty.

"It's time for me to leave," Kirov was saying. "Let's talk about your book and research materials. You must bring them here yourself, because I will need your help in explaining them to my commission. I want you to bring them here two weeks from now."

Kirov listed the titles and authors of the studies he wanted, weaving a spell with his voice. "Can you remember them all?" he asked.

"They are burnt in my brain. This kind of meditation gives me a photographic memory."

"Then I shall see you tomorrow. Let me know if you have trouble getting passage to the States. Our people in the San Francisco consulate will help you get return tickets to Moscow."

Their meeting had accomplished several things, Kirov thought as he left the hotel. Kozin's men would bear witness to their collaboration; Fall would travel through Russia safely; and Fall would learn from this that one could speak with immunity about God and his angels in the midst of the strictest surveillance. So many results confirmed the Way's surprising fruitfulness in action.

Time was running short, however. Strelnikov's deadline was less than three weeks away.

26 Kozin's surveillance teams operated from a headquarters outside Moscow. In his office there, Kozin reviewed the tapes of Fall's meeting with Kirov in the National Hotel. He was both angered and impressed; there was no denying Kirov's talent for hypnotizing a man on the spot. "No one else has this ability," he told his assistants. "No wonder people compare him to Rasputin."

Listening to this effortless recruitment, Kozin decided to follow the American. With coercive hypnosis, results declined with distance from the hypnotist. Continuing surveillance of Fall might reveal a flaw in Kirov's methods.

The KGB had an effective residency in San Francisco. From it, Fall and his friends could be followed, and their phone calls tapped. But the operation would do more than check on Kirov's methods. It might uncover additional CIA links to Lester Boone and Western parapsychology. Kirov hadn't ordered such surveillance, Kozin believed, because he trusted Fall too much. The way the two men were becoming friends should make the KGB suspicious.

27 For three days Atabet, Corinne Wilde, and Kazi Dama had reviewed Fall's adventure with amazement. Like him, they believed Kirov had told the truth about his aims. Fall's experience in the mosque and its extraordinary resemblance to Atabet's own recent visions convinced them. The entire episode, beginning with Fall's dreams about Kirov the previous November, was a strange and unexpected validation of their work.

But sharing their work with the Soviet government seemed another matter. How might the military use Darwin's book or Atabet's understanding of bodily transformation? Would some secret lab try to apply their insights to the training of pilots and soldiers, Kazi asked. Psychic warfare had been tried in Tibet for centuries.

"Nothing I've written is classified," Fall said, holding up his catalogue. "The Greenwich Press papers on parapsychology are available to the public, and have found their way to the Soviets already. My book would be the same. Kirov's practically memorized my summary of it."

It was the first of November, and the four friends were gathered in the kitchen of their Olema farmhouse. The painting of a winter sun stood beside the hearth. "I think you should give him your book," said Atabet, gazing at the painting. "But we should also give copies to people like Gorski who could pass them around over there. None of our work should be controlled by a government body."

"But Kirov's study is sponsored by their Academy of Sciences.

He says the book would circulate among psychologists and medical men before it reached the army."

"Then let's make sure," said Atabet. "Give it to your other friends there. And we should think about publishing it here."

Kazi Dama had a troubled look. "Kirov is in danger," he said. "I can feel it. His study has risen too high."

Silently, the four friends thought about the Russian. For each, he had become a vivid presence in the room.

After a long silence, Atabet turned to Fall. "Darwin," he said. "I'm still not certain how that mosaic resembles my painting. Would you tell me again how they're alike?"

Going to the painting, Fall ran his finger along the contours of Russian Hill. "This slope is almost identical. But the buildings are different in detail. This high-rise, for example, is almost the same as a minaret. These houses are brick huts. Yet the two produce the same overall impression. In both, the buildings suggest living cells. The composition's the same, they both give a sense that the hill might be part of a human body, and they both have this same winter sun shining through the earth around it."

Atabet slumped in a chair. "It was eleven years ago," he said. "In the winter of 1961. A phrase kept running through my mind—'the sun within the sun.' The light in Turner's work obsessed me. Then I sat on my deck one day, looking at the city, when Russian Hill seemed upside down! It seemed the setting sun was rising. That's how the image appeared."

He closed his eyes to remember the experience more deeply. In some way, it was connected to his realizations of these last two weeks. The Russian's larger Earth, with its extra vistas and central density, was a powerful image of the world he might open into.

But a shadow clouded his memory. "The moment I saw that sun, I thought of Hiroshima. I knew at once that sun could kill me." He paused. "So Kirov says that the mosaic shows the end of ordinary history. Do you think they foresaw the bomb?"

"In some symbolic way they might have," Fall said. "They could have sensed the danger of the Light's miscarriage through a wrong turn human culture might take. According to Kirov, the school that based itself there—whether it was shamanistic, Zoroastrian, or Islamic—always believed in the spiritual transformation of the body. They were clairvoyant about it, he says, even three thousand years ago. At the start of the Muslim era, they already talked about wrong turns people could take as they discovered the secrets of matter. Given so much insight, they might have had an intuition about the atomic bomb, though they wouldn't have the details right. Kirov dates the icon to the Bronze Age."

Atabet didn't answer, and Fall turned away exhausted. The power of Atabet's realization, coming with this rush of events, had numbed him. Corinne, too, felt spent. To both of them now, as it had for Atabet, the painting seemed to throb with pain. What was it saying to them? According to Kirov, some of the prophecies had said that the sun would rise in the West because the ordinary earth was setting.

As Atabet sat by the hearth, the painting seemed to split in two. On his eyelashes were spidery lights in which the winter sun divided. The association he felt to Hiroshima and the bomb was part of a larger web, he suddenly realized. There were a thousand more suns in the earth, like the eggs of a tormented mother, a thousand suns pressing in on him . . .

He stood, balancing himself deliberately against this sudden recognition. Like a sleepwalker caught in a nightmare, he went to the kitchen table. Spread out before him were two maps of the USSR that Fall had used to trace his journey, and across them both small luminous points were flashing. "Darwin," he whispered. "I'm having one of my spells. Will you come here?"

Alarmed, Fall and Corinne stood by him while he bent over the table intently. "I can locate their atom bombs," he said. "If I could see them all and prove it, wouldn't that give Kirov more ammunition?"

"What are you talking about?" Fall asked, placing a hand on his back.

Atabet did not answer. Instead he touched the map where one of the lights was flashing. "Some of their missile sites are here," he said. "They're buried on some kind of island."

"But that's in the mountains," Fall said quietly. "And there aren't any rivers where you're pointing."

"Yes, an island," Atabet said, closing his eyes to focus on the image he saw. "With a perfect coast. But it's not in a river. It's an island in the snow." In his vision, a woman's breasts were heaving through the ground. Were they the breasts of a woman in labor?

As he asked himself the question, the mounds turned into metal structures. Instead of breasts there were two, white radar domes. And to their side, shrouded by a stand of birch trees, there was a missile silo. Inside it something was flashing. Letting his finger find the thing's tenderest center, he took a pencil from a pocket and made a circle where the bomb might be.

"Kirov told you we had to find ways to show how our nations are joined in the Light's miscarriage," he said. "If I can get these right, maybe we can help."

"We're already joining forces," said Kazi Dama. "Listen—in the jars."

Corinne sat up abruptly. There was a ringing in the shelves by the sink, the sound they had heard the night before, and a rattling of the window that faced the eucalyptus.

"They're out there," Fall whispered, turning away from the window. "It's that goddamned microwave device. They'll keep track of us until I leave for Moscow."

"Good," Atabet whispered. "If they see me make these guesses, they won't think it's a CIA plot. Why don't you go see what they're doing, Kazi?"

Kazi Dama went outside, while Atabet let his mind return to the buried suns he sensed. Sparks of light were flashing from the Ukraine to Vladivostok.

To locate each warhead precisely, he waited for his image of each site to come into steady focus: breasts would turn to radar domes, and islands into well-fenced sites. With his eyes closed, he moved his hand across the map. He saw a sandy ocean, and an island like the first. Waiting for the image to clear, he saw ten missile silos. Marking a line of sites near Kirghizia, he moved his hand north until another bright image appeared. There was a silver bucket and apples sliding on ice. Metal cranes were sinking in a bog.

"Apples," he murmured. "What have apples got to do with atom bombs?"

"Maybe they're building silos there," Fall said. "You're pointing to Lake Baikal."

In Atabet's shifting vision, the apples turned to red metal spheres. Were they some kind of transport device? Or did they shield the warheads from the cold? He felt something round and smooth. Where the sensation was strongest, he made five circles with dots.

It was one in the morning when Atabet stood up from the maps. "This is madness," he sighed, looking around at the others. "But I think I did it. I'll go over tomorrow to check." He ran his hands across both maps. Each had several hundred *x*'s marked in red. "I can't tell exactly how many warheads each cross represents," he said. "But this should give them a good idea about the general layout. The dotted circles, especially these by Lake Baikal, are a little less certain. Maybe they're building them now."

He stood unshaven in the firelight, his blue denim shirt hanging over his belt. "What were you seeing?" Corinne asked. "You haven't said a word since eleven o'clock."

"I hope I was imagining it." He shuddered. "But the horror is closer than we think. It seems to be happening *now*, in fact. It's as if the bombs are going off already."

28 Four days after Atabet made his missile maps, Fall brought them to the Soviet Union. When Kirov came to his rooms at the National Hotel, they were spread on a table in full view of the hidden cameras that Kozin had installed. Fall told him about Atabet's guesses, and Kirov had him repeat the story to make sure it was filmed and taped. If the guesses were even partly correct, they would provide astonishing confirmation of his argument that clairvoyance should be studied in depth.

When Fall finished his account, he gave Kirov his book and papers. Kirov had him describe them carefully for Kozin's microphones. Then he set a date for their next meeting and took the documents to his commission's new office in the Academy's headquarters on Leninskii Prospekt.

At first Atabet's maps were greeted with amusement. As news of the incident spread from the commission's office, members of the Praesidium staff began to say that Kirov would be a laughing stock by nightfall. By six o'clock that night, however, the jokes had turned to alarm and suspicion. A check with the military showed that Atabet had located more than a hundred Soviet missile sites, including silos east of Lake Baikal that were not yet finished. These and other unfinished sites were marked with dotted circles. Fall and Atabet must be instruments, unwitting or not, of U.S. intelligence, some of Kozin's people argued. But if that were the case, why would the Americans want the Soviets to know? At eight o'clock the San Francisco KGB Residency was queried for information. At ten o'clock a coded message from California referred Kozin to material sent by diplomatic pouch three days before, material that his team had not yet reviewed. In it was evidence that Atabet had made his guesses without CIA help. There were films and tapes to show that.

When Kozin reviewed the films from San Francisco, he was

forced to admit that the California team was among the KGB's best. It was amazing that they could have made them from a hill four hundred yards from the target. This was a virtuoso performance, he told his staff.

At 5:30 the following morning, Strelnikov studied the maps. After reviewing the entire affair and consulting with Kozin's people, he decided to let Kirov include the event in arguments before his review committee. He granted the permission in a formal written statement, knowing that most of his colleagues would interpret his decision as a concession to the proponents of parapsychology. But he felt he had no other choice. To suppress the incident might ultimately bring it even more attention.

Atabet's maps, meanwhile, had upset Kozin badly. His own surveillance people, boasting about their success in tracking the Americans in California, inadvertently strengthened Kirov's case. One had even said he was convinced that clairvoyance was sometimes an effective intelligence tool, one that their team might use. Hearing one of his own men voice such an opinion, Kozin concluded that Kirov was turning each effort to debunk him into a victory. Strelnikov's decision to put Atabet's guesses before the review committee confirmed this. If he wasn't stopped soon, Kirov's influence in the Academy might increase dramatically. The only way to hurt him now was through a scandal. Fortunately, Kozin's surveillance people had found out something he could use to cause one.

At three o'clock that afternoon, Kozin came into Strelnikov's office. "I hear you've seen Kirov's latest find," he said. "What does the military say about it?"

"The Defense Ministry says it is accurate," Strelnikov said with a shrug. "But they are not worried. The Americans get more information than that from their satellite pictures."

"But what do you think?" Kozin folded his hands on his lap to compose himself. "Is it some kind of trick?"

"Your staff says it isn't. They told me about the movies your team in San Francisco made. I congratulate you."

"But the movies don't prove that American intelligence is not involved. The whole thing might be part of a plan."

"According to your staff, that is highly unlikely. At least the part your people filmed. The American's spontaneity in making his guesses is obvious, they say."

"I've seen the films, but something about this alarms me. I hope you won't give this material to Kirov's review committee."

"And why not?" Strelnikov's strong features softened. "What does this episode prove?"

"So you *are* giving the American's maps to the review committee!" Kozin smiled sardonically. "Don't you think you're taking a risk, showing everyone our missile sites?"

"Not in the least. The Defense Ministry has given its approval. No one on the committee works for Western intelligence, and even if they did they wouldn't learn anything new. General Gradov laughed about it when we talked today. If you're concerned, go talk to him."

Kozin checked the anger he felt. "It is unfortunate," he said, choosing his words with care, "that you have put Muhammad Khan on the review committee. My people have found some alarming facts about him."

"What alarming facts?"

"He might belong to a secret Sufi group with separatist aims for Islam, a group connected to the Naqshebandi clans of Central Asia. One of my people heard him pass secret signs to members of a group here in Moscow. It seems that the militant sheiks have taken an interest in Kirov's commission. Some of us think they are working with Kirov himself."

"Are you sure of this?" Strelnikov veiled his alarm. "The faculty of the Institute for Islamic Studies said he knew more about esoteric Islam than anyone else, and we need someone on the committee to check that side of things."

"Unfortunately, this might be the wrong someone," Kozin said with discouragement. "Have you heard the phrase, 'Tamerlane's Angels'? It's a code name for his group. Or the 'Way by Kyzyl Kum'? Another one of their codes. One of my staff heard Muhammad Khan use both phrases with another member of the Islamic Directorate for Central Asia yesterday. We are trying to learn what they mean."

"Then we should drop him from Kirov's committee," Strelnikov said quietly.

"No!" Kozin leaned toward the desk. "Please, these are only suspicions. If they are plotting something, this is a good chance for us to see. Kirov's commission might draw them out."

Strelnikov nodded gravely, raising his hand to signal an end to their talk. "Yakov," he said. "I am watching this whole thing carefully. Nothing will get out of control. But if you don't moderate your worries and stop bothering me like this, I will have to complain to the Committee for State Security."

Kozin was stunned. This rebuke proved that Strelnikov was on

Kirov's side. "I am only doing my duty," he said, veiling his alarm. "I will keep you informed about our surveillance of Kirov and the sheik."

Strelnikov nodded, but did not reply. He could no longer hide his dislike for Kozin. "Please go," he said. "I'm sure you will do your duty."

Later that afternoon, Strelnikov sat alone in his office looking at Rozhnov's book. For three weeks he had studied it with fascination, wondering who its anonymous author might be.

The book was a commentary on a Persian poem, "Golshan-e Raz,' The Rose Garden of Mystery, that focused on the ascent of the soul to *fana fi-llah*, its reabsorption in God. Strelnikov reread a passage that described the *visio smaragdina*, the Green Vision at the summit of the Mystery, the ecstatic union within the emerald labyrinth of the 'luminous night.' He was amazed how closely the words resembled the cries of Boris Marichuk in his final agony. The cosmonaut might have been shouting the words of this passage.

Strelnikov put down the book and started pacing the office. His restlessness had grown as he fought his fascination with the complexities of the space-capsule crash. Slapping the desk, he cursed his state of confusion. Was he suffering that turn to religion he had so often joked about? The failure of nerve that afflicted so many aging scientists? Or was he on the edge of extraordinary insight? He cursed Kozin for warning him against Kirov, the person who might help him most with his dilemma.

29 Kirov placed his files on the table, straightened the lapels of his formal gray suit, and surveyed the conference room. Its cool businesslike atmosphere, he hoped, would contribute to a dispassionate meeting. The bare white walls and green carpeted floor had a quieting effect that was reinforced by the dignity of the room's location on the Praesidium's second floor. The sobriety that pervaded the building might restrain the passions his report would invite. That would be fortunate, given the potentially volatile make-up of the group. A fight during his first review would not sit well with Strelnikov and his colleagues.

Kirov took a seat to gather his composure. In spite of his

elaborate preparations, the review committee's dynamics were impossible to calculate. Muhammad Khan's remarks that morning had only increased his uncertainty about the committee members.

Kirov recalled their chance encounter, the second one in which the sheik had mentioned Tamerlane's Angels. The old Sufi passwords sometimes meant that friends would help in a crisis. Was the sheik an ally after all? There were rumors that the government's Islamic Directorate for Central Asia, of which the old man was vice-chairman, had been infiltrated by a Sufi group. Did Muhammad Khan have an allegiance to it? Conceivably, he had tried to say there would be allies at this meeting.

Kirov reviewed the committee list. Present at this first meeting would be: Sheik Muhammad Khan, as an expert on esoteric religious psychologies; Leonid Karpov of the KGB's Department A, the disinformation section of the First Chief Directorate; Boris Alexeyev, an anthropologist who studied shamanism; Yevgeny Strugatsky, a medically trained director of the space-flight program; two psychologists from Moscow State University; and a secretary to record the proceedings. Had the sheik signaled that there would be friends in this critical group? Though he could not be sure, Kirov was prepared for such a possibility.

He had assembled several studies for this meeting. For each one he had passed a summary page the day before to every committee member. He thumbed through them now, rehearsing his arguments. He would begin by saying that the Soviet leadership faced a triple challenge: from the Western world's research into mental process, from the irrepressible interest of the Soviet people in such mysteries, and from certain inexplicable events like the capsule incident. He would then review Soviet intelligence reports about Western parapsychology, work with "hidden reserves," and research in altered states of consciousness. These and other studies, he would argue, contained overwhelming evidence that humans possessed untapped capacities that commanded the interest of people all over the world. Interest in the mind's farther reaches was irresistible and could be harnessed through the kinds of programs he would eventually propose. He would present a mass of supporting material, including several KGB studies (one on UFOs), transcripts from the 1966 Commission on Soviet Values, summaries of Soviet successes in parapsychology and Darwin Fall's two-thousand page study of the human organism's neglected powers. As further evidence for his argument, he would describe the apparent connections between the cosmonaut incident that had triggered this study and the extraordinary possessions of an Argentine boy at Project Elefant. In conclusion, he would reveal Jacob Atabet's successful guesses about the placement of Soviet missiles. To support this revelation he would use the written confirmation of Ivan Strelnikov that the American had made his maps in California.

As Kirov reviewed his summaries, the recording secretary came into the room. He was a man in his sixties, tall and ascetic-looking, with a command of Central Asian languages. Kirov had seen him before in meetings of the Council for Affairs of Religious Sects. The tall figure bowed with a look of apology. His tape machine had just broken down, and he wouldn't bother to find another. But Kirov shouldn't worry: the Academy official in charge of this review had given him permission to take shorthand notes. Kirov joked that there would be enough for everyone to read without another lengthy transcript.

The secretary seated himself behind the chairs at the conference table. As he did, a voice echoed in the hall. Boris Alexeyev came through the door, wiping his sweating forehead and hitching up his corduroy pants. He had gained fifty pounds since they had seen each other last, Kirov guessed. "Vladimir!" he said with a booming voice. "I hear that you will lecture on the secrets of angels!"

Alexeyev laughed loudly, his red beard bouncing on his chest. "Be prepared for some extraordinary tales!" he said to the secretary. "I did not think I would ever hear something like this at an Academy review committee!" Alexeyev's disarming presence would lighten the discussion, Kirov knew, but the man would shrewdly track each nuance of his presentation. No one in the Soviet Union knew more about Siberian shamanism, but Kirov was never sure what credence Alexeyev gave to the putative powers of the shamans he studied. His attitude toward Kirov's studies was unclear.

As he and Kirov traded pleasantries, the two psychologists entered, dressed in dark blue suits. They were thin, with glasses, and looked to be in their thirties. Neither was familiar to Kirov, though he had heard that one was an expert in reinforcement theory and an acquaintance of B. F. Skinner. They took their seats quietly, a little shy it seemed in Kirov's presence. He guessed that they had never participated in a Praesidium review. Alexeyev winked at Kirov, his playfulness a vivid contrast to the psychologists' formal demeanor. One of them forced a smile for the anthropologist, while the other studied Kirov's summaries.

Then Leonid Karpov arrived. He was a stocky, broad-faced man who had been a protégé of General Agayants, the first director of the KGB's disinformation department. Karpov helped circulate misleading information abroad about Soviet work in parapsychology, and he decided which psychic researchers could be seen by Westerners. Kirov was glad he was on the committee, for the man knew better than anyone else which Soviet efforts in these fields were supported by government funds and which were amateur efforts.

Yevgeny Strugatsky came next, carrying a briefcase under his arm. He was a director of cosmonaut training whom Kirov had seen before at the Baikonur Cosmodrome. They had occasionally talked about the psychological aspects of space flight, Strugatsky asking Kirov's opinions on concentration exercises to control the nausea caused by zero gravity. Kirov wondered if he knew of the telepathic experiments conducted on the ill-fated flight. Strugatsky nodded pleasantly and shook hands with the others. There was an unencumbered intelligence about him that felt refreshing to Kirov, a clarity of mind that would help this group when passions ran strong.

Looking around at them, Kirov relaxed. Face to face, the group was not as forbidding as he had thought it might be. Whoever had chosen its members had been lenient, thinking perhaps that other reviews would be more critical in the weeks to come. Tougher questions would be asked higher up, especially in the Academy's ruling Praesidium.

But one of the psychologists broke the genial atmosphere. "Have you confidence in this UFO study?" he asked Kirov with clear disdain. "Your interviews with peasant ladies were criticized at our institute. We were surprised to find them here. The hypnotic regressions you used are quite suspect. . ."

But his words were interrupted. Muhammad Khan came in, bent but stately in an Uzbek robe, his lined, bearded face shining with humor and kindness. He smiled at each person in turn, fixing them with his shrewd green eyes. Kirov felt a thrill. How a man of such presence could thrive in the politics of the religious boards was a testimony to Islam, he thought, or to some Sufi path he must follow. The two psychologists avoided his glance, and Karpov seemed slightly annoyed. Only Strugatsky and Alexeyev returned the sheik's look with steady faces.

"Kirov," the old man sighed. "What entertainments do you have for us? I am intrigued by your summaries." He took a roll of papers from his robe and shook them sternly. "But I have written warnings on them with some lines from the Koran you might not like." He nodded toward the psychologist who had been speaking. "But I interrupted you," he said. "Please go on."

The psychologist continued with his objections to the UFO study, then deferred to his colleague from the university. With a flat, metallic voice, the second psychologist began to criticize psychic research. He reminded the group that throughout its long history the field of parapsychology had produced uncertain results in the Soviet Union and the West. Kirov could see by the reactions that this would be a lively discussion. The two psychologists, it was clear, would oppose him.

"The *tone* of these summaries is disturbing," continued the second psychologist, who appeared to be the senior of the two. "One gets the feeling in reading them that psychic research produces consistently positive results. But that is not the case. The American, Rhine, gets only—what is it?—a one percent positive result after forty years of work. And he has been criticized for not reporting his negative findings. Vasiliev's work was the same. There is general agreement at the university that such research cannot be trusted. Our colleagues are adamant about it."

"And yet there is enormous interest in these fields," Leonid Karpov said with ostentatious irony. "You must know how many Westerners come to the Soviet Union in search of our psychic discoveries!" He held up an American book on the subject that he had indirectly helped to write. "Some come from Western intelligence agencies. Other governments are interested in these matters."

"But not Western scientists," the senior psychologist said. "In a poll of academic opinion in the United States, seventy to eighty percent of the scientists interviewed said there was no such thing as ESP. Most of the others were neutral. It is not *governments* that are interested, only a few members of them. Without meaning offense, I must say that there are superstitious people everywhere. That book is an excellent example. As disinformation, of course, it was a masterpiece."

Karpov seemed unoffended at the psychologist's remark. "It is not hard," he replied with a smile, "to convince Westerners that Russia is doing mysterious things. It isn't hard to guide them to people like Edward Naumov." The mention of Naumov brought smiles from the psychologists. The man was famous in Moscow for his attempts to rally support for parapsychology among both Russians and Westerners. Soviet academics had tried to silence him on several occasions.

"But Comrade Karpov," Kirov said. "We do have projects like those the Americans imagine: Project Elefant, the Yoga Institute in Tashkent, our psychokinesis projects at the universities. Foreign intelligence is not stupid in these matters. I even hear that our space program is conducting experiments." From Strugatsky's look Kirov knew he was aware of the experiment on the Marichuk flight. "So we must keep this in perspective. Our government has been committed to work in these fields for more than fifteen years, and now the Americans are in it, too. You have our espionage reports. Our academicians do well to remind us about the uncertainty of psychic research, but they must not forget our government's continuing interest in the subject."

Having appraised each man at the table, Kirov had decided that Alexeyev, Karpov, and Strugatsky were the three he would try to persuade. All would have influence in the Academy's Praesidium. The psychologists would aid his arguments by their predictable negativity. It was as if this committee had been chosen by someone friendly to his cause.

"We are not questioning people's belief in the subject." The senior psychologist frowned. "We are only saying that ESP is a phantom effect."

"Our concern in this study," Kirov answered affably, "goes beyond ESP, of course. You have our summaries. I think it will help our discussion, though, if I develop the lines of our thinking." He looked around to them all for agreement that he should proceed. Muhammad Khan's nod held a hint of reassurance.

"We may disagree," Kirov began, "about the extent of foreign governments' support for psychic research, but none of us can deny the growing interest abroad in the mind's greater mysteries. To keep track of foreign work with hypnosis and parapsychology, our Academy and universities now employ several translators. At least one hundred articles a month on these subjects are translated from English, French, and German into Russian. And more translators are needed for work on biofeedback, meditation, sports psychology, super-learning, creativity, and the physiology of altered states. These fields are developing swiftly abroad, and are beginning to attract interest here among people in all walks of life. Students in all our universities are calling more attention to them." Kirov glanced at the psychologists. "And some of our professors, too. Even now, the Academy of Social Sciences is proposing a study of traditional cultures like those in the Caucasus to see what their shamans might teach us. At Kazakh State University, studies of the bio-field are well advanced.

Everywhere, students and professors alike are considering issues like those now before this commission. What is the nature of our hidden reserves? they ask. How may we harness our powers for health and creativity? How may our self-imposed limits be overcome? We deny this call by our students and academics at our nation's risk. If we do not respond, they will pursue these interests in private, often in bizarre and destructive ways. By sponsoring such explorations, though, the government and the Academy would stimulate our people's creative energies rather than deny them. They would demonstrate our scientific and cultural innovation for all the world to see. To that end, I have proposed the all-union institute on hidden reserves described in my report. It would sponsor research in the fields I have mentioned, and help coordinate similar programs at various universities and institutes. Are there any questions so far?"

Alexeyev's small blue eyes had a sly look. "Eminently sensible," he said, pulling at his beard. "What you have said so far cannot be argued. But I expected something more interesting, about our cosmonauts' visions perhaps!"

Kirov couldn't tell whether Alexeyev was trying to be helpful or not. "The visions will come later," he said. "And you will find them entertaining, indeed. But the mandate of this commission calls for practical proposals first. We are asked to find ways in which unusual capacities like those revealed through hypnosis and parapsychology might be understood and developed. The Committee for Science and Technology asks if such an effort might contribute to the solution of our larger social problems. They have suggested that the study of creativity, for example, might help us develop more gifted scientists and engineers, more teachers and diplomats. They ask if the study of ancient healing methods might help the sick, or if the study of the bio-field might increase our understanding of will and emotion. In their mandate to the Academy they list fourteen disciplines neglected by conventional science that might contribute to the national good. The Soviet Union, they argue, leads the world in some of them—like the study of the bio-field. It is a national disgrace if we do not support them simply because they cause controversy among our academics. You may read the Committee's statement if you like. It is included in the files I will give you."

Kirov stood and handed each member of the group documents to supplement his report. There was silence while everyone examined them.

The two psychologists looked sullen and a little confused. "I think you are exaggerating the scientific status of parapsychology abroad," the older one said. "I have never met a European scientist who believed in ESP. You are wrong to call the subject a challenge from the West."

"That is what many Soviet scientists said about cybernetics," Kirov said. "We were ten years late getting into the field, as everyone at this table knows, and that has cost us dearly in computers and navigational systems. We've been wrong about new findings in genetics and in the field of general relativity. By avoiding controversial work, Soviet science often fails to capitalize on its native strengths. This is especially true with hidden reserves. Our nation could lead the world in this field, but our academics neglect the subject and some campaign against it. But why? If something interests our people and stimulates their creativity, why not trust it? Our people seem gifted in fields like parapsychology . . ."

"You are talking about *my* field," Alexeyev interrupted. "Given our ethnic richness, the study of shamanism should be more advanced here than anywhere else in the world. But we are crippled by the desire for respectability. If I were to publish my observations of Siberian shamans, the Academy would reprimand me and discourage the circulation of my articles abroad. The truth is, I would be nervous telling *this* group what I've seen. Our cosmonauts' apparitions would be everyday events for some of the sorcerers I've seen."

Again there was silence. The senior psychologist picked up one of Kirov's files and read it with irritation. Everyone but the sheik studied the documents on the table.

Muhammad Khan, however, was absorbed in meditation. "In your written summaries," he murmured, "you said there were certain 'inexplicable events' that prompted this study, events 'alarming to our ordinary view of the world.' Could you give us examples of them? So far, what you have said is not alarming, though it might make some of us unhappy." He glanced at the psychologists. "Kirov, your study is very careful—I have seen it all before. But the results of research in these fields are modest. What are the inexplicable events you referred to?"

Muhammad Khan was opening the way for an account of Marichuk's visions. Kirov decided to follow his lead. Emphasizing the caution he felt about the incident, he told the story step by step: his contacts with Lester Boone and the German industrialists, their loan of Ramón to Project Elefant, and the boy's possessions during his attempts to contact the capsule. As he described the incident, he reached for papers by his side. "This story is so incredible," he said, shoving a folder to the center of the table, "that you might want to see this statement from the directors of the cosmonaut mission confirming the telepathic attempts."

"Is this story true?" Karpov turned to Strugatsky. "It sounds like one of our disinformation efforts."

The space scientist made no attempt to qualify Kirov's remarks. "The story is correct," he said without emotion. "Though our interpretations of it may differ."

"I would like to hear yours," Kirov said. "You have studied the space-capsule tapes more than we have, and you know about the cosmonauts. Is there any connection between the mens' visions and the apparitions in Novosibirsk? Three people at Project Elefant saw something like Marichuk's apparition. The coincidence is striking."

"I haven't talked to the people in Novosibirsk," Strugatsky answered coolly. "Though these papers make a case for the similarity. Yet it is all so far-fetched. I am not clear about the connection you see. You think there were something like ghosts involved?" He smiled with genuine amusement. "Or what? Certainly you don't mean that."

"It is extremely far-fetched." Kirov returned Strugatsky's look of amusement. "But we must stay with the facts. You can find them in the protocols of Project Elefant. No one there knows about the capsule incident, even now. You have heard the tapes yourself. Everyone here should do that. Both men were convinced they saw a luminous 'humanoid' shape that wanted to communicate. Marichuk watched it for nearly three hours! But how to understand it? I would like to suggest a straightforward answer—that *some kind* of force was involved, a force with extension in space and a guiding intelligence. Remember, it appeared to six people: Marichuk, Doroshenko, the boy Ramón, and three people at Project Elefant. The similarity is undeniable."

"The tapes are terrifying," Strugatsky said gravely, looking around at the others. "I think each of you should hear them. They are much more vivid than the transcripts in Kirov's report."

"This incident," Kirov said, "is strange beyond belief. But as scientists we should remember how often such visions occur to stable and unsuspecting people. Most of us are ignorant of this. That is why I have included our UFO study; not to argue that men in spaceships come from other planets, but to demonstrate the frequency and intensity of these visions among all sorts of people here and abroad. Of course, this does not prove that there is an objective reality to the things these people have seen, but it is suggestive. And thirdly, our older traditions bear witness to such phenomena." He leaned back with an ironic smile. "I know this violates all our modern instruction, but undeniable correspondences exist between the ancient descriptions of such events and the naïve perceptions of people like our cosmonauts. Many people we've interviewed over the last ten years have seen things like Marichuk's apparition. We are dealing with something that will not go away, something intrinsic to human nature, something that transcends cultural conditioning and common sense. Surely it deserves study."

"You are forcing a big pill down our throat," the senior psychologist said. "These things may be worthy of study, but to leap from there to 'older traditions'—I hope you don't mean angels. I'd like to hear what our representative from the space program says about these men."

"It was a shock to us," Strugatsky said. "Marichuk had been a pilot for fifteen years and had no nervous problems. I have studied his file for weeks. There was nothing to warn us about this incident. *Nothing*. Our entire staff has reviewed it. Since the early 1960s we have not accepted anyone into the cosmonaut program who has had a mental breakdown, because we learned in our first flights that any kind of instability might worsen in space. We have been extremely careful. I invite you to review our files."

"Now, Kirov," the senior psychologist said with a frown, "what connection do you see between these apparitions and the telepathy experiment? You believe the Argentine boy awakened some kind of 'disembodied entity'? I hope you realize how preposterous that sounds."

"Able scientists entertain these notions," Kirov answered. "Several have confided their interest to me. If we count bodies, of course, you will win. But science does not progress by taking votes. It proceeds on the basis of facts and helpful theories. I am simply proposing that our government encourage a more thorough study of these things. These questions, finally, are forcing themselves upon us."

"You can't count bodies to do science," Boris Alexeyev said wearily. "And you can't count angels to understand God. Do you know that saying, Kirov?"

Kirov nodded, puzzled at the anthropologist's intent.

"You cannot count angels," Alexeyev said with a resonant voice. "But counting them is only one problem. How can you get them to sit still? Shamans have tried to show them to me, but they have always moved too fast." He blinked as if some imaginary form had just flown past him, and everyone except the psychologists smiled.

"These scientists who have confided in you," the senior psychologist said with contempt, "what have they said about disembodied entities? Have they seen them?"

"At the Yoga Institute in Tashkent," Kirov answered, "a study of yogis is underway. Psychologists there have produced illusions among unsuspecting subjects, and attribute them to telepathic suggestion. They have also discussed the possibility that such efforts might empower energies we know nothing about. In the yoga tradition, there is a distinction between hallucination and subtle entities, the same kind of distinction that exists in Islam." He nodded toward Muhammad Khan. "And in every other traditional psychology."

"Not only is there such a distinction," the sheik said quietly, "but even finer differences between the kinds of apparitions one might see in contemplative practice." The old man fixed the gaze of each psychologist in turn, then turned to Strugatsky. "The point is clear, I think. This incident raises questions that must be answered. It is good that our government has asked for this study."

Karpov and Strugatsky nodded their agreement. Would they back his proposal, Kirov wondered. The chemistry of the meeting, it seemed, had put them on his side.

It was time to end his presentation by showing them Atabet's maps. Kirov briefly described the incident and held up Strelnikov's note of confirmation. But as he did, there was a noise at the door. An argument had started in the hallway. Then, without warning, Kozin came into the room. "Comrade Kirov," he said with a shaking voice, "you did not give me the correct time for this meeting. And the man at the door doesn't have my name on his list! What is the meaning of this?"

Though Kirov felt a sense of shock, he did not show it. "You are not on the committee," he said calmly. "It must be *your* mistake."

Kozin stood trembling by the secretary, holding a paper for them all to see. "Then explain *this*!" he said. "This is the original committee list. I was never told about my removal from it!"

Kozin's name had never appeared on the list, yet he wouldn't storm into a meeting like this without some legitimate authorization. "Has anyone seen a committee list with Kozin's name?" Kirov asked.

No one said they had. "Has there been a mistake?" Kirov asked the secretary.

The thin, ascetic figure took a sheet of paper from his briefcase.

174

"There is no mention of Comrade Kozin here," he said, passing it around.

"Then we have *two* lists!" Kozin said, his hands shaking. "Does anyone have an explanation?"

Everyone at the table masked his reaction except Alexeyev and the sheik. "Internal surveillance is not my specialty," Alexeyev said with a resonant voice. "You should talk to the people in those departments."

Taken aback at this hint of ridicule, Kozin glowered at the anthropologist.

"Have you something to bring to this meeting?" asked the sheik, almost in a whisper. "Are you responsible for some of these reports?"

"I am responsible for Comrade Kirov's surveillance." Kozin brought himself under control. "The Committee for State Security has assigned me to this project."

Kozin's mad strategy was suddenly apparent to Kirov. By storming in like this, he would plant just enough doubts in the minds of the committee members to influence their recommendations.

"I think he should take a seat," Kirov said quietly. "The question of his membership can be settled later. It seems he has something to contribute."

Everyone at the table was embarrassed by Kozin's behavior. It might be possible, Kirov thought, to reveal his instability. "You come at a propitious time," he said, while Kozin took a seat. "I was about to show the American's maps of our missile locations." He held up Strelnikov's note again. "This is a confirmation from Ivan Strelnikov that these documents have been reviewed in his office. Such a note seemed necessary because they are so hard to believe." He passed the statement to Alexeyev while Kozin looked on with contempt.

Spreading Atabet's maps on the table, Kirov felt his confidence rising. The American's extraordinary gifts, so evident in Kozin's films, seemed instruments of the same power that ruled his life, a power that was working even now to overcome every resistance. Atabet's maps confirmed his sense that these events were somehow destined . . .

"But who are these Americans?" Alexeyev asked. "Is this something they do all the time?"

"Darwin Fall is in Moscow," Kirov said. "He is in contact with people all over the world interested in parapsychology and hidden reserves. He is also an important scholar and has contributed his unpublished work to our commission. But these maps were totally unexpected. He gave them to me at the National Hotel just two days ago, under the cameras of our surveillance people. Strelnikov's office reviewed them, because they identify most of our intercontinental missile sites, and some we are only planning. The circles with dotted lines represent silos we haven't built yet. They are not on the satellite pictures, but Atabet found them out!"

"I smell disinformation," Karpov sighed. "This could be a CIA job. Perhaps they are using these people."

"No," Kirov said. "Though that is the most plausible theory. By happy circumstance—or rather by the foresight of Comrade Kozin—we have followed Fall and his friends in California. Some of Kozin's people filmed the American making his guesses. That is why there is such alarm. *We have seen them do this and have it all on film!*"

"Does American intelligence know we have these maps?" Strugatsky asked.

"We aren't sure yet, but our people in Washington are trying to find out. In spite of our surveillance in California, we don't know what Fall and his friends have told their government. They seem more intent to share their work with us."

"Are you sure about these dotted circles?" the senior psychologist asked with dismay.

" You have Strelnikov's note," Kirov answered. "He says that almost every one identifies a site on the planning boards."

"But this is impossible!" The psychologist looked to Karpov. "The Americans must have a spy in our military."

"You think they would tell us, then?" Alexeyev said with contempt. "That is a stupid remark."

"But these 'guesses'!" The psychologist was visibly upset. "Where do you propose they come from? I don't understand this at all."

"Neither do I," said Kirov. "That is why we have proposed more study of these matters. No one yet has given an adequate explanation of clairvoyance. Conventional science cannot comprehend it."

"You are right," said Alexeyev. "Though I have nothing so dramatic as this, I have seen Siberian shamans do things I can't explain. I, for one, will second your proposal."

"Let me look at this confirmation." Karpov took Strelnikov's note. "Astonishing. Simply astonishing!" The disinformation expert started walking back and forth across the room.

The others stood around the maps, while the senior psychologist examined Strelnikov's note. Kozin sat back in silence. Alexeyev's bass voice sounded above the rest: "Yes, I will second your proposals! These events are extraordinary!"

Kozin stood abruptly. "This is insane!" he shouted, slamming a fist on the table. "I cannot believe what I am seeing, giving credence to such superstition. This committee is a farce!"

"But we have made no findings," Alexeyev said. "We have not written a thing. This is our very first meeting."

Kozin looked at the anthropologist with contempt, then turned to Muhammad Khan. "I suppose you agree with all this," he said.

The sheik wagged his head enigmatically, his face and gestures conveying more innuendoes than Kirov could comprehend. The psychologists were plainly embarrassed by the surveillance man's behavior. Kirov guessed that they would mention his outburst in their reports, with an unfavorable opinion of his character. Everything seemed to be working in his favor.

"Comrade Kozin is partly right," said the sheik. "Perhaps we are getting too excited."

Everyone was looking at the maps, but they turned to the old man. A force in his wavering voice commanded their attention.

One by one, the group returned to their seats. Only Kozin remained standing, his arms folded in a gesture of defiance.

When the group was seated, the sheik began to speak. "Kirov," he said, "I want to commend you for introducing these difficult subjects so boldly. I fear two things, however. You know as well as I the dangers of religious enthusiasm. It has been the greatest danger to the Way." He paused, as if waiting for acknowledgment.

Startled that he had mentioned the Way so openly, Kirov glanced around the table. The secretary wasn't recording the sheik's remarks.

"If your proposals were suddenly made public"—the sheik paused for effect—"there would be just this sort of enthusiasm. We saw that in the 1960s both here and in the West. Our people are inflamed by ideas and give way to impulse easily. So we must be careful to make this knowledge public by degree. We must proceed with care. I presume you will recommend that."

Kirov nodded, uncertain as to what the sheik was driving at. "I have not thought about timetables," he said. "The studies I propose will take decades."

"Good," the old man said. "But there is a second thing. We have seen your evidence. The American's guesses about our atomic weapons—if they're as accurate as Strelnikov says—show how effective these powers can be. But here is the difficulty. They could be used by our dissidents! We have seen the success of Project Elefant, however limited, and success in places you have not had time to mention. What would prevent our malcontents from using these powers against our leaders?"

Surprised by these remarks, Kirov wondered what the sheik intended. Was the wily old man concealing his role in the meeting?

"Through the entire history of Islam," the old man continued, "there have been groups that practiced sorcery. For every angelic circle, there was a demonic one. It could happen again. That is what we see, after all, at Project Elefant. They have cursed one gulag after another, according to these reports. What is to prevent someone from doing the same thing to our leaders?"

Kirov did not answer. If he argued against the old man's admonitions, he might weaken his case that these powers could be effective. "So we should go slowly," Muhammad Khan said, his gaze moving down the table.

Kirov followed his glance. Alexeyev seemed reflective, Kozin contemptuous, and the psychologists dismayed by these remarks. But Karpov and Strugatsky agreed with Muhammad Khan's warning. Kirov suppressed his anger. Had the old man weakened their support?

"We must take infinite care," said Muhammad Khan, "because we are playing with powers we don't understand. That is what Comrade Kozin is trying to tell us."

"I have no special knowledge," Kozin said with annoyance.

"But your surveillance teams are the best we have." The old man smiled warmly. "Without them it would be harder to believe this evidence. You have seen the dangers in religious cabals."

"There are cabals," Kozin whispered, "at this very table! I am afraid we are witnessing one now."

Kirov felt sudden fear. Did Kozin know something he wasn't telling?

"You know what I'm saying," Kozin said, walking away from the table. "I think we are surrounded by Tamerlane's Angels!"

The secretary leaned forward and asked him to repeat the remark. "Tamerlane's Angels!" Kozin whispered. "Comrade Kirov will explain what I mean."

"I do not know what you mean," said Kirov. "You will have to do the explaining."

"You don't know what it means?" Kozin looked to the sheik. "Then why has our representative from Islam used the phrase so frequently? And why has he referred to 'the Way'? They are not telling us everything they know. 'Tamerlane's Angels' is a password used by secret groups in Central Asia that Kirov and Sheik Khan belong to."

"It is the name of a group that was disbanded ten years ago." The sheik looked around at the others. "Have I been using the phrase as Kozin says? Do any of you remember?"

Kozin looked at the secretary. "Examine the transcripts," he said. "Sheik Khan has used the phrase in a very peculiar way."

The secretary thumbed through his pad. "I will look," he said. "But it will take a moment."

The group sat in silence while the secretary searched his notes. Was the ascetic-looking figure another secret ally, Kirov wondered, remembering there would be no tapes. "Does anyone remember our using the phrase?" Kirov asked. "I have no idea what Comrade Kozin is trying to tell us."

No one remembered, it seemed.

"*You* remember," Kozin answered. "And you do." He looked at the sheik. "And I think you know, too." He nodded toward Alexeyev.

"Me?" Alexeyev exploded. "This is outrageous! Are you accusing me of something?"

"And I remember what?" asked the sheik serenely. Kozin refused to go further. He folded his arms to suggest that he had revealed the entire cabal.

"If you don't tell us what you mean," Alexeyev fumed, "I will demand a hearing."

Kozin had missed the mark in regard to Alexeyev, Kirov saw. But what did he know about Muhammad Khan? "So you think we form a cabal?" the sheik said with an ironic twinkle. "I don't think you really believe that."

"But, Comrade Kozin," Kirov said, "since you've raised this issue with such vehemence, I think you should tell us what our cabal consists of. What are we supposed to be doing?"

"You know perfectly well," the sallow figure answered, his arms folded defiantly.

"If you don't want to explain your remarks," Kirov said, "we will continue."

Kozin shrugged, as if the proceedings were compromised now. "The matter I am referring to," he said, "will emerge as these meetings go on. But there is another thing. My assistants are preparing a report to explain Cosmonaut Marichuk's apparition in more sensible terms. It appears that the man was homosexual. His 'angel' was Doroshenko."

"That is absurd!" Strugatsky exclaimed. "We have questioned

every one of his friends and coworkers, and that never came out."

"I have examined your studies of him," Kozin said. "Perhaps you should look at them again."

"I have studied them carefully." The even-tempered space scientist regained his composure. "If you are referring to his admission of adolescent homosexual feelings, you have a very slim case. It is a long way from a few fleeting urges twenty years ago to panics and apparitions."

"Comrade Kozin's report should make interesting reading." Boris Alexeyev shook his head with amusement. "I did not realize that the Committee for State Security had advanced so far in its study of human motivation."

"We shall let the Praesidium decide when I present my report." Kozin fixed his gaze on a portrait of Lenin above the conference table. "I refuse to say any more."

"Then we will proceed," Kirov said. "Unless there are other objections."

Glances were traded around the table. Karpov and Strugatsky were angry at Kozin, and both the psychologists embarrassed, but everyone nodded for Kirov to continue. He finished his summaries and introduced the proposals he would make to the Academy while Kozin looked on with contempt. Kirov guessed that the others now believed the surveillance man to be imbalanced.

His presentation done, Kirov adjourned the meeting. Kozin stood in a corner, watching suspiciously as everyone left the room. He must be suffering some kind of breakdown, Kirov thought.

But for whom was Muhammad Khan working? His admonitions might have weakened Strugatsky's and Karpov's support. And how would Strelnikov react to this preliminary meeting? It was not a good sign that so many complexities had appeared in a group whose dynamics were fundamentally helpful to him.

30 Waking, Ivan Strelnikov felt a strange elation. The yellow chair at the foot of his bed, the old wooden chest of drawers, the curtains waving by the window pulsed with energy. Everything seemed filled with the buoyancy his dream had produced.

Rising carefully, as if any sudden movement might disturb his pleasure, he stood beside his bed. In his dream he had discovered a magnificent stone—a piece of quartz, perhaps, or a giant uncut diamond—and had carried it up a passageway into an emerald hall. There, a single ray of laser light had streamed into the stone, forming a brilliant rainbow.

Standing naked before his bathroom mirror, Strelnikov examined his face. It seemed the face of a stranger—the prominent cheekbones, well-formed jaw looked too fixed and heroic to be his own. The cool, gray eyes did not convey the fullness he felt. Alarmed, he stood back. The man in the reflection was not him—his essential self did not have these boundaries. Washing his face, he remembered another part of the dream...

Vladimir Kirov had come to his office at the Academy to help him remember the secret of his experience in the emerald hall. Then, to Strelnikov's amazement, Kirov had turned into a panther and led him out to the street. Now, washing his hands, Strelnikov realized the dream had been erotic. Quickly he rinsed his mouth and shaved, shaking in the cold. The soft, gray hair on his muscular chest stood erect, he shivered so badly.

In five minutes he dressed and called his driver, forcing all memory of the dream aside. He wouldn't have coffee this morning, he decided. A limousine ride would ease his agitation.

Monday through Friday, the driver came on duty at 7:30 and could reach Strelnikov's apartment a few moments after being called. This morning the call came before 7:30, but the driver had been up early. At 7:35 Strelnikov rode in his long black Chaika toward Leninskii Prospekt.

Snow had fallen in the night, producing a radiance in the streets around him. "It's early," he told the driver. "Drive past the Kremlin before you go to the Academy."

The driver slowed the limousine and Strelnikov leaned back for the view. But as he settled into the cushioned seat, he remembered his dream again.

Strelnikov took pride in facing upsetting truths. In the dream there had been something almost sexual. Kirov's handsome figure had become a panther, and Strelnikov had willingly ridden it. Riding in this limousine, he felt the way he had felt on the panther's back: there was the same pleasure-filled surrender, the same sense of being carried through the morning darkness toward a splendid place. He looked at the snow-covered sidewalk, brilliant in the silvery light of the towering streetlamps, and gazed up at the gold-leafed cupolas above the Kremlin wall. The view was dazzling, and charged with energy. It held layer upon layer of the past joined in one enormous moment. Feudal, czarist, revolutionary pageantry hovered in the air. The city was unfolding like his dream, he thought—carrying the past toward a marvelous future.

Strelnikov could not remember an experience like this. He wondered if its significance would unfold as the day proceeded.

Patiently, Kirov waited outside an office in the KGB Center on Dzerzhinsky Square. Two KGB officers, Konstantin Smyslov and Fyodor Karel, had been chosen by Directorate T to review Kozin's charges. Inside, they examined their files on Kirov and Muhammad Khan. "There is no real record of the sheik until he was forty," said Smyslov, a large, craggy-faced Russian in his fifties. "We don't know what he did until 1937. It simply says he was a farmer near Tashkent."

Fyodor Karel made a sour expression. Neither man was satisfied with the records of Muslims on the religious boards; there were always such gaps in their past. "He is a good soldier, it seems," Karel sighed. "Without him, we wouldn't have uncovered this subversive group—this Tamerlane's Angels."

Karel, the smaller of the two, was a KGB veteran who had risen to power under Stalin. "Tamerlane's Angels . . . " He shrugged. "Kozin must be confused. Doesn't he say that Kirov and Muhammad Khan belong to it? Or is there another group with that name?"

Smyslov shook his head. The affairs of Islam's sects had always confused him. "Maybe *several* groups," he said. "The tomb of Tamerlane is one of their important shrines." He turned to their secretary sitting across the room. "Record all this," he said, "even if the sheik says something Uzbek."

The gray, ascetic figure nodded. But Muhammad Khan spoke Russian well, he said. He had heard him at the meeting of Kirov's committee.

Smyslov turned to Karel. "Fyodor," he asked, "what do you think of Kozin's charges? He claims that six members of Tamerlane's Angels are in Moscow, drawn here by Kirov's commission. Here is a list of their names. As you can see, not one works for the religious directorates. They're all Party bureaucrats or academics."

"There are two problems with his charges." Karel frowned. "First, we have no certain evidence against these people, though two might belong to the Naqshebandi brotherhoods of Dagestan. And second, Kozin has done this before. It is his third alarm about Islamic plots, and the first two caused investigations that only proved the innocence of everyone involved. What *does* worry me is Kirov's performance this year in Europe. He's traveled erratically, producing nothing with intelligence value. And we know he has friends in Sufi groups all over Central Asia."

"But *his* group is not political," Smyslov said. "That has been proven again and again since he won his Order of Lenin. Directorate T has sent agents to check his friends, and they have always found them opposed to Islamic separatism."

Karel looked as if he wanted to spit. "This is a mess!" he said. "If Kozin cannot back his claims, he must be reprimanded. To cry wolf three times is too much!"

There was a knock on the door. "Sheik Khan and Vladimir Kirov are waiting," said a female secretary, looking into the office.

"Tell the sheik to come in," said Smyslov. "We want to see him alone."

Muhammad Khan looked sad and tired. He seated himself carefully, as if his bones might break. "It is wearisome," he said softly, "to answer such misguided charges. Comrade Kozin, I fear, is confused."

"He is not the only one with doubts," said Karel. "It seems you have had some too—about the dangers of Kirov's proposals. We have reviewed the comments you made before the Academy's review committee."

Muhammad Khan's gaze receded as if toward some distant horizon. "I do not question his motive," he said. "It is only the wisdom of his ideas for Soviet Central Asia. The kind of permission he seeks for religious activity there might be welcome at another time, but not now. Not when interest in Islam is growing. New freedoms might encourage fanatics. It might bring out elements that scorn stability, elements that use religion for political change. It is simply the *speed* of liberalization I object to. There is a saying in Islam about not going faster than the Lord."

"Rumor has it that more is involved," Smyslov said, lying to test the sheik. "Some say you think Comrade Kirov is involved in a deliberate conspiracy."

"No, not a conspiracy." The sheik made a weary gesture. "These rumors are fantastic. I only said Kirov has allies interested in liberalizations like the ones he proposes. That is no secret. I was trying to answer Kozin's accusations that we are part of Tamerlane's Angels, a group I helped eliminate two or three years ago."

"Is there anything else you want to tell us?" Karel asked, his small face thrust forward intently. "Anything about Comrade Kirov we should know? You have known him for many years?"

"I do not know him well," the old man sighed. "We met through the religious boards, at a few committee meetings. I have nothing more to say about him."

Smyslov and Karel studied the tired-looking figure. Then Karel opened Kirov's file. "Please wait," he told the sheik.

No one spoke while the two men studied KGB records of Kirov's work. Smyslov reread Strelnikov's note confirming the validity of Atabet's maps. "Extraordinary," he whispered to himself. "There is no doubt we should study this more, as Kirov is telling us. How can Kozin object to that?" At length he pushed a button in his office intercom and asked his secretary to show Kirov in.

As he entered, Kirov nodded at Karel, Smyslov, and the sheik. Then he glanced at the figure bent over the recording machine, recognizing the secretary who had taken notes the day before. Had a secret benefactor seen to this?

There was silence until Kozin came in. He seemed more sallow than ever, Kirov thought, as if his rage had turned to bile. Kozin sat down and waited for Karel to acknowledge his presence.

"So then," Karel said. "We will try to keep this precise. We want to hear your accusations one by one, Comrade Kozin. When you have presented them, Kirov and Sheik Khan will reply."

The surveillance man laid a folder on Karel's desk, removed several papers, and arranged them before him. "This will take time," he said, "because my claims may be hard to believe. That is why I have this documentation.

"I was assigned to follow Kirov during the sensitive study ordered by the Committee for Science and Technology. Through that surveillance I found the following alarming facts. First, Comrade Kirov took the American Darwin Fall to a mosque near Samarkand to meet members of a secret Islamic group. One of the group has told us that they discussed plans for an Islamic revival in Uzbekistan. Second, I have information that Comrade Kirov was on the verge of defection in Prague last month, and appealed to this American for help. This we know through Darwin Fall's conversations in California, which we have monitored. Third, there is another secret group in Central Asia that goes by the name of Tamerlane's Angels, to which Muhammad Khan and Kirov belong. Fourth, a special analyst for the Committee of Science and Technology, one Georgi Baranov, is in league with secret groups working for a religious revival, a fact we have clearly established. He and Kirov are in constant touch about their plans in this regard. And fifth, there is evidence that the American

Jacob Atabet's so-called clairvoyant guesses about our missile sites were actually obtained through Kirov, who passed them to Fall, who gave them to Atabet in an effort to mislead us. It seems they are working in concert to promote Comrade Kirov's proposals." Kozin paused dramatically, fixing in turn Smyslov's gaze, then Karel's. "So you see why I am unhappy. The final proof that something sinister is happening was my deletion from the committee appointed to review Kirov's study. Is it possible that he has allies in the Praesidium of the Academy of Sciences? And on the State Committee for Science and Technology? It is time to find out."

"Are those your accusations?" Karel asked.

"I have more," Kozin said. "But I think I have presented enough to begin with. These transcripts contain evidence you will need to examine."

"Kirov," said Karel, "would you like to answer first?"

Despite his fear, Kirov felt power and serenity forming like an island around him. "I will answer each point," he said quietly, "and then try to explain why Kozin has been so deluded. For I have discovered some things he hasn't told us, things that have caused his recent erratic behavior. Let me take his five points in reverse order. First, about the American Atabet—Comrade Kozin's accusations are wild conjecture. I do not know where our missile sites are placed, so I could not pass them on to Fall. If we fail to appreciate the American's guesses, we will have failed as intelligence people. Kozin is undermining his own men by making this accusation, for they *filmed* the American as he was making his guesses. Seeing him do it was a coup. Beyond that, we have recruited these Americans for our cause. Fall said he would give us his studies before they were published in the United States. Does that sound like a plot against us? Admittedly, the entire affair is strange, but that is all the more reason to be calm about it.

"We will have to ask Comrade Baranov to answer the second point. I can only say that Kozin's charge is absurd on the face of it because Baranov's record for loyalty is impeccable. It is easy to check his KGB files. His personal life has been checked again and again, given the sensitive nature of his work, and no charge of Islamic plots has ever been made against him. Comrade Kozin, I'm afraid, has sounded another false alarm about Muslim conspiracies, something he has done before.

"And in answer to the third point, *several* groups might be called Tamerlane's Angels. Tamerlane is an Islamic hero, after all. I have not heard the name, however, since the group in Tashkent was eliminated two years ago. Perhaps Kozin's cabals only have two or three members! I can assure you, though, that I do *not* belong.

"A soccer club in Tashkent goes by that name," Muhammad Khan said softly. "They are angry because two other groups want to use it. And I have heard that a basketball team in Samarkand has the name printed in gold and silver on their shirts. Comrade Kozin, it seems, does not understand our Central Asian love of history."

"And fourth," Kirov said, "I have not planned to defect. The conversations Kozin refers to, evidently, were recorded in California between Fall and his friends. I *did* tell Fall I was sympathetic to his studies and that I wanted to visit the United States. But I never told him I wanted to defect. You will find, when you study Kozin's transcripts, that his accusations are based on conjecture." He turned to Kozin. "What would I gain from such a course? Imprisonment and years of surveillance? Torture, possibly? Do you think the CIA would honor my work at Orly Field?" He turned back to Smyslov and Karel. "You must study the transcripts of Fall's conversations. I think you will find that Comrade Kozin has made up a story about his remarks.

"Regarding the final point, we will have to hear from the man at the mosque. If anyone has made the accusations Kozin claims, he might be trying to undermine my position. I did take Fall to see the place, as part of our work together. He is a student of religious history and was excited by the trip. His assistance has been worth the effort, it seems." He turned to Kozin. "You must produce this man and let us question him. No Islamic revivals are being planned in that place, and you know it. The people who care for it are peasants, with no education or political aspirations of any kind. Do you think they can mount a threat to the Soviet State?

"None of these accusations has any substance whatsoever. But they do tell me something about *you*." He tried to hold Kozin's gaze, but the sallow figure looked ahead resolutely. "Strelnikov tells me that you're threatened by this study. Why? Is it because you failed to give credence to Lester Boone's work in Europe with his German friends? Or to the successes of Project Elefant? From the beginning you have opposed parapsychology, even when some of your people warned us that American and German and French and British and Dutch researchers were providing information about these things to their own intelligence people. Are you trying to cover your bad judgment?" He turned to Smyslov and Karel. "I leave it to you to decide. To make his accusation understandable, you should review his long opposition to psychic research. His bad judgment has impeded our recognition of Western work in these fields for many years."

Kozin started to laugh—a flat, sinister laugh, full of confidence. "Ah, Kirov," he said, looking at the ceiling. "What a spectacle you are! Do you realize that you are the butt of jokes among academicians and intelligence people? The laughingstock of scientists all across the Soviet Union? Do you realize that I only take you seriously because of your Islamic plots?" He came forward on his chair to face Karel and Smyslov directly. "Comrade Kirov is not dangerous because he advocates parapsychology. He is dangerous in his advocacy of religious freedoms. We know that interest in Islam is a catalyst for political unrest. He would be harmless if there weren't trouble in Central Asia from groups like the Naqshebandi. Don't you agree, Sheik Khan? You have already told the Academy's review committee that you feared his innocent plans. Perhaps you should repeat your statements here."

Muhammad Khan adjusted his robes, his long, gnarled fingers playing with a string of beads. For a moment he gathered himself, then laughed with surprising pleasure. Kozin's anger and contempt, it seemed, did not faze him at all. "This reminds me of an ancient saying among our people," he said. *"Angels work in ignorance.* It means a number of things, among them this: that in the mysteries of human governance we are groping, beating our wings in the faces of friends and allies, confusing each other as we confuse our enemies."

The words ran through Kirov like a knife. "Angels work in ignorance" was a password of the Sufi Way. Had the sheik delivered another signal to him?

"We should not fight," Muhammad Khan said. "The remarks that you, Comrade Kozin, refer to—my remarks before the review committee—were given in the spirit of friendship. Kirov is the most able intelligence man working with religious groups in Central Asia. He is an intelligence genius. There is nothing to be upset about, though there is counsel to be given." He touched Kozin's shoulder with a kindly look. "And I can tell you with complete certainty that no Islamic revivals, conspiracies, or soccer teams can rendezvous in that dusty old mosque. It is the least-frequented place in Uzbekistan."

For a moment no one spoke. Then Smyslov asked Kozin if he wanted to answer. Kozin glanced at Kirov, then at the sheik. Finally he threw up his hands as if to say any answer would be futile.

"We shall investigate the mosque," Karel said impassively. "That will be easy to check on. And we shall study each of your charges carefully. Now you all may go."

Kirov was startled by this abrupt end to the hearing, but the sheik stood up at once. Bowing with dignity, he turned to leave the room. Kozin watched him, while Karel and Smyslov arranged their files. Kirov waited for Kozin to stand. It would not be wise to leave first, for there was no telling what story he might fabricate next. Finally Smyslov looked up. "You both may go now," he said. "Unless either of you has something more to say."

Kozin stood and looked dumbly at Kirov, his expression strangely vacant. Then he started for the door. Smyslov seemed embarrassed by his behavior, but Karel was irritated. Kirov saw that both of them sensed his instability. But would they dismiss his charges?

31 After leaving the hearing with Karel and Smyslov, Kirov went out into Dzerzhinsky Square. Muhammad Khan stood waiting for a car. Among the plainly dressed people coming and going from the KGB Center, he seemed a regal figure in his Uzbek robes.

Kirov greeted him.

"Kozin has no friends," said the sheik. "Not a single friend in the world. Is it possible for you to make peace with him?"

"It will be difficult," Kirov answered. "But I can try. Angels work in ignorance."

The sheik signaled toward a Volga sedan coming down the street. "You read thoughts well," he said. "You must have had good teachers. Try to befriend him. Otherwise there will be another battle." He opened the sedan door, said something to the driver, then turned to touch Kirov's arm. "With patience, we will see an end to ordinary history."

An end to ordinary history—Kirov was stunned to hear the phrase. How could the sheik have known it? There must be conspiracies he knew nothing about, conspiracies that could provide a sheik from Uzbekistan with some of his most intimate thoughts. He started to walk down the street, trying to compose himself. In the growing confusion, clarity was all-important . . .

"Volodya!" a voice called. "Come here!"

Startled, Kirov turned to see a small sedan parked beside the curb. Behind the wheel sat Baranov.

Kirov took a seat by his side, and they drove out of Dzerzhinsky Square. Baranov's large, dimpled face was pale and unshaven. "Rozhnov just talked to me," he said, glancing into the rearview mirror. "He is helping dispel Kozin's stories. But we have other problems. Muhammad Khan, it seems, is trying to undermine our proposals."

"But he was a friend just now in the hearing," Kirov said with a sinking sensation. "He called me the best intelligence man in Central Asia."

"Rozhnov knows him. They met in Tashkent forty years ago. Now, listen. We don't have very much time. Rozhnov said five or six Islamic leaders are in Moscow this week trying to discredit us. They are very tough people, he says, well hidden in the Party and government, with a long-range plan for Muslim independence. They think there will be more Soviet Muslims than Russians by the end of the century, and they don't want them seduced from Islam. Our proposals look dangerous to them because so many Islamic young people are drifting away from the faith, some influenced by subjects our proposals encourage."

"But they can't turn back the clock."

"Rozhnov says they are old and tough and determined. They want a separate Islamic nation."

But what is Rozhnov's role in this? Is *he* part of some secret group?"

"I don't know, he hasn't given me a single clue. His information about the Islamic leaders came from the Moscow militia."

"From the Moscow militia!" Kirov said with disbelief. "How would *they* know about it?"

"I don't know. Everything's confusing now. I am worried, Volodya. Did Kozin say anything about me to Karel and Smyslov?"

"Yes, but his stories sound crazy. They will dismiss his charges."

"Unfortunately, his charges have already reached my staff. We are having a meeting in my office to review them. But you should go back to the Praesidium now and wait for Rozhnov's call. He wants to talk to you." Baranov's large eyes, magnified by his thick glasses, looked frightened. "There are too many plots, Volodya. This is getting to be a mess."

Baranov drove off, and Kirov walked toward Leninskii Prospekt. Everything looked desolate. For every ally in their work, it seemed, there were new enemies. Was their project finally hopeless? Half-closing his eyes, he struggled to control his dejection. "*Al-Allah, al-Allah,*" he whispered. "It is up to God."

All the way to the Praesidium he prayed for help, but his discouragement only deepened. By now, Kozin's stories about him were being passed from office to office through Academy headquarters. It would be best, he thought, to avoid more confrontations with Kozin and wait for Rozhnov's call. Maybe Rozhnov knew a way out of the growing confusion.

But as Kirov approached his commission office in the Praesidium, he heard a loud voice inside. Opening the door, he saw Kozin bent over a desk berating a frightened secretary. As Kirov entered, Kozin turned with a look of fury. "Karel and Smyslov do not believe you!" he exclaimed. "And neither does Strelnikov. You think you made a fool of me this morning, but your lies are obvious to everyone."

Recoiling from the shock of this unexpected encounter, Kirov stood by the door. "It's better if we talk by ouselves," he said, almost in a whisper. "If we go over your charges calmly, you'll see that they're all mistaken."

"I'm tired of your stories, Kirov." Kozin's hands were shaking. "Don't you see that your schemes are finished? I'm here to tell you that. Your schemes are finished, do you understand? Your commission will be disbanded."

They stood facing each other in silence, then a look of fear crossed Kozin's face. Suppressing a sudden intense anxiety, he picked up a phone. "Get me Strelnikov's office," he said with a shaking voice.

Kirov made a gesture toward his secretary that they shouldn't interfere.

"Strelnikov!" Kozin exclaimed, "there is an emergency. My people have uncovered new proof that Kirov is running a major conspiracy. I must talk to you!"

Kirov watched without intervening, sensing that Strelnikov recognized Kozin's breakdown. He stood motionless while the distraught figure hung up.

"He will see me!" Kozin said, his hands trembling with fear and anger. "You will be arrested. So will Baranov. And Rozhnov and Darwin Fall and Muhammad Khan! They all will be exposed. Your so-called friends from Bukhara are here, ready to reveal your plots."

A wave of fear passed through Kirov's silent equanimity. Was Kozin telling the truth? As if in answer, a uniformed KGB guard came into the room with an old man from Bukhara whom Kirov recognized. The man often came to the mosque to perform the *zikhr*.

"You will tell us everything," Kozin said when the door was shut, glowering at the frightened old man. "The entire story of your plots. Tell us everything you told me this morning. Everything about the things you heard the traitor Kirov say."

Kirov could see the old man had been beaten. Kozin, it appeared, had penetrated the circle in Bukhara that came to the desert mosque.

Before the old man could answer, there was a knock on the door. Then a uniformed militiaman came into the room.

"What do you want?" Kozin asked impatiently.

"I have a message from Strelnikov's office," said the man, a middle-aged officer from the Moscow Police. "He wants you to see Doctor Petrovsky's staff. People there will hear your accusations."

"Doctor Petrovsky?" Kozin exclaimed. "But I want Strelnikov! This is a conspiracy against the State. What will I do with these traitors?"

"I only have this message." The militiaman brought himself to a slightly menacing attention.

Kozin faced him in cold fury. "Petrovsky!" he fumed, turning away from the crowd that had gathered by the door. "Petrovsky has nothing to do with this!"

"Do you understand the message?" The militiaman held Kozin's arms. "Petrovsky's office is a block from here."

Kozin did not answer. Instead, he reached for a phone and asked for Strelnikov's office. Kirov guessed he was bluffing. "Yes, Lomov!" he said loudly, repeating the name of Strelnikov's assistant. "You say he will see me? Good! I will come at once with the man from Bukhara." He hung up the phone and gestured for the old man and his guard to follow. Then he shouldered his way through the crowd and hurried down the corridor. Kirov and the others followed.

In an effort to keep up with the rest, the KGB guard hurried the man from Bukhara along, while the militiaman ran ahead to intercept Kozin. "Come with me," he said, grabbing Kozin's arm. "If you don't, I'll put you under arrest!"

"Do you know who I am?" Kozin shook the man's hand away. "I work for the Secret Police. Come with me, I will explain everything."

Kirov watched them disappear into the anterooms outside Strelnikov's office. Even thirty feet away, everyone heard them

191

talking loudly. In the quiet of this corridor, the outburst was alarming.

As Strelnikov came to his office door, he remembered his erotic dream. Somehow Kozin had appeared in it, too. "And what is happening?" he asked, glancing at his startled assistants. "What is wrong, Yakov?"

Kozin had trouble replying. Seeing Strelnikov so close was a shock, something he had not fully expected. Suddenly he seemed to be outside his body. The entity below him, the thing named Yakov Kozin, was running like a wild machine. "Everything is wrong," he said hoarsely. "There are enemies all around us."

"Enemies?" asked Strelnikov. "What kind of enemies?"

"Vladimir Kirov. Muhammad Khan. Georgi Baranov. Alexander Rozhnov." He recited the names in a practiced litany. "And members of the Praesidium itself. You are surrounded, and I am trying to help you!"

"I have heard about your claims," said Strelnikov. "That is why I want you to review them with Doctor Petrovsky. Didn't you get my message?"

"I suspect Doctor Petrovsky," Kozin whispered. "He is a *psychiatrist*. Many psychiatrists are in league with these people!"

"Not Doctor Petrovsky," said Strelnikov softly, "He is my very good friend. You go see him."

Kozin returned to his body, seized by another fear. Was the Chief Scientific Secretary involved in the plot? Was he an ally of Kirov? Staring into Strelnikov's eyes, he struggled against an impulse to say so, an impulse to shout the fact to everyone. But that would be too dangerous. Now, more than ever before in his life, he had to control himself. Summoning a crooked smile, he bowed slightly and turned to leave.

But Strelnikov sensed his thought. "Yakov," he whispered. "Come here. I know what you are thinking. Please don't think like that. It will only make matters more confusing."

Seeing that Strelnikov could read his mind, Kozin was filled with a new kind of terror. Escape might be impossible now. But no one had stopped him so far, not Kirov, not Rozhnov, not their friends in the government. Despite his terror, he made a vow: he would take his story to every high official he could reach. He would save the State all by himself. "Yes," he bowed. "I agree. I will try to compose myself. Maybe Doctor Petrovsky can help."

"Take Comrade Kozin to Petrovsky's office," Strelnikov told the man from the Moscow police. "They are expecting him." He stepped back into his office. Poor Yakov had gone crazy, he told himself, but even so his charges should be checked.

In the corridor, Kirov watched Kozin come past, walking like a zombie. It was clear he had been sent to Petrovsky. Kirov turned to the old man from Bukhara. Cowering against a wall, the pathetic figure pointed to his ankles. "They beat me," he whispered. "I had to tell them something." Kirov gave him a reassuring look, then turned and walked away. This was the time to see Strelnikov, who would be checking on Kozin's claims by now.

His intuition was confirmed when he reached his office. A message had arrived that Strelnikov wanted to see him.

Strelnikov had a weary look as Kirov came into his office. "Kozin's paranoia is out of control," he said. "I had a militiaman take him to a doctor. People at the Committee for State Security are worried about him too."

"Yes, he is disturbed." Kirov chose his words with care. "There are parts of this affair he can't comprehend and they seem to be driving him crazy."

Looking at Kirov now, Strelnikov remembered the stone in his dream. Kirov had known its secret. "You will have to explain this," he said. "What is it that's driving him crazy?"

"His inability to control events," Kirov said. "He cannot fathom the mysteries my study implies. Perhaps he is struggling against something he secretly wants."

Strelnikov watched him with fascination, memories of his dream flooding back. Once again, he felt a powerful attraction to him. Kirov's courage, his intelligence, his vision were rare and valuable. This was a man he would like for a friend. Masking his feelings, Strelnikov took off his glasses to clean them.

Kirov felt a strange intuition. Strelnikov, he thought against his better judgment, was entering a mystical state. He might be vulnerable to an encouraging phrase. "Have you heard the old Muslim story about the net of precious stones?" Kirov asked, citing an image Sufis used to test one's understanding. "It is one way to understand Kozin."

Readjusting his glasses, Strelnikov said he had not.

"It means that each of us reflects the other, to the end of space and time. It refers to mystic states in which one sees their essential unity with all others. Kozin, I think, is struggling against that kind of perception. He spends most of his time, you know, appraising other people, watching movies of them, listening to them carefully. Studying people so intently, one begins to identify with them. One secretly feels their life as your own. That is why spies sometimes have a change of heart about their enemies. Kozin, however, doesn't understand this. Some of his colleagues say he has been obsessed with me. Maybe his paranoia about me comes from a secret identification."

"That each of us reflects the other," Strelnikov murmured, "to the end of space and time. Yes, I could see how one might struggle against that." He remembered riding a panther through the streets, a panther like this Kirov. In the dream he had hovered between pleasure and panic.

Kirov saw that Strelnikov understood. Was he a member of some practicing group? "Have you heard of Tamerlane's Angels?" he asked, carried away by this amazing possibility. "Or the Path by Kyzyl Kum?"

Strelnikov felt a dagger stab. "Tamerlane's Angels" and the "Path by Kyzyl Kum" were the passwords Kozin had ascribed to Kirov's group. Was there truth in his paranoid claims? "No, I don't know what they mean," he said with weariness. "But I would like to."

To Kirov, Strelnikov's face seemed to form a single tear, dropping from the eye of some larger countenance. Now another person sat before him, a person bound to do his awful duty. "So what do these terms refer to?" he heard the Scientific Secretary ask.

"They are old Sufi passwords," Kirov said, attempting a retreat from his blunder. "They are used by groups that practice a mystic way leading to illumination. I thought you might know about them."

Strelnikov saw that Kirov was suddenly embarrassed. "And what are you after?" he asked with a sad expression. "What do you seek in your ambitious proposals?"

Kirov paused before answering, uncertain now what this complex man was asking. "I am hiding nothing," he said at last. "Everything I want is there in my proposals. A careful tolerance of religious groups, more study of the mind, a possible revising of our Marxist understanding that could lead us toward a more interesting future. I am not hiding anything in the sense that Kozin claims. There are no plans to overthrow the State."

Strelnikov felt profound weariness beneath his cool demeanor. Everything Kirov said was true, all his instincts told him, yet he must have comrades who answered to code words like the ones he had just repeated. Even though this man embodied something his heart reached out to, he could not allow secret scheming. "I believe you," he said. "But we must continue our inquiry into

Kozin's claims. It will not interrupt the review of your proposals."
He avoided Kirov's glance. "I am glad we have had this talk, and
perhaps we shall have another."

Masking his fear with a formal nod, Kirov left the office.

Strelnikov started pacing, struggling against an impulse to
shout with anger. The complexities of these events were increasing in a way that would cause a scandal. He crossed and recrossed
his office trying to calm himself. Then he cursed out loud. Kirov's
use of passwords like "Tamerlane's Angels" meant he was allied
with subversive groups. That felt like a stab in his heart. For if
Kirov was, then who else might be a secret schemer? Was the
whole world breaking down? Gradually he calmed himself and
poured a glass of vodka.

Five minutes later, he was numb and cold and detached. In his
coldness he made a resolution. He would no longer be charmed
by this Vladimir Kirov. The erotic element in his feeling for the
man was turning to disgust. He shuddered as he remembered the
panther.

The episode had shown him that mysticism like Kirov's was no
guarantee against treachery and falsehood. He would search out
Kirov's past as if he were a proven traitor to the state. But as he
made this decision, Strelnikov felt a sudden grief. Another vodka
did not help. A pressure was growing inside him now that
threatened to tear him apart.

32

Walking toward his apartment on Ujinsky Pereulok,
Kirov felt a sense of suffocation. Having recognized
the secret phrases, Strelnikov would distrust him
now and be suspicious of all his proposals. He had never blun-
dered like this before. Had he been deliberately trapped? That
was impossible, he decided. Strelnikov had been in an exalted
state, however well-controlled, and had wanted to be a friend. As
he reviewed the exchange, Kirov felt a pressure in his chest. He
and Baranov were in jeopardy.

One thing was certain: he must reassure Directorate T and the
State Committee for Science and Technology that his commission's proposals were designed in part to promote social harmony.
He must make the point in such a way that no one could possibly
doubt its validity. In the next few hours he must find a way
through the labyrinth he had stumbled into.

In his apartment a handwritten note lay on the bed, placed there by the cleaning woman. Written in an emergency code that he and Baranov used, it said that friends were taking steps to protect him. More instructions would arrive that afternoon.

Kirov looked at his watch. His meeting with Strelnikov had taken place only an hour before, at roughly one o'clock. The message must have arrived in the last few minutes. He went down to the building's entrance hall, and asked the lady who watched the door when the note had been delivered. About ten minutes before, she said. A messenger had brought it from Baranov's office. Kirov was amazed. The note was not in Baranov's hand, but who else knew their code?

Concealing his elation, Kozin left Petrovsky's office. He had answered the psychiatrist's questions sensibly, with no sign of anxiety or rage. When Petrovsky had asked what his problems were, he had said that his colleagues simply felt he was working too hard. He appreciated the Scientific Secretary's concern, and would sleep a little more that night, but he had never felt more energetic in his entire life. The real problem, he joked, was a female assistant who took an overly protective attitude toward him. She had caused Strelnikov's worry. The story had satisfied Petrovsky. When he phoned the Praesidium, an assistant said that Strelnikov would return his call within the hour. Thinking the matter settled, the doctor let Kozin go.

Walking to his office, Kozin felt a new confidence. With perfect clarity, he saw every move he would make. There were people he could trust in the midst of this stupendous intrigue, and he would talk to every one within the next few hours.

Kozin was certain now that he would finish Kirov's career, but exposing Strelnikov would be more difficult. He had not watched over the elite, however, without learning ways to compromise them. There were things to reveal about anyone, including the famous academician. In this moment, all his years of sacrifice and all his unrewarded labors would come together. The heroic act he now foresaw would win him the gratitude of Soviet leaders for many years to come.

Half an hour later, Kozin had arranged separate meetings with four highly placed KGB men. By five o'clock that afternoon he would plant enough rumors about Kirov and Strelnikov to keep them on the defensive for weeks. Once that was accomplished, he would do something even more audacious.

Smyslov and Karel guessed that Kozin's paranoia was part of a nervous collapse, but after they talked to Kirov's superiors they decided to check some of the surveillance man's charges. There were just enough suspicions about Kirov in the KGB offices to lend Kozin's stories credence. With Strelnikov's consent, they put Baranov under surveillance, had several Muslim leaders in Moscow followed, and ordered the arrest of Darwin Fall.

Strelnikov was relieved at these developments, for he felt increasingly divided. In the hours after his exchange with Kirov, his agitation was offset by a crippling detachment. The intensity of this division had produced what seemed two separate entities, forcing a choice upon him. Was he the wounded figure hiding his emotion, or the one who seemed so free? As he waited to meet with Rozhnov, the split was painfully acute.

Strelnikov crossed his office slowly, counting every step. He had to be careful, for his state was dangerous. He stood by a table—like a figure frozen in a photograph, his thoughts growing more and more distant.

He walked unsteadily to his desk, struggling for composure. Had someone in his office drugged him? He sat with his head in his hands, remembering Kirov's words about a net of jewels. Had Kirov tried to tell him something about this extraordinary state?

"Come in," he heard himself answer a knock on the door. "Rozhnov, have a drink while I finish this business."

"Are you all right?" he heard Rozhnov say. "Can I get you something?"

"A vodka," he said faintly. "Then bring a chair and sit down."

To compose himself, Strelnikov stared at a photograph on the wall above his desk. It showed one of his most famous inventions, a laser for the spectroscopic analysis of living cells.

"Did you say a vodka?" Rozhnov asked.

"Yes. Thank you. I need it badly." From the photograph now came an emission of light that seemed to fill the room.

Rozhnov crossed to the desk looking as if his body were suspended in air. Had he been drugged, Strelnikov wondered, or had he suffered a stroke? But as Rozhnov handed him the glass, he felt thankful, felt grateful for the gift he was given. Without drinking, he looked into the face across the desk. It seemed to hold centuries of wisdom.

"Kirov's commission is causing a scandal," he said. "Everything's turned upside down . . ." His voice faded. Rozhnov's face seemed ugly and close, the face of a witch from a Russian fairy tale. But then it was sweet and friendly, an elfin center of beneficence.

"That is when we need friends most," Rozhnov sighed. "When the rest of the world is going crazy."

The old man's complex face was a welcome point of reference. Strelnikov watched it with childlike wonder, savoring new insights about the character it revealed. He felt vaguely omniscient. "I have been in a peculiar state." He forced a smile. "It started just this morning. I don't entirely trust my judgment." As the admission came forth, Strelnikov checked himself. Rozhnov might be part of Kirov's plot.

"I've never seen you looking better," Rozhnov said. "Why don't you trust your judgment?"

Strelnikov studied the old man's countenance. There were depths and nuances in it he hadn't seen before. This was a profound and exceptional man, someone he would like to confide in. But he hesitated. The man might also be an enemy of the State.

"Is there something embarrassing?" Rozhnov asked.

With all his suspicions, Strelnikov liked and admired the old bureaucrat. But still he checked himself. Should he talk about Kirov freely?

Rozhnov, however, was not burdened with contradictory thoughts. Strelnikov's divided state was something Rozhnov had wrestled with for years, until he had achieved his present integration. "You don't want to answer," he said. "What are you hiding? Some new discovery, one the world won't understand?"

Strelnikov smiled at the old man's sly inflection. "Not a scientific discovery," he said. "But a philosophical one. It has something to do with that book you gave me."

"Something about the secret of light?"

"Yes, the secret of light." With a handkerchief, Strelnikov wiped perspiration from his upper lip. From the photograph of his laser invention, a subtle light was streaming.

"I thought the book might bear on the issues raised by Kirov's commission," Rozhnov said. "It is good to see how enduring these insights are. That book is very old."

The light from the photograph filled the space between them. Strelnikov looked down at the desk. "Do you know the people in Yakov Kozin's surveillance group?" he asked at last.

"Not very well," Rozhnov said, framing his next revealing statement. "But this afternoon I heard about Kozin's claims. It seems he has named us *both* traitors to the State."

Strelnikov gathered himself. "Named us *both*?" he asked, lifting his vodka carefully and placing it on the desk. "I hadn't heard that we were part of the plot."

"I heard it from the office of Secretary Brezhnev himself. They asked me if the man had gone crazy."

Strelnikov looked at the intercom on his desk to make sure that no one could hear. "We had him sent to a doctor this afternoon," he whispered, "for a medical check. I am sure his superiors will recommend he get some rest."

"Perhaps you should check with the doctor. According to Brezhnev's people, Kozin is passing his stories now to anyone who'll listen."

"Even to Brezhnev? Impossible."

"I heard it from people I trust, just an hour ago. Maybe you should check."

Turning to the speakers by his side, Strelnikov flipped a switch and asked an assistant to place a call to Petrovsky. "We shall hear in a moment," he said. "I find this all surprising."

While the phone connections were being made, Strelnikov held back his fear. Absurd as it seemed, there was a bond between him and Kirov that others might perceive, a bond that Kozin had sensed.

"Petrovsky here!" The doctor's voice came over the speaker.

"Petrovsky? What happened with Kozin? How did he seem to you?"

"He's all right," the doctor said. "I recommended a little rest, but there is nothing wrong with him. No strange ideas or reactions."

"You gave him a medical clearance?" Strelnikov was astonished. "But he was acting like a madman here!"

"Like a madman? I'm surprised. He was completely rational in my office. I wish you had told me that."

"I had a guard escort him. He was out of control here at the Praesidium. Didn't you talk to the man I sent with him?"

"No, I didn't see him. In fact, there was no guard with him. He came here all alone."

"If you see him again, give him a longer examination. The man is very sick." Strelnikov's voice was filled with displeasure. He hung up and rose to his feet. "Rozhnov, what else is he saying? What did the people in Brezhnev's office tell you?"

"Only that," said Rozhnov gravely. "That you and I and Kirov are involved in some incredible plot. No one believes it, of course."

Strelnikov composed himself with effort. "Then you don't think there is anything to his stories? Kirov said something to me about secret Muslim groups, something about 'Tamerlane's

Angels' and the 'Path by Kyzyl Kum.' Do you know anything about that?"

"Those Muslim passwords are getting to be an open secret. All sorts of gossip are floating around about them."

"All sorts of gossip!" Strelnikov was surprised. "I thought they were guarded secrets."

"These Muslim groups generate a thousand rumors," Rozhnov said with disgust. "'Tamerlane's Angels' must be totally ineffective as a signal, given all the ways it is used. No, I think Kozin is crazy."

Strelnikov felt a sudden relief. If Kirov had no allies who answered to these passwords, there might be no truth at all in Kozin's claims. But would the people in Brezhnev's office call for investigations? "I will check on Kozin," he said, his husky voice faltering. "Perhaps we can talk about this tomorrow."

Seeing that Strelnikov was too distracted for more conversation, Rozhnov stood and left. He had accomplished what he had come to do.

33 A light snow was falling as Avram Berg approached the National Hotel. Rubbing his hands for warmth, he scolded himself for being nervous about seeing the American. Fall would like his proposal. The only problem was getting to see him.

Adjusting the collar of his overcoat and wiping the snow from his beard, Berg went through the hotel door into the outside foyer. "I am here to see a friend," he said to the doorman.

"Your name, please?" the uniformed figure asked.

"Avram Berg. Darwin Fall is expecting me."

The doorman, a stocky, red-faced Russian in his sixties, looked at the list of people permitted to enter. "There is no Avram Berg on this list," he said. "I will have to phone his room."

Berg was afraid Fall might not remember his name. "That is not necessary," he said impatiently. "Mr. Fall is expecting me. Someone has forgotten to put my name on your list."

"Stay here, please," the man said with a scowl. "I will phone his room."

Berg followed the doorman into the main foyer and stood by while he picked up the house phone. His beard and scruffy overcoat had not made a good impression. "Stand outside," the doorman said with a threatening look. "Or I will not make this call."

"I am a television producer," said Berg, raising himself on tiptoe so that his five feet seven inches might equal the doorman's height. "He is expecting me."

"He is *not* expecting you!" the scowling figure answered. "Get out of here!"

Seeing that the man was about to grab him, Berg backed away. As he did, Fall came down the carpeted stairs from above. Seeing Berg, he waved.

"Darwin Fall!" Berg called out. "I am here to see you about that television show. My producer wants to see you!" He shouldered past the doorman, stepping on a toe for revenge, and held Fall's shoulders as if they were dear old friends.

"It's good to see you," Fall said with a worried look. "I need someone I can talk to. Do you want to go for a walk?"

Berg hestitated. "It's snowing," he said. "We will be more comfortable in your room."

"But I need some exercise." Fall pulled Berg away from the angry doorman. "I've been stuck here since the weather got bad."

Berg nodded, and they went outside. Pulling their collars up against the falling snow, they started down the sidewalk. "I'm stranded," Fall said. "The man I'm here to see hasn't called for two days, and I haven't been able to reach Gorski. None of my other friends answer their phones. How did you know I was here?"

"Gorski said you were coming. I talked to him a few days ago."

"Then why doesn't he call me? Is he all right?"

"He has been sick with the flu," said Berg, placing a hand on Fall's shoulder. "But I must tell you about my program. Will you talk to my boss about it?"

"What do you want me to talk about?"

They had turned off Marx Prospekt onto Gertsena Street and were walking more rapidly now. "I want you to describe your own research and talk about Soviet parapsychology." Berg waved his arms expansively, shaking the snowflakes out of his long black hair. "My producer is crazy to meet you."

Fall did not reply. A man was running down the sidewalk toward them, waving desperately. "Who is that?" Berg asked. "He seems to know you."

The man wore a reclaimed army coat and looked frightened. "Darwin Fall," he said breathlessly, handing Fall a folder. "These papers are from Vladimir Kirov. Please! Read them carefully. They contain secret information about Soviet psychotronics. Take them to your colleagues in the States."

The man disappeared through the falling snow, and Fall started to open the folder. "Don't open it!" Berg whispered. "This might be a trick!"

"A what?" Fall asked with disbelief.

"A police setup. Drop that folder, and let's go."

As he spoke, a black Volga sedan pulled up to the curb ahead and three men seized the man in the army coat. Then two of the men ran toward Fall.

"You are under arrest!" said one in broken English. "You please give us that paper." He was a short, angry-looking man with a flattened nose. Before Fall could protest, he took the folder.

"But I haven't done a thing!" Fall gasped. "You can't arrest me!"

The second man came up beside him. With an abrupt gesture he signaled another sedan.

"What is this?" Fall shouted. "You have to give me some explanation!"

"You know what you have done," said the first man. "We don't argue you." They both shielded him from Berg and two curious passers-by.

"I will tell my producer about this," Berg said to Fall, turning away to hide his face. "He will call the authorities."

"We are from the Moscow Police," said one of the men as he shoved Fall toward the car. A moment later Fall was seated between them as they drove off. The other sedan had gone in the opposite direction.

"The American Embassy knows I am here," Fall said angrily. "I had an appointment there this afternoon."

The two policemen looked straight ahead, neither of them giving the slightest sign they heard him. The car was slowing as it passed through Dzerzhinsky Square. To his horror Fall recognized the KGB Center. The car had parked by an entrance of the Lubyanka Prison.

Five minutes later he sat alone in a room with bare walls, three chairs, and a table. Someone would come to see him, his accosters had said—he had no choice but to calm himself. Had Kirov been arrested too? Visions of torture crossed his mind, and his anger turned to acute anxiety.

The door opened and two men came in. One, blond and wearing a light blue suit, looked more Swedish than Russian. The other was a thug like the men in the Volga sedan, a muscular man about six feet tall who wore a fixed look of contempt. In broken English he asked Fall for his overcoat and jacket. While he emptied their pockets, the Swedish-looking man asked Fall to describe his Moscow visit. "What are you really doing here?" he asked with even good humor. "We know about your meetings with Vladimir Kirov."

Fall said that he would not answer until he had talked to someone from the U.S. Embassy.

"You will only make trouble for yourself this way," the man said quietly. "The more you cooperate, the sooner you can leave. Personally, I don't like this kind of thing, but it appears you might be in trouble. We have seen your missile maps."

Again Fall refused to answer. At this, the second man ordered him to take off his clothes. When Fall refused to comply, they told him they would use force. Fall saw that they meant it. A minute later he stood naked while the two went through his pockets. The man in the blue suit inspected Fall's passport and wallet, removing each credit card and holding it up to the light. For ten minutes Fall sat on his chair and shivered. It might be weeks before his friends in California realized he was missing. Did the Russians know that?

"So you have a meeting at the U.S. Embassy," said the blond interrogator. "We will check on that. Somehow I don't believe you." He continued to scrutinize Fall, looking him up and down with apparent good humor. The other man handed back his clothes, and both Russians watched him dress.

At the National Hotel two KGB agents searched Fall's rooms. After looking through all his belongings, they placed his books and an unfinished letter to Atabet into cases they carried. Then they ordered the maids to rearrange everything in the suite as if they had given the place a special cleaning. A half-hour later, they delivered their finds to the KGB Center.

Smyslov and Karel had not confirmed any of Kozin's stories. Because Kirov's work in Central Asia involved his winning the confidence of Muslim groups, he had to learn their secret signs and passwords. Nowhere was there evidence of his plotting against the State or signs of cabals he might be engineering. The most damning thing against him in the wake of Kozin's scandal was his heightened visibility.

But their inquiry had taken a startling turn. Several people reported rumors of Strelnikov's role in the "Kirov plot." Prominent members of the KGB might also be involved. One of Smyslov's assistants had heard the rumor at the Kremlin. Upon learning this, Smyslov and Karel finally decided that Kozin had gone on a paranoid rampage or worked for a conspiracy himself. The man would have to be detained.

Some fifteen minutes after ordering Kozin's detention, Smyslov and Karel examined the materials from Fall's hotel room. There was a diary entry in which Fall described Sergei Aitmatov as "a new kind of Russian patriot" involved in a "transformation of Soviet society." What had Kirov told him to promote such an extravagant opinion? This could be an important lead. But more interesting—and confusing—were strange markings in Fall's copies of two books: Nabokov's *Lolita* and *Love's Body* by Norman O. Brown. It seemed the two volumes held a secret code.

Handwritten notes in the page margins contained frequent notations that "A. said." "A" must stand for Aitmatov, they decided (not thinking of Atabet), and the notations bearing this designation added up to an elaborate scheme for restructuring the Soviet State. Several passages in *Love's Body*, especially in chapters seven ("Head") and fifteen ("Freedom"), appeared to provide philosophical support. "The real apocalypse comes," one passage read, "not with the vision of a city or kingdom, which would still be external, but with the identification of the city and kingdom with one's own body ... Kingship is fornication—the identity of politics and sex." This was doubly underlined and in several places the notation "A. agrees!" was marked. Was this the kind of thing Kirov was telling his American friends?

That the citation in *Love's Body* was related to Kirov's concerns was proven by a diary entry. "Aitmatov links bodily transformation to the withering away of the state," Fall had written. Then, in the most outrageous statement of all, Fall concluded his summation of "A.'s vision" by paraphrasing Norman O. Brown: "The Kremlin is the Penis of the Soviet State, A. says—the Monarch refusing polymorphous liberation!" Both Karel and Smyslov were disturbed that Kirov would talk about the government with such derision. The passage convinced them that these materials should be studied carefully. Given their potential importance, moreover, they would have to be analyzed for invisible writing.

There was a problem, however. The United States Embassy had just lodged a formal complaint about Fall's arrest with the Foreign Ministry. But if invisible inks were involved, the study of his diary and books would take several days to complete. If Fall were released he would miss them, and if he missed them he would cover his tracks. They might lose these precious leads to conspiracies they could only guess at.

Darwin Fall, however, had not learned about the embassy protest. While his books caused alarms at the KGB Center less than a hundred yards away, he sat alone in his cell wondering how long it would take his friends in California to see that he was missing. There was no way he could know that he had protection here in Moscow, some of it based in the Center itself.

Fall's diary and books had been delivered to Smyslov and Karel at five o'clock. News of the embassy protest reached the Center at six. At seven the cleaning lady came to Kirov's flat to deliver a second message. When she told the old lady at the building's entrance that she had returned for her belongings, the KGB man sitting in the small foyer hardly noticed her. On the second floor she looked for signs of more police, then pushed a note from Baranov under Kirov's door. Fall had been arrested, it said, and would be released at eight o'clock. Kirov could see him in safety at the National, for in response to the United States embassy protest, the police were about to end Fall's special surveillance. He should go to Fall's room at once, however, for it might be his last chance to see him.

34 At eight o'clock that night, Fall was released. With no apology or explanation, his blond interrogator told him that he had been cleared of all charges. Because of suspicions generated by his meetings with Kirov, however, he would have to leave the Soviet Union within twenty-four hours. A ticket to London on Aeroflot would be sent to his room in the morning.

A guard led Fall out to Marx Prospekt and showed him the way to the National Hotel. A light snow fell. He buttoned his overcoat and hurried down the street as if he might be chased. Conceivably, the police were not finished with him yet.

He reached the hotel ten minutes later and went up the stairs to his room. Would he be under surveillance now? The old lady who signed in the guests on his floor smiled winsomely, showing no sign that she regarded him with suspicion. With genuine warmth, she asked if he wanted some tea.

While he lay on his bed, the lady brought in a samovar. Shaking a motherly finger at him, she went into the bathroom and turned on the bathwater taps. When she returned to the bedroom she pretended to shiver. "Too cold," she said in heavily accented English. "Hot bath now!"

He poured a cup of tea and drank it, reviewing his ordeal. His arrest had been a setup, he knew, but for what purpose? Had Kirov gotten into trouble?

The memory of the Lubyanka filled him with disgust. The bath would help wash it away. He undressed and got into the long claw-footed Victorian tub, stretching out to full length. Closing his eyes, he let the heat sink in. But instead of relaxing, he started to shake. First fear, then anger rose in him. Sitting up, he swore out loud. When he got back to the States he would make formal complaints to the CIA, the State Department, and his senators.

He got out of the bathtub and dressed in clean clothes. But as he looked through his dresser drawers, he saw that his room had been searched. Some of his books and papers were missing; both his suitcases had been repacked. He tried to compose himself. He had to think of a way to see Kirov before he left.

As if to answer his thought, Kirov's voice called out. "Darwin," he said as he entered, "we don't have very much time. I want you to listen carefully."

He stood by the floor lamp, unshaven and haggard. "Sit down," Fall said with alarm. "Are you in trouble?"

Kirov sat in a chair facing him. "I know about your arrest. But we can talk freely now. This room is no longer bugged." He hesitated, for it was hard to frame his next remarks. "You are leaving tomorrow," he said with an expression of shame. "This is the last time I will see you. I must tell you how to reach Umarov and other members of our school. First, however, let me tell you exactly what my work has been. You must hear every part of it."

Listening to Kirov now, Fall remembered him greeting his friends in the mosque. He thought of his face at the *zikhr* and his presence in the Well of Light. That this brave and selfless figure, bearing witness to a power and love all humans were meant to enjoy, should be justifying his life with this look of embarrassment filled him with both sadness and rage.

Kirov appeared to be asking forgiveness. "I did not seek this life," he said. "It seemed I was led to it by a special destiny. I had to protect our school and work for this land's rebirth."

"But it isn't over," Fall said. "Russia's spiritual awakening is just getting started."

"My projects are finished, though. Now they will stop the Academy study and forget about the space-capsule crash. Our study has caused a scandal." He bent forward, his face in his hands. "Tonight I feel as I did in Prague, that this time of my life is over. If our dreams are to be realized, they must emerge in the light of day—not in secret studies by the State Police.

"Our two nations owe the world their collaboration," Kirov said.

"The things we love cannot flourish until the Soviet Union and America are partners. I see that clearly now. Everything falters—agriculture, industry, science, the Way—as long as we fight one another. You must work for that. You must work for the joining of our nations in every way you can." He handed Fall a scrap of paper bearing Umarov's address. "You must write to Misha. He will tell you about people in the States who know about our school."

"But what will happen to you?"

"No one knows." Kirov looked at the floor. "The whole thing's still in chaos."

"But can't you escape?"

"No. They are following me. A man is waiting in the hall. They don't know what to do yet." He closed his eyes to restrain his emotion. "But here," he said, taking a book from his coat. "It is a collection of Pushkin's poems. I have sealed something in it, my account of Ali Shirazi with a study of angels and the Mind that you and your friends might find useful. I try to join some science with the Way of Hurqalya. That is where many discoveries wait, I think, where the old and new worlds meet."

He stood, his face trembling with grief.

"We will help you," Fall insisted. "I can't leave you here like this."

"There has been guidance so far," Kirov said. "Even though our projects have failed. The next step will make itself known to us."

They embraced, then Kirov shook himself free and left. Fall started to follow, but a figure came down the corridor trailing Kirov closely. Fall stepped back in the room. Struggling with his emotions, he went onto the balcony. The Kremlin shone in the floodlit snow, and beyond it St. Basil's Cathedral.

With tears in his eyes, Fall watched the street below hoping for a last glimpse of his friend. A moment later, Kirov left the hotel flanked by men in overcoats. It appeared he was under arrest. As Fall watched with grief and anger, the three figures got into a car and drove away.

35 Leonid Brezhnev rode to his apartment in Kutuzovsky Prospekt. It had been a trying day. He gave his assistant a glass of vodka from the bar built into the rear of his Zils limousine, then drank a glass himself.

"These stories!" he said. "Where do you think they come from?"

His assistant, a young man from the Party Secretariat who would be available for emergency duty that night, did not answer. To render any opinion about such a delicate matter could get him into trouble: better to sip his vodka like the General Secretary and shake his head with disgust.

"But who started them?" Brezhnev swore out loud. "They damage Strelnikov's standing and the reputation of the Academy. And they are totally absurd. This episode with the American was uncalled for. Have they released him yet?"

Again the assistant shrugged. For the last two hours he had relayed messages between the Foreign Ministry and the U.S. Embassy in an effort to clarify Fall's arrest. "They were not ready to release him the last time we talked," he sighed. "They thought his books were filled with codes."

"It is all connected to those stories about Muslim plots," Brezhnev snorted. "They are making an international incident out of someone's delusions. Even our television people are complaining. Do you know what that is about?"

"The American was going to appear on a television show with Soviet scientists." Brezhnev's assistant sounded exhausted. "They were going to film the show tomorrow."

The long black car turned toward the entrance of the building, stopping beside two militiamen ready to escort Brezhnev inside. "When we get upstairs, tell Strelnikov to come here at once," Brezhnev told his assistant. "I want to hear his account of this Kirov commission." Then he hurried past his guards and rode the elevator to his floor. But as he stepped into the corridor, a stranger came out of the shadows. "I'm here to save your life!" the man whispered. "Your enemies are staging a coup!"

Two bodyguards grabbed the stranger's arms, pulling him back down the hallway. Brezhnev watched with horror. "Help search him!" he said to his assistant. "See if he has a gun!"

"Ivan Strelnikov and Vladimir Kirov!" the struggling figure shouted. "They are your enemies!"

"Who are you?" shouted one of the guards.

"Yakov Kozin. You have seen me. I work in the Committee for State Security!"

"He is a surveillance expert," said Brezhnev's assistant. "I recognize him now."

The General Secretary stood transfixed as Kozin went down on his knees. "Comrade Brezhnev," he pleaded, "I must tell you what they are planning. It has been my job to find out. I have information you can check!"

"Bring him in," Brezhnev said with anger. "Let us hear what he has to say. It may be the quickest way to find the source of these rumors."

Shivering with a fear that threatened to erase his will and coherence, Kozin was led into Brezhnev's rooms. Once inside, the two bodyguards searched him carefully, then kept his arms pinned to his side. A third guard had come in from the hallway. "Tell us what the plot consists of!" the assistant demanded. "Strelnikov will answer your charges."

"Vladimir Kirov!" Kozin gasped. "Remember that name— *Vladimir Kirov*. You must not forget it. And Rozhnov, Alexander Rozhnov. And the sheik Muhammad Khan! They are all in it together!"

"I have heard those names all afternoon," Brezhnev said fiercely. "But tell us what they are *doing*. These stories are insane!"

"They are plotting a takeover," said the desperate figure. "The Academy study of the mind is their front. They are all in league with Muslim groups. Remember 'Tamerlane's Angels.' That is a name to watch. *Tamerlane's Angels!* It is one of their passwords..."

"But how can such a group take over the government?" Brezhnev demanded. "They don't have a single tank. Or any votes on the Politburo!"

Kozin saw the General Secretary's growing impatience and realized that his time was short. "Strelnikov can read your mind!" he whispered. "And so can Vladimir Kirov. They all know what you think."

"They sound like supermen," a resonant voice said. "What other powers do they have?"

Kozin turned to see Strelnikov standing behind him. Shocked, he backed away into one of the guards.

Strelnikov was the calmest person in the room. Brezhnev paced up and down, fingering his jacket nervously, then turned to study Kozin. Kozin, meanwhile, tried to return Strelnikov's gaze.

"*This* is the source of the rumors," Strelnikov said to Brezhnev. "He has started them all." He looked with menace at Kozin. "Your people in Department Ten have told us all about it. They think you have gone crazy."

Kozin was incapable now of strategic thinking. "Yes, I have done this alone!" he gasped. "No one else has the strength or knowledge. But that does not make me wrong. You know that, comrade, don't you?"

"Take him away!" said Brezhnev gruffly. "The man is a lunatic!"

The bodyguards hauled the protesting figure toward the door.

But with a burst of manic energy, Kozin loosed himself and headed for Strelnikov. One of the guards tackled him, banging his head on the floor. A second jumped on his back. Together, they carried the unconscious figure out into the hall.

Pacing up and down, Brezhnev spoke with nervous gestures. "Strelnikov, we cannot have this. I blame it all on that study. It has raised a hundred rumors about the Academy and has damaged your reputation. It has ruined Vladimir Kirov and embarrassed the State Committee for Science and Technology. It's as if you had all taken whores to the Kremlin and had an orgy in Georgievsky Hall! Finally some people cannot stand it, and like this Kozin, they will snap. For the Academy to study apparitions in such secrecy, with a committee headed by a famous espionage agent, is not a good idea. People are joking that the CIA put drugs in our vodka!"

For the first time Brezhnev saw the humor of it. "Let's have a cognac," he growled. "And agree to call off the study. The Committee for State Security will have to decide what to do with Vladimir Kirov."

"I never wanted that study," said Strelnikov. "I warned everyone about it the day it was conceived."

"*Da!*" The General Secretary grinned with bearish good humor. "Let us leave the mysteries of the soul to our priests and poets! The rest of us can find illumination enough with good cognac like this!"

36

Waking from his nightmare, Strelnikov sat straight up. Though the room was dark, he could see from the clock at his side that it was six-thirty. He had slept for less than five hours. He tried to calm himself, but the dream was too upsetting. He could not dispel a sense that his mind would vanish in the light he had seen. Its radiance still threatened to overwhelm him.

Throwing the covers back abruptly, he got out of bed, washed his face, and dressed. To his relief, there were sounds of dishes rattling and the smell of coffee. His maid was already up.

Sitting in his kitchen, Strelnikov felt the dream receding. With a sigh of gratitude, he buttered the toast on his plate and drank a cup of coffee. The warmth of the stove had never been more welcome.

Turning to his maid, Strelnikov asked if she dreamt. A sturdy, intelligent woman of sixty, she seemed to have wisdom in these matters.

"Ah, dreams!" she said. "People talk to me sometimes in them and tell me surprising things."

"Is that right!" Strelnikov studied her face. "What kinds of things do they tell you?"

The woman bit her lower lip as if to suppress a smile. "Sometimes sad things, sometimes naughty. Sometimes they foretell the future."

"Foretell the future?" Strelnikov asked. "Tell me one like that."

The lady looked at the ceiling. "There's one I'll never forget," she said, refilling Strelnikov's cup. "In it, a stranger gave me a necklace, then two days later a relative died and left me her favorite jewels. They looked exactly like the necklace in the dream."

As she spoke, Strelnikov remembered that in his dream Kirov had told his story about the endless net of jewels. In it, each diamond reflected all the others.

"It's a necklace I wear at dinners here," she said. "You must have seen it."

"I don't remember, but I'm often preoccupied. Next time I want you to show me. And you have naughty dreams? I didn't think you'd have dreams like that, Marina."

"Sometimes," she said with a blush. "Once I dreamt I was a spy."

"A spy? And what were you doing?"

"Watching everyone, and having a marvelous time! I could go anywhere I wanted. And everyone was watching me as if they knew all my secrets. Every person in the dream was a spy. There was something naughty about it."

Strelnikov sat back thunderstruck. There had been something like that in *his* dream, a sense that everyone secretly knew one another.

Strelnikov emptied his cup. "I will look for that necklace," he said politely. "We will have to talk about this more."

In his spacious front room Strelnikov telephoned his driver. Then he paced back and forth to control the anxiety his talk with Marina had triggered. There seemed no way to suppress his dream. . . .

It had started with someone whispering a line from Rozhnov's book, "everyone is given a way without knowing the destination," as there began a thorough review of his scientific work. Watching a long faded movie of his past, he had carefully re-examined his development of coherent light. He had stood for what seemed an eternity, puzzling over each turn his work had taken, over each idea, each invention, until the horror of the dream had finally dawned on him. Suddenly he saw that his mind was the same laser light he had worked so long to perfect. It was as well-defined, as pure, as hard and focused. To his horror, he was trapped in a single beam that bounced from mirror to mirror in a machine he had invented. He was trapped in a brilliant labyrinth that turned on itself forever.

Strelnikov tried to remember: had he gotten up from his dream in the dark, his arms paralyzed, before he fell back exhausted? He wasn't sure, because all he could recall now was a sense that Kirov had come to his rescue. Kirov had entered the labyrinth to show him that every mirror was a luminous face. Instead of mirrors, there were faces everywhere that seemed to know and support his every thought and feeling. For an exhilarating moment he saw that each person he faced was a unique and marvelous entity within a single radiant light, every one reflecting and somehow embracing the others. All of it was brimming with a joy and power that could annihilate him.

Standing by a table for support, Strelnikov cursed his inability to control these extravagant thoughts. His weakness must come from the strain of these last four weeks and the trauma of Kozin's scandal. To restore his confidence, he remembered his talk with Brezhnev the evening before. The General Secretary's quick dismissal of Kozin's charges had been a great confirmation, a gesture of trust that would serve him for years to come. Brezhnev had even told him that his work on lasers deserved more state support. Remembering their talk, Strelnikov felt his strength returning. His position in the Academy, his status in Soviet science, were more solid than ever now. In a few weeks the Kirov episode would be largely forgotten.

By the time his driver arrived, Strelnikov was almost back to normal, and ten minutes after that, seated in his limousine, he felt completely restored. With a sense of relief, he decided to destroy all the files of the space-capsule crash. When he reached the Praesidium, he would eliminate every trace of Kirov's commission.

As the day wore on, Strelnikov erased sign after sign of the scandal. He threw Rozhnov's book away, and ordered the removal of every document Kirov had used to support his study. The UFO report, Fall's book, the tapes of the capsule incident. Atabet's maps were sent to the KGB center in Dzerzhinsky Square. By five o'clock that afternoon, no remnant of Kirov's investigation remained in the Academy files.

Kozin, meanwhile, was sent to a well-guarded spa in Georgia, Baranov was assigned to a lab in Minsk, and Kirov was given leave in Tashkent until the KGB decided how his compromised talents might be used in the future. All this was accomplished while Strelnikov's dreams sealed over. Whatever truths they might have delivered were erased just as surely as Kozin's unfounded stories.

AUTHOR'S NOTE

But the story is not over. In the ten years since these events, several Americans have joined with Soviet citizens to explore those vast uncharted territories the Soviets have taken to calling "our hidden human reserves." Their ventures include a comparative study of exceptional capacities that appear in various cultures, an analysis of ancient and modern disciplines for personal growth and illumination, and some projects to demonstrate the promise of their findings.

A new generation of political leaders, either here or in the Soviet Union, could end this adventure of the spirit. But we can be hopeful. Sometime in the next few years, Darwin Fall may write a book about these matters. With their Soviet friends, he says, he and Jacob Atabet are finding unexpected vistas beyond the labyrinths of ordinary history.

San Francisco, 1982